A Guide for
HAJJ AND 'UMRA

By

Anis Daud Mathews

KITAB BHAVAN
NEW DELHI

A Guide for Hajj and Umra

KITAB BHAVAN
Publishers, Distributors, Exporters & Importers
1784, Kalan Mahal, Darya Ganj,
New Delhi - 1100 02 (India)

Phones : (91-11) 23277392/93, 23274686, 32906494
Fax : (91-11) 23263383

Website : www.nusratalinasri.com

Email : nasri@vsnl.com
: nusrat@bol.net.in

1st Edition : 1993
5th Edition : 2011

ISBN : 81-7151-149-X
Book Code No. : G00059

Printed & Published in India by :
Nusrat Ali Nasri for KITAB BHAVAN
1784, Kalan Mahal, Darya Ganj,
New Delhi - 1100 02 [India]

Bait Allāh

TRANSLITERATION OF ARABIC NAMES

The following system has been used in this book:

Consonantal	ا	a		ط	ṭ
Sound				ظ	ẓ
Long Vovel	آ	ā		ع	'
	ب	b		غ	gh
	ت	t		ف	f
	ث	th		ق	q
	ج	j		ك	k
	ح	h		ل	l
	خ	kh		م	m
	د	d		ن	n
	ذ	dh		ة ه	h
	ر	r		و	w
	ز	z	Long Vovel	و	ū
	س	s	Diphthong	و	au
	ش	sh	Consonant	ی	y
	ص	ṣ	Long Vovel	ی	ī
	ض	ḍ	Diphthong	ی	ai
Fatha	ـَ		Short Vovel		a
Kasra	ـِ		Short Vovel		i
Dhamma	ـُ		Short Vovel		u

NOTE

1. No distinctive sign is used for Hamza (ء)
2. The 'h' preceded by a short 'a' in Arabic names is seldom pronounced hence has been left out; e.g. 'Umra for 'Umrah as required in Arabic spelling.

CONTENTS

APPENDIX

FOREWORD

It gives me great pleasure in introducing the author of this book, Anis Daud Mathews, who very kindly agreed to devote some of her precious time in compiling this guide for Ḥajj and 'Umra for intending Pilgrims from English speaking countries.

Born in Pakistan, she was awarded her B.S. and M.S. Degrees at the University of Panjab, Lahore. She taught for a while in Medical College, at the University of Baghdad. Having completed her experimental work at A.E.R.E. Harwell, she was awarded an M. Phil in Nuclear Physics by the University of Surrey (England). In 1974 she came to Saudi Arabia with her husband where they presently reside.

In addition to providing useful information to help prepare the Pilgrim for the Sacred Journey, she has compiled a beautiful collection of prayers for each occasion, in original Arabic, along with their Transliteration and Translation to help those who cannot read or understand Arabic. These prayers are only a guideline, generally derived from the Holy Qur'ān and from the sayings of Prophet Muhammad (may peace and blessings of Allāh be on him). It will be according to the Sunna to recite these, if time permits, otherwise one can pray in any language, as Allāh is the best of Listeners.

There is a stepwise explanation of each ceremony of Ḥajj or 'Umra with flow diagrams, maps and pictures of various sacred places to prepare the reader mentally and spiritually for the greatest occasion of his life, the PILGRIMAGE TO MECCA.

Thanks are due to innumerable sources from which this information has been compiled. The Ministry of Hajj and Auqāf and the Ministry of Information of the Government of Saudi Arabia, the Managers of various Hotels, Saudia-Airlines, Rabita-tal-Ālim-al-Islāmi, Mecca Mukarrama, and P.I.A. are the prominent ones who deserve most sincere appreciation and acknowledgement for the information provided in this book from their sources.

Also, grateful acknowledgment is due to ARAMCO, their Public Relation's Chief, Mr. 'Abdulla Jum'a and their Photographic Department for providing all the pictures included herein by their world famous Photographer, S.M. Amin of Pakistan. These photographs have really beautified this book.

May Allāh reward Ismāil Amīralī and Ḥāmid Alī for their selfless efforts in typing and retyping the manuscript in the shortest possible time. May Allāh also bless my brother in Islām, Daud Mathews, for checking and rechecking the manuscript and providing useful suggestions all the time to improve the contents of the book.

Because of a deadline to bring this book to intending Pilgrims before Ḥajj this year, there may be errors and omissions here and there, which we regret and pray to Almighty Allāh to forgive us. However criticism and suggestions to improve this book are most welcome and when included in the second edition will make this book worthy of reading by every Muslim.

May Allāh bless all those who have contributed in the compilation of this book, and May Allāh help the readers to take full advantage of its contents and thus attain His Grace and Blessings in the Holy Land for a beautiful life in this world and in the Hereafter. May Allāh accept our humble contribution to further His Cause, and reward us all, Ameen.

M.A. Qazi,
U.P.M.
Dhahran (Saudi Arabia).

August, 1977

GLOSSARY

ابيض	Abyad	White
عذاب	'Adhāb	Anger, Torment
اذان	Ādhān	The call for the prayer pronounced loudly to indicate that the time of praying is due.
آفاقى	Āfāqi	The Outsider. That Muslim who has come with the intention of Ḥajj from outside the Miqāt Boundary.
احكام	Aḥkām	"Orders", According to Islāmic Law, there are five kinds of orders: (1) Compulsory (Wājib واجب) (2) Orders without obligation (Mustaḥab مستحب) (3) Forbidden (Moḥarram محرّم) (4) Disliked but not forbidden (Makrūh مكروه) (5) Lawful and allowed (Ḥalāl حلال)
اهل الحرم	Ahl-e-Ḥaram	The people living within the boundaries of the Sacred Valley.
عين	'Ain	The eye
اخضر	Akhḍar	Green color
الله اكبر	Allāh-u-Akbar	Allāh is Great.
الوداع	Al-wadā'	Farewell, Good-bye
عرفات	'Arafāt	Name of the mountain and adjacent plain located 7 miles from Minā, where Pilgrims spend the 9th of Dhul-Ḥajj, Rukn-e-A'ẓam.
اسمر	Asmar	Brown, Brown-skinned.
عصر	'Aṣr	Afternoon prayer time.
اسود	Aswad	Black
ايام	Ayyām	Days
آية	Āya(s).	Verse(s) of the Holy Qur'an
بدنة	Badana	(Plural: Budn) the whole Camel or cow offered as a sacrifice.
بيت	Bait	The House
بيت المقدس	Bait-ul-Maqdis	It is a famous mosque in Jerusalem which is regarded as the third greatest Mosque in the Islāmic World; the first and second being Al-Masjid al-Haram at Mecca and the Mosque of the Prophet at al-Medina respectively

بيت الله	Bait-Allāh	The House of Allāh (at Mecca). .
بركات	Barakāt	Blessings of Allāh
بنت	Bint	Daughter, Girl.
دم	Damm	Blood; the sacrifice of a goat, a sheep, or one seventh part of a Cow or a Camel in order to compensate for failing to perform a Rukn for Ḥajj or 'Umra, correctly.
ذو محرم	Dhi Maḥram	A male whom a woman can never marry because of close relationship e.g. brother, father, an uncle or her own husband.
ذوالحجّة	Dhul-Ḥijja	The twelfth month of the Muslim Calendar.
ذوالحليفة	Dhul-Ḥulaifa	The Miqāt of people of Medina now called "Bir 'Alī".
ذوالقعدة	Dhul-Qa'da	The eleventh month of the Muslim Calendar.
فجر	Fajr	Dawn prayer or early morning before sunrise.
غُسل	Ghusl	Taking a bath in a special ceremonial way. This is necessary for one who is Junub, and also on other occasions.
هدى	Hadī	An animal (a camel, a cow, a sheep or a goat) offered as a sacrifice by a Pilgrim.
حديث	Ḥadīth	The traditions of the Prophet i.e., his sayings and deeds.
الحجرالاسود	Ḥajar-al-Aswad	The Black Stone implanted in one of the southern (Yemenite) corners of the Ka'ba. It is a Sunna to kiss this during Ṭawāf for 'Umra or Ḥajj
حجّ	Ḥajj	The Pilgrimage to Mecca.
حجّ التمتع	Ḥajj-Tamattu'	Ḥajj performed with 'Umra preceding it.
حل	Ḥal	The place outside the boundaries of Ḥaram.
حلال	Halāl	That which is allowed, permitted or permissible, lawful. That which is recommended in the way of Allāh.
حرام	Ḥarām	Forbidden, prohibited, Sacred, holy.

حرام	Ḥarām	The valley in which a non-Muslim is not supposed to enter; also used for the Ka'ba, Mecca or Medina. It is forbidden to fight, to kill a person or hunt within these sacred boundaries.
حرمان	Ḥaramain	The two sacred Mosques in Mecca and Medīna.
حطيم	Ḥaṭīm	The semi-circular northern wall of Bait-Allāh, included in the Ṭawaf, and supposed to be part of the Greater Ka'ba.
الحجر	(Al)Ḥijr	The unroofed portion of the Ka'ba which at present is in the form of a compound towards the northwest of the Ka'ba i.e. (within Ḥatīm).
حدود	Ḥudūd	Allāh's boundary limits for Halāl and Ḥarām.
حكم	Ḥukm	A judgement or legal decision, especially of Allāh.
عيدالاضحى	'Īd-al-Adhā	The three day festival of Muslims starting on the tenth day of Dhul-Ḥijja.
عيدالفطر	'Īd-ul-Fiṭr	The three day festival of Muslims starting from the first day of Shawwāl, the month following Ramaḍān. Fiṭr literally means breaking the fast.
اضطباع	Iḍṭibā'	To wrap one of the sheets of Ihrām in such a way that it comes below the right arm and hangs over the left shoulder so that the right shoulder remains uncovered.
افراد	Ifrād/Afrād	Ḥajj-e-Ifrād is to go and stand in the valley of 'Arafāt and do Ṭawāf-e-Ziyāra i.e. to perform Ḥajj only without performing 'Umra in Iḥrām.
احرام	Ihrān	The state of ritual consecration (of a Mecca Pilgrim) During this the Pilgrim, wearing two seamless woolen or linen, towels or sheets usually white, neither combs, nor shaves

	Ihrām (Con't)	and observes sexual abstinence to please Allāh; Garments of the Pilgrim.
امام	Imām	The person who leads others in the Prayer or Muslim Caliph.
اقامة	Iqāma	The statement of the Ādhān is recited reduced so that the statements that are repeated twice in the Ādhān are recited once in Iqāma except the last occurrence of "Allāh-u-Akbar". The Prayer is offered immediately after Iqāma has been proclaimed.
عشاء	'Ishā	Night prayer, the time for which starts about one and a half hours after sunset.
استلام	Istilām	To kiss Ḥajr-al-Aswad (the Black Stone)
اعتكاف	I'tikāf	Seclusion in a mosque for the purpose of worshipping Allāh only. The one in such a state should not have sexual relations with his wife and one is not allowed to leave the mosque except for an urgent necessity e.g. answering the call of nature or to join a funeral procession etc.
ازار	Izār	A sheet worn below the waist.
جبل	Jabal	The mountain
جبل الرّحمة	Jabal-e-Raḥma	The mountain of Mercy in the plain of 'Arafāt where Prophet Muḥammad ﷺ delivered his last sermon (Khuṭba). To pray near it is is Sunna and has a special degree of acceptance with Almighty Allāh.
جلّ	Jalla	Exalted.
جلال	Jalāl	The attribute of Allāh, Sublime, Exalted.
جهنّم	Jahannum	The Hell.
جمع بين صلاتين	Jam'a bain Ṣalātain	To pray two Prayers together such that one is delayed and the other is in time e.g. Ẓuhr and 'Asr are combined in 'Arafāt at 'Asr as Sunna.

جماعة	Jamā'at	Congregation specific for prayers.
جمرة	Jamra	Three places between Muzdalifa and Mina depicting the points of stoning the Devil.
جمرة العقبة	Jamrat-al-'Aqaba	One of the three stones (pillars) situated in Minā. One of the ceremonies of Pilgrimage is to throw pebbles at these stones which stand as symbols of Satan.
جنابة	Janaba	The state of a person after having sexual intercourse either with a person or in a dream etc. A Muslim in such a state is not allowed to pray or do any other kind of worship unless and until he performs Ghusl (have a bath) or Tayammum.
جنازه	Janāza	The Dead, funeral.
جنايه	Janāyat	A mistake in performing the Arkān (Steps) of the ceremonies of Ḥajj. To compensate for this, Damm is recommended, which is sacrificing an animal during Ḥajj.
الجحفة	(Al) Juḥfa	The Miqāt of the people of Shām (Syria)
جُمعة	Jum'a	Friday or Friday prayer.
جنب	Junub	A person who is in a state of Janāba.
كعبة	Ka'ba	A stone building (cube) in the Great Mosque at Mecca towards which all Muslims turn their faces in prayers.
خطبة	Khuṭba	Sermon.
كفر	Kufr	Disbelief including the refusal of anything of what the Prophet Muḥammad (P.B.U.H) brought
لبّيك	Labbaik	I respond to your call.
مبرور	Mabrūr	(Ḥajj) accepted by Allāh for being perfectly performed according to the Prophet's traditions.
مغرب	Maghrib	Sunset Prayer.
مغسل	Maghsil	Washroom, Toilet.
محسّب	(al) Maḥassab	A valley outside Mecca sometimes called Khaif Bani Kināna.
محرم	Maḥram	See Dhi Maḥram

مكروه	Makrūh	Not approved of, undesirable, unpleasant, from the point of view of religion although not punishable or rewardable. Not encouraged in Islām.
مناسك	Manāsik	The Arkān (steps) of the ceremonies of Ḥajj.
منحر	Manḥar	The place of sacrifice in Minā.
مقام ابراهيم	Maqām-e Ibrāhīm	The station where Prophet Ibrāhīm stood while he and Ismā'īl were building the Ka'ba.
مروة	Marwa	The hill near the Ka'ba.
مسجد	Masjid	The Mosque; the placeof prostration
مطاف	Maṭāf	Round trip, area of circumambulation round the Ka'ba.
مواقيت	Mawāqit	Certain positions specified by the Prophet (P.B.U.H.) for the people from which to assume Iḥrām on their way to Mecca when intending to perform Ḥajj or 'Umra.
ميلين اخضرين	Meelain Akhḍarain	The two green pillars in Mas'a (where Sa'ī is performed)
منى	Minā	A place outside Mecca on the road to 'Arafāt. It is five miles away from Mecca and about 10 miles from 'Arafāt.
ميقات	Miqāt	Boundary of the area around Mecca, before entering which, a Pilgrim has to be in Iḥrām. It is forbidden to enter Miqāt without Iḥrām during the Ḥajj or for 'Umra.
مؤذن	Muadhdhin	A caller who pronounces the Adhān loudly calling people to come and join the Prayers.
مؤكده	Mu'akkida	Insisted upon, necessary.
معلم	Mu'allam	Pilgrīm's guide in Mecca.
محل	Muhlil	One who is not Muḥrim.
محرمة	Muḥrima	A female in the state of Iḥrām.
ملتزم	Multazim	The door of the Ka'ba.
مصلى	Muṣallā	A place for praying.
مستحب	Mustaḥab	Commendable, desirable worship
متمتع	Mutamatti'	A pilgrim performing Ḥajj-e-tamattu'.

مطوّف	**Mutawwaf**	A Pilgrim's guide inside the Holy Mosque
مزدلفة	**Muzdalifa**	A valley between 'Arafāt and Minā where the Pilgrims returning from 'Arafāt spend a night between the ninth and tenth of Dhul-Hijja after performing Maghrib and 'Ishā prayers together, leaving for Minā after sunrise on the tenth. This night is one thousand times better than Lail-atul-Qadr.
نافلة	**Nāfila**	Optional practice of worship in contrast to the obligatory (Farīda)
يوم نفر	**(The day of) Nafr**	The 12th day of Dhul-Ḥajj when the Pilgrims leave Minā, after performing all the ceremonies of Hajj at 'Arafāt, Minā and al-Muzdalifa.
نحر	**Nahr**	The 10th of Dhul-Hajj, the day of sacrifice.
نمرة	**Namra**	The mosque in 'Arafāt where Ẓuhr and 'Asr are combined at 'Aṣr on the 9th of Dhul-Ḥajj.
نيّة	**Niyya**	The Intention.
نسك	**Nusuk**	The sacrifice of a goat.
قباء	**Qabā'**	An outer garment with full length sleeves
قدوم	**Qadūm**	The preceding, Ṭawāf-e-Qadūm, the first Tawaf in Ḥajj.
قارن	**Qārin**	One who performs Hajj-al-Qirān.
قرن المنازل	**Qarn-al-Manzil**	The Miqāt of the people of Najd. It is situated on the way from Tā'if to Meçca.
قصر	**Qaṣr**	To shorten, to lessen, to cut (hair)
قبلة	**Qibla**	The direction towards the Ka'ba in Mecca, in which all Muslims turn their faces in Prayer.
قران	**Qirān**	Ḥajj performed along with 'Umra in the same state of Ihrām: Hadī is to be brought by the Pilgrim along with him and offered when performing this type of Ḥajj
قيام	**Qiyām**	The posture of standing in prayer; Overnight prayers

قنوت	Qunūt	Invocation in the Prayers
ركعة	Rak'a	The Prayer of Muslims consists of Rak'at (Singular Rak'a) which comprise one bowing and two prostrations.
رمضان	Ramaḍān	The month of Fasting. In this month the Holy Qur'ān started to be revealed to our Prophet and in it occurs the Night of Qadr.
رمل	Ramal	Fast walking accompanied by the movements of the arms and legs to show one's body health. This is to be observed in the first three rounds of the Tawāf of the Ka'ba, and it is to be done by the men only and not by women.
رمى	Rami	The throwing of pebbles at the Jimār at Minā.
ركن	Rukn	Support, Corner, Nook; First, primary or important principle.
ركن يمانى	Rukn-e-Yamani	The sourh-western corner of the Ka'ba facing the Yemen. It is Mustahab to do Istilam (to kiss this) or touch it with both hands.
سعى	Sa'i	The ceremony of walking and partly running seven times between Ṣafā and Marwa, performed during the Ḥajj or 'Umra; meaning effort.
صدقة	Sadaqa	Anything given voluntarily in charity.
صفا	Safā	A mountain near the Ka'ba.
سهو	Sahw	Forgetting (here it means forgetting how many Rak'at) One should perform two additional prostrations of Sahw.
السجدة	(As) Sajda	To prostrate, or prostration.
		A sura by the recitation of which prostration becomes essential when certain verses are read.
صخرة	Sakhura	Rock, Boulder
شام	Sham	Syria, Palestine and Jordan (region comprising of).

اشواط	Shawāṭ	Plural of Showṭ; seven Shawāṭ constitute one Ṭawāf of the Ka'ba.
شوّال	Shawwāl	The 10th Month of the Muslim calendar.
شوط	Showṭ	To circumambulate the Ka'ba once is called a Showṭ (starting from the Black Stone and ending at the Black Stone).
سواك	Siwāk	A piece of a branch or a root of a tree called Al-Arāk used as a tooth-brush.
سبحان الله	Subḥān-Allāh	To honour Almighty Allāh from all what (unsuitable things) is ascribed to Him.
سحور	Suḥūr	A meal taken in the early morning before Fajr prayer on the nights of Ramaḍān, the month of fasting.
سنّة	Sunna	All the Traditions and Practices of the Prophet that have become as models to be followed by all Muslims.
تهجّد	Tahajjud	Optional night prayers offered at any time after the 'Isha prayer and before the Fajr prayer.
تكبير	Takbīr	Saying "Allāh-u-Akbar" (Allāh is Great).
تكبيرة	Takbīra	A single utterance of "Allāh-u-Akbar"
تلبيد	Talbid	To glue the hair or the beard during the Ḥajj so that no hair is broken or fallen.
تلبية	Talbiya	Saying "Labbaik, Allāhumma Labbaik" (O Allāh ! I am present to respond to Your Call.)
التّنعيم	(At-) Tan'īm	A few miles from the north of Mecca from where Meccans may assume the state of Ihram to perform 'Umra.
تقليد	Taqlīd	To tie a collar or a chain to the neck of the sacrificial animal; putting colored garlands round the neck.

تراويح	Tarāwīḥ	Optional prayers offered after the 'Ishā prayer on the nights of Ramaḍān. They may be performed individually or in congregation.
تروية	Tar- wiya	The 8th day of Dhul-Ḥajj, when Pilgrims start going to Minā.
تشهّد	Tashahhud	The recitation of the invocation: "At-taḥiyyātu lillāhi .....(upto) wa ash-hadu anna Muḥammadan Rasū-lullāh" while in "Qu'ūd" (i.e. sitting posture) in prayer.
تسليم	Taslīm	On finishing the prayer, one turns one's face right and left saying "Asalām-u-Alaikum....."This is called Taslīm.
طواف	Ṭawāf	The circumambulation of the Ka'ba (seven times).
طواف الافاضة	Ṭawāf-al-Ifāḍa	The Ṭawāf performed after coming from Minā on the 10th day of Dhul-Ḥajj. This is one of the essential ceremonies of Ḥajj.
طواف الوداع	Ṭawāf-al-wadā'	The last Ṭawāf before leaving Mecca
تيمّم	Tayammum	To put or lightly strike the hands on clean earth and then pass the palm of each on the back of the other, blow off the dust and then pass them on the face. This is performed instead of ablution when water is not available or when one is too sick to use water.
ثواب	Thawāb	The Divine reward
عمرة	'Umra	The Pilgrimage of Bait-Allāh during the year at any other time than Dhul-Ḥajj, the month of Ḥajj. In reward two 'Umras are said to equal one Ḥajj.
واجب	Wājib	Obligatory, requisite
وقوف	Waqūf	Staying in 'Arafāt anytime between the morning and sunset on the 9th of Dhul-Ḥajj constituting the major Rukn of Ḥajj.

وتر	Witr	An odd number of Rak'at with which one finishes one's prayer at night or after 'Ishā prayer.
وضوء	Wuḍū	The act of ablution in order to purify oneself for offering prayers, reading the Holy Qur'ān, performing Ḥajj or 'Umra or any other kind of worship of Allāh.
يلملم	Yalamlam	The Mīqāt of the people of the Yemen
زكاة	Zakat	A certain fixed portion (2-1/2%) of the wealth of every Muslim to be paid for the benefit of the needy in the Muslim community. The payment of Zakāt, as it is one of the five pillars of Islām, is obligatory on all Muslims.
زمزم	Zam-zam	The sacred well inside the Ḥaram (the Great Mosque at Mecca). Its water is supposed to be healthy and blessed.
ظهر	Ẓuhr	Noon, Mid-day prayer.

MAP OF SAUDI ARABIA

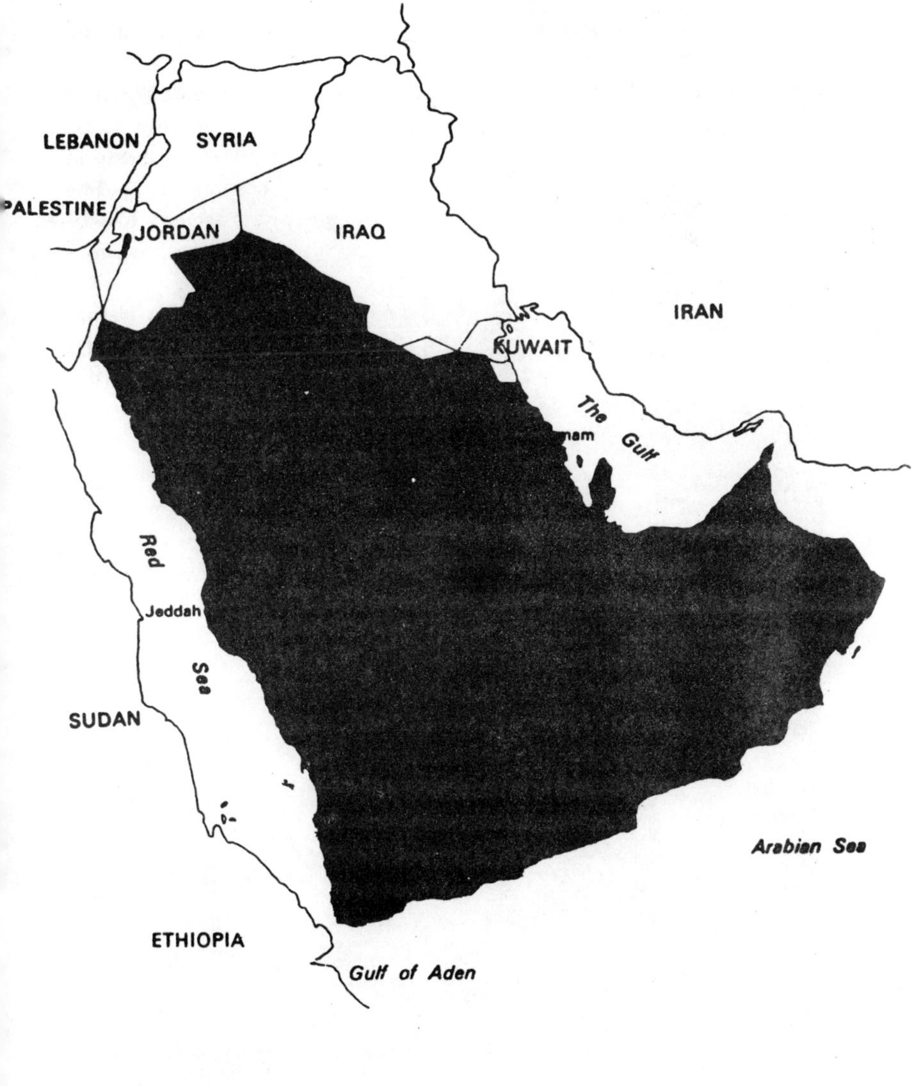

House of Allah at Dawn

CHAPTER ONE

GENERAL INFORMATION

ENTRY VISA

Entry visa must be obtained from a Saudi consulate in your country before beginning a journey to Saudi Arabia. It will be a Pilgrimage Visa either for Ḥajj or for 'Umra. The application forms and fees etc. can be requested by writing a letter to the Ṣaudi Consulate. (Addresses are given in Appendix I)

At least 2 months before the date of departure, you should contact the consulate. When applying for a pilgrimage visa, please transmit the following to the Saudi Consulate, along with the necessary application forms for a visa and visa fees:

1. A document or statement from appropriate officials or agencies certifying to your and your wife's (if accompanying you) religious faith or affiliation.
2. Photocopy of marriage certificate.
3. At least two passport size photographs of each of you.
4. A self addressed envelope for return mail (stamped).

And please do not forget the application forms and payment for visas.

Please do not leave your country unless you have a Pilgrim's visa stamped in your passport. You cannot obtain this at the airport, seaport or enroute.

Plenty of time should be allowed both when getting an Entry visa or Exit visa. The passport office is usually crowded with very many people specially during Ḥajj season. Rather than spend a couple of hours there, it would be wiser to employ a messenger. Likewise, the hotels will, if asked, usually send someone to register arrivals. Visitors must register within three days of arrival. If you plan to apply in person for a Visa in New York City or London or Beirut, you must expect to devote at least one week in the process, at your own expense. Consulates will not issue visas in less than 24 hours, and more time may be involved if documents are not in order.

Therefore it will be wise to plan well in advance and take advantage of the less expensive alternative of obtaining a visa by mail. This is generally not productive unless a stamped self-addressed envelope is sent to the Consulate.

TRANSPORTATION

Cheap excursion fares up to a maximum of 45 days are available both during Ḥajj season and off season. It is again advisable to book your seats well in advance to avoid disappointment due to very heavy demand in the Hajj season.

Cheap Ḥajj trips are arranged by various groups in USA, Canada and Europe, which also include ground arrangements in Mecca, Medīna and Jedda. It may be more economical to avail yourself of one of these during the Ḥajj season. Your airline agent can help you in visas, hotels, stop-overs etc. Remember to reconfirm your flight within 24 hours of your departure. Also reconfirm your onward flight at each stopover again within 24 hours of your departure time. Travel within the country is provided by Saudi Airlines (3-4 flights every day), (For address and phone, see appendix II)

No one with an entry visa to Israel will be allowed into Saudi Arabia.

HEALTH REQUIREMENTS:

The Saudi Arabian Government requires evidence of recent Cholera immunisation within the last six (6) months. It is also advisable to have small pox immunisation with a validity of 3 years on an International Health Certificate duly signed and endorsed by appropriate Health Authorities.

PASSPORT PHOTOS

Wallet size photos (24) should be brought with you. Also bring a good negative from which additional positives, if required, can be made here. You will need these for various purposes immediately upon your arrival in Jedda.

CURRENT EXCHANGE RATE

Rate for buying Saudi Riyals

One US Dollar	=	SR 3.54
One UK Pound Sterling	=	SR 6.00

Saudi Riyals can be bought at Banks and money exchangers in all Middle Eastern cities at reasonable rates of exchange. They are also available in Banks and Foreign Exchange dealers in New York and London at a small discount. It is recommended that you bring with you at least 100 Saudi Riyals in change for porter's tips, taxis, etc. No banking or exchange facilities are available inside Jedda Airport and international flights usually arrive at odd hours when these facilities in the markets are closed.

ACCOMMODATION:

A list of hotels in Jedda, Mecca and Medīna is given in the Appendix III. The prices begin at about 50 Riyals per night for a single person and may be as high as 250 Riyals per night. The rates are doubled during the month of Ramaḍān and quadrupled during Ḥajj Season.

It is advisable to write to these Hotels for reservations at least two months in advance. These will be for the complete season i.e. about one month and they expect from 50% to 100% of the full amount in advance to reserve a place for you on your arrival.

It may be cheaper to ask your Mu'allam (the official Ḥajj guide appointed by the Government), again well in advance of accommodation that you want and also settling the rates before your arrival here. If you have a friend in Mecca or Medīna it will be quite useful to ask him to rent one or two rooms with a family in a private house for you. This is the cheapest way of living in Mecca or Medīna. These rooms are reasonable in price and usually have moderate living facilities.

DEPARTURE

A list of Airlines and/or their agents in Jedda, Mecca and Medīna are given in the Appendix IV. It is advisable that you should reserve your seat at least two weeks in advance (or get a return seat confirmed before you reach here to avoid undue delay and last minute disappointment). It is customary to reconfirm your seat within 24 hours of your departure or your name will not be on the manifest.

MAJOR CITIES IN THE KINGDOM

Jedda

The chief seaport of Saudi Arabia and the gateway for most of the Pilgrims to Mecca, some fifty miles to the east. The early history of Jedda is not well known but it seems to have been made a port for Mecca in A.D. 646 by Caliph 'Othmān. At its present site, however, Jedda only dates from the 17th century.

In 1916 the British occupied the City and from the end of the World War I till 1925 it was ruled by the Hashemite ruler of Mecca. In that year it was captured by Ibn Saūd and became part of the Saudi Province of the Hejāz.

The city at present, has excellent port facilities on the Red Sea, and a large International Airport. The city has been largely built in the last forty years, and a modern water system, brought some thirty miles from the Wādī Fāṭima, supplies Jedda with ample water. Over 1,000,000 pilgrims pass through Jedda each year enroute to Mecca or to Medīna and hard surfaced roads lead to each of these cities. The population of Jedda was estimated in the late 1960's at about 250,000.

Mecca

The most Holy city in Islām and the centre of annual pilgrimage from all over the world. Situated in the central Hejāz, Mecca is below the escarpment that provided Mecca's sister town and agricultural supplier, Ṭā'if, with a pleasant climate. In Mecca itself, temperatures often become ovenlike and the area is rather barren.

Mecca was well established in pre-Islamic times. It was well known to the geographer Ptolemy as Macoraba, and by the sixth century A.D. was an important centre on the spice road from Southern Arabia to the Mediterranean world and was perhaps- the most important centre of culture in Northern Arabia. In Prophet Muhammad's time, the tribe of the Quraish dominated the life of the city; Prophet Muhammad ﷺ himself was a member of the Hashemite clan of this tribe. Although the Prophet of Islām left Mecca for Medīna in A.D. 622 and, indeed, is buried in that city, Mecca was designated the primate city of Islām and the centre of that city, Ḥaram, with the legendary well of Zamzam and the Ka'ba, became and remains the major pilgrimage point of Moslems from all over the world.

Throughout the history of Islām, Mecca was usually under the control of one or another outside power, but in the period of the Ottoman empire, it maintained a considerable measure of autonomy under the rule of the Qitāda family, Hashemite rulers or Sherifs of the city. Mecca was twice part of the Saudi empire, once from 1803 to 1813 (though the city was disputed with the local Qitada ruler) and again when the forces of King Ibn Saūd entered the city in October 13, 1924.

Since the incorporation of Mecca into Saudi Arabia, the city has been generally enhanced by a building program that began in 1955, following the completion of reconstruction of the Prophet's Mosque at Medīna. The region around the Ka'ba, the Holy Mosque Area, was greatly enlarged, allowing some 300,000 pilgrims to pray together, all with a good view of the sacred structure of the Ka'ba. At Mecca are situated the Saūdi College of Education and the Sharī'a and Islāmic Studies College. The city is on a major highway that runs from Jedda to Riyadh. Present population is estimated at 200,000.

Medina

The second (after Mecca) most holy city of Islām. Medīna is located in the Northern Ḥejāz, some 300 miles north-east of Mecca in a large oasis. It is surrounded by six valleys, the best known being the Wādī Al-Aqīq. Originally titled Yathrib, the city was prosperous at least by the sixth century A.D., being on one of the main spice routes from the area of Southern Arabia to Syrian and Palestinian areas. According to traditional accounts, the city was originally settled by members of Banū Qaila, a tribe from what is present day Yemen. At the time of Prophet Muḥammad it was controlled by two main pagan tribes, the Aws and the Khazraj, plus a number of Jewish groups, probably judaised Arabians or Aramaeans. In Islāmic tradition, the name Yathrib was changed to Medīna (Arabic for "the City of the Prophet"), after Prophet Muḥammad's arrival in A.D. 622; however, the name may have been introduced by Aramaec speaking Jews and may have been originally the Aramaec word "Medinta"

Medīna became the centre of Islamic political power and Prophet Muḥammad himself lies buried there. The first three Caliphs ruled from Medina but following the rise of the Omayyad Dynasty political power passed from Arabia. At present the city of Medīna is an important agricultural centre, being noted for date groves. It was the southern terminus of the old Damascus-Medīna railroad destroyed in World War I. Today Medīna is connected by modern road southward to Jedda and Mecca, northward to Tabūk, and eastward to Riyāḍ. A road northeastward to Hail is presently being completed.

The city is famous for its historic spots, the best known being the Mosque of the Prophet, where Muḥammad lies buried. This structure was begun in A.D. 622 and is the prototype of all mosques. In 1946 King Ibn Saūd announced his plan to enlarge and this project was completed under King Faiṣal in 1955.

Medīna is the site of the famous Islāmic University with students from more than sixty countries. At present it has a television station, and several new hotels. The population of Medīna is approximately 100,000.

HISTORY OF THE SACRED MOSQUE IN MECCA

The Holy House of God, originally built by the Prophets Abraham and Ismā'īl, was in an open area of Mecca, where no other building existed.

Later Quṣay ibn Kilāb allowed people to build their houses around the Ka'ba. They encircled it with houses leaving only the narrow clearance known till now as al-Maṭāf (the place of circumbulance.) Every house was separated from the next one by a road giving access to al-Mataf.

In the Period of the Orthodox Caliphs

'Umar ibn al-Khaṭṭāb, the second Caliph, expanded the Mosque, provided it with lamps to be illuminated at night, and surrounded it with compound walls with gates. He also constructed a dike to protect it from flooding streams.

'Uthmān ibn 'Affān, the third Caliph, renovated and enlarged the Mosque, and added to it a roofed porch.

In the Reign of 'Abd Allāh ibn al-Zubayr

The Holy Ka'ba was renovated and the Mosque was enlarged.

In the Umayyad Period

al-Walid ibn 'Abd al-Malik, the Umayyad Caliph, renovated and expanded the Mosque. He covered the porches with embellished oak wood and supplied them with marble pillars.

In the Abbasid Period

Abū Ja'far al-Mansūr, the Abbasid Caliph, enlarged the Mosque and added one porch. His son al-Mahdī expanded it and enlarged it further Al-Mu'tadid Billāh, another Caliph, expanded the mosque in the place now known as Bāb al-Ziyāda (the expansion door) which includes the site of Dār al-Nadwa (the council-hall). Caliph al-Muqtadir Billāh expanded it in the place now known as Bāb Ibrāhīm (Abraham's Gate). With this expansion the total area of the Mosque was 29,127 sq. m.

In the Circassian Period

Sulṭān al-Nāṣir Faraj ibn Barqūq renovated the Mosque's building.

In the Ottoman Period

Sulṭān Salīm undertook the renovation of the Mosque's building and covered its porches with the domed roofs which still exist. The construction was completed in the reign of his son, Sulṭān Murād.

In the Saudi Period

In 1955 orders were issued to move all machinery and equipment used in the expansion of the Mosque of the Prophet to Mecca to start the expansion project of the Holy Mosque.

Within the same year placing the cornerstone of the expansion was celebrated. We should praise God Almighty that this Holy Mosque has been expanded as it never was before. From 29,127 sq. m., its area has been expanded to 160,168 sq. m. The new Mosque is a two-story building whose walls are covered on the inside and the outside with locally made marble. Al-Ṣafā and al-Marwah, between which pilgrims must perambulate, are now within the Mosque. Seven 90-meter high minarets have been added. The Mosque now can accommodate more than 300,000 worshippers. The total cost of the project was approximately 700 million riyals. The old Mosque has been retained and the new Mosque surrounds it making the whole view a wonderful architectural design.

IN SAUDI ARABIA

DRESS:

Conservative dress is necessary for all to visit the surrounding areas of the Ḥaram. Iḥrām, two pieces of towels or white linen sheets, for men and a plain white maxi and a scarf to cover the head for women can be brought with you or these can be bought both in Jedda and Mecca at reasonable rates.

FOOD AND DRINKS:

There are a number of dining facilities available in Jedda. Hotels around Mecca do have restaurants while roasted chicken and other food and drinks can be bought from vending kiosks around Masjid-al-Haram.

HEALTH:

The Ministry of Health in 1969-70 had a budget of some $37 million. In 1970 there were 49 hospitals in the kingdom, 6299 hospital beds, 180 health clinics, and 271 health units. There were more than 3600 medical and para-medical personnel in the kingdom in 1970.

RED CRESCENT SOCIETY:

Equivalent of Red Cross. In 1969 some 139 health personnel including 13 physicians were on the Red Crescent staff.

MEDICAL FACILITIES:

During Ḥajj time free medical facilities are provided to all Ḥājīs by the Saudi Government. In addition mobile health facilities and Ambulances are contributed by all the Muslim countries. Hospital facilities in Saudi Arabia are free for the public.

There are plenty of Drug Stores and Chemists in Jedda, Mecca and Medīna, and unless it is a highly specialized drug, most of the common ones are available without prescription.

POSTAL SERVICE:

In 1970 there were approximately 400 post offices in the kingdom, and some 1400 villages served on 35 delivery routes. Mail boxes, primarily in large cities, are estimated at some tens of thousands.

TELEPHONES:

In 1970, Saudi Arabia had 28,000 telephone lines. A project has just finished at the cost of more than $50 million adding three automatic exchangers and 76,600 new lines in ten major cities.

TELEGRAPH:

Since early 1960's there has been rapid development of telegraph services with the replacement of wire by wireless equipment, the installation of teleprinter equipment at major cities, use of underground cable (linking Jedda, Yanbu and Medīna) and installation of telephone booths.

TRANSPORTATION:

Roads:

In the fiscal year 1969-70, the kingdom spent $118 million in various road and port projects, 81 million dollars on air facilities, and $9.00 million on major roads alone. In 1962, there were 1,950 miles of trunk roads in Saudi Arabia and by 1969 mileage had increased to 4,600 miles. Agricultural roads as such began to be constructed in the year 1964-65 with the completion of 900 miles during that period. By 1969 there were nearly 1,100 miles of agricultural roads.

Ports:

In the year 1969, a total of 8,349 ships called at Saudi Arabian ports, more than a third of them at the eastern port of Ras Tanura. For the Red Sea ports, Jedda handled the most ships reflecting the pilgrimage situation and general trade demands of Ḥijāz.

Airports:

Saudi Arabian Airline traffic has shown a dramatic increase in the period 1969-70. In terms of seat miles produced, the rise has been from 160 million to over 700 million. There are major airports at Medīna, Jedda, Riyāḍ, and Dhahrān, the latter three being International Airports.

Railroads:

The railroad from Damascus to Baghdād was destroyed during the first world war. It is deserted now. In late 1940, a railway line was completed between Dammām and Riyāḍ, a distance of 370 miles and is still operative. Between 1960-69 the amount of freight hauled declined from 140 million ton miles to 27 million ton miles. The actual number of passengers carried increased during this period from 58,000 in 1960 to 115,000 in 1969 and actual tonnage carried from 721,000 to 941,000 representing overall increase in personal and economic activity in the eastern sector of Saudi Arabia.

NEWSPAPERS:

Organized under the Ministry of Information, there are at present about 10 daily and weekly newspapers in the kingdom. Arab News and Saudi Gazzette both from Jedda cater to the needs of English reading people. In addition, most of the booksellers carry imported American, British, French and German magazines and Daily Newspapers.

CUSTOMS DUTY & IMPORTS:

3% minimum duty payable on all imports. Machinery, Personal effects, Gold and Silver coins, Jewelry & currency and display merchandise is exempt from this.

The following goods can not be imported into Saudi Arabia:

1. Articles contrary to Islāmic religion or culture
2. Alcoholic drinks of any kind, and any article containing in whole or in part of heroin, morphia, cocaine, hashish, opium or any other narcotic substance except those imported under license for medicinal purposes.
3. Arms, ammunition, war material etc.
4. Articles of food for human consumption found to be unfit or injurious to human health
5. Plants or animals, or animal skins or parts that do not carry a certificate from the authorities that they are free of disease.
6. Hunting arms that do not carry the appropriate license.
7. Articles made in or shipped from occupied Palestine (Israēl).

TIME:

Arabic Time:

The clock is set to zero (12 hours) at sunset every day. The time of sunrise therefore is irrevelant in practice. Arabic time is kept for all prayers and by the businessmen, also.

Sun Times:

This is merely Arabic time plus or minus six hours. It is used by some Europeans and other expatriates. Sunset is at 6 O'Clock. GMT + 3. This is based on local time anywhere else. It is three hours later than Greenwich Mean Time.

GMT:

Saudi Arabian Airlines, their timetable and some of their employees use GMT, the same time as at Greenwich (England).

A table of Prayer Times in Arabic is available in Stationary shops.

SHOPPING:

It is true that you can buy any thing in Jedda. There are all kind of stores offering a variety of goods at very reasonable prices due to low customs duty and strict price control by the Government. Souk is a traditional Arab market where you can strike a bargain if you know Arabic or are accompanied by an Arabic speaking friend, preferably a Saudi.

All makes of Cameras, Radios, Cassettes are available in the market. Photographic equipment, most recent like Polaroid and films for the same, are readily available in all major cities at very reasonable prices. Electrical household goods, stationary items, typewriters etc are readily available and may cost anything from 10-50% more than what one will pay in UK or USA.

FOOD:

Food is sold in the open market, both fresh and canned qualities are available. There are supermarkets in all major cities and products from all over the world except those from Communist countries (and Israel) are easily available. Imported fine quality Cheese, Lamb, Beef, Chicken (both fresh & frozen) can be bought. All kind of baby food and diapers etc, are also available in any quantity

CLOTHES:

A wide choice, rather expensive, is available for the family both for the summer and winter. A shirt may be purchased from 10 rials to 75 rials and a pair of trousers from 35 rials to 170 rials.

CARS:

According to Saudi Law, one must have a valid Saudi Driver's Licence to drive in Saudi Arabia. It is therefore not advisable to take a chance because it will be a violation of the law.

TAXIS:

The cheapest mode of transportation in the city premises. The rates are fixed by the Government at 3 rials per trip. From a foreigner they may charge 5 rials within the city limits. Airport charges and late night charges are always more. It is advisable to fix the rate with the driver before entering the taxi.

Service taxis are older models and cost only a few Qursh. They run on fixed routes and between fixed points. The buses are Volkswagon or similar mini-buses holding ten or more. They cost a standard 4 Qursh in Jedda. The bus station is near the Post Office.

A seat in a service taxi to Mecca costs SR 10 and to Medina upto SR 30.00 The prices are usually doubled in peak hours and during the Ḥajj season. A taxi will charge about SR 35 for taking pilgrims around for Ziārạ both in Mecca and Medīna. It is cheaper to get 4-5 persons in a Taxi and share the fare. Usually the taxi driver accepts 10-15% tip, with thanks.

ELECTRICITY SUPPLY:

Nominal supply voltage is 110 V (60 cycles) and 220 (50 cycles), but it fluctuates rather more than most European supplies around these values, perhaps by as much as 15%.

COST OF LIVING:

Due to inflation round the world, Saudi Arabia has also been affected although not to the same extent due to strict government controls. Food is still cheaper because it is heavily subsidised by the Government and there is strict control on rents, taxi fares and gasoline prices. On the average a family of four in an average size city can live on between 3-4 thousand rials. This covers the basic minimum necessities of life.

Residential quarters are available at rents of not less than 1000 Rials per month for a one bedroom apartment. This does not include services and usually one year's advance is expected. No maintenance is provided for the house.

Rial is the minimum possible unit for buying any item or for a tip.

COST OF VARIOUS COMMODITIES:

			Riyals
Rice (Kilo packed)			2½ – 4
Milk – 1 litre.			3.00
Eggs – Dozen			7.00
Meat	Beef	Kilo	18.00
	Lamb	Kilo	15.00
	Chicken	Kilo	10.00
Potatoes		Kilo	4.00
Tomatoes		Kilo	4.00
Condensed Milk			3.00
Sugar (Kilo)			1.50
Oranges (Kilo)			3.00
Apples (Kilo)			5.00
Grapes (Kilo)			7.00
Cauliflower (Kilo)			5.00
Beans (Kilo)			4.00

Carrots (Kilo)	5.00
Cucumber (Kilo)	5.00
Cheese (Kilo)	12.50
Lettuce (Kilo)	5.00
Crisco (Shortening)	8.00
Vegetable Oil (Gal)	20.00
Fruit Juice (3 lb)	4.50
Cigarettes (Packet of 20's)	1.50
Bread Loaf	1.00

and Arabic bread is sold at a controlled rate of 8 pieces for one Rial. These prices are based on an average of 4 seasons. There are seasonal variations and the prices are governed by the general economic rule of supply and demand as anywhere else in the world. The increase in prices with time is inevitable.

CLIMATE:

Jedda is very very hot. Visitors arriving by Air will feel it immediately on stepping down from the plane. Even in winter (December to February), the temperature does not drop below 60°F., and a light weight tropical suit is more than enough.

During the summer, temperatures often exceed 100°F, a jacket is intolerable. A simple shirt and that too of cotton is the most comfortable thing to wear. Pants of trousers of light weight cotton are also desirable. Nights are usually pleasant and in summer a shirt is enough. In winter one may need a sleeveless sweater or a medium warm winter suit.

Maximum temperature in Jedda and Medina is 100° and 80°F during summer while it drops to 39 and 43 degrees, respectively, during the winter season.

DISTANCE BETWEEN CITIES

From	To (Kilometres) Jedda	Mecca	Medīna
Jedda	—	72	424
Mecca	72	—	447
Medīna	424	447	—

PUBLIC HOLIDAYS

Friday is weekly day of rest and worship. The Hijra Calendar provides for two government holidays

1. From end of Ramaḍān to the beginning of Shawwāl .... 2nd week of September, 77
2. From 5th to 15th of Dhul-Ḥijja .... 3rd week of November, 77

These are only three to five days long respectively in the private sector.

WORKING HOURS

Government Office hours are 8:00 am to 12.00 noon and then from 4.00 pm to 6.00 pm.

Banks

8.00 am to 12.00 noon (till 12.30 on Thursdays) Some banks also open for a couple of hours in the afternoon

Shops

8.00 am to 12.00 noon
4.00 pm to 9.00 pm.

During Hajj season in Mecca, Medīna and Jedda, shops keep late hours for the convenience of the Pilgrims.

Best months to perform 'Umra are December, January, March to May, and September or October; the last two months are pretty busy because the Pilgrims start coming in but one really enjoys the 'Umra in the Month of Ramaḍān, the blessed one.

CHAPTER TWO

INTRODUCTION

بِسْمِ اللّٰهِ الرَّحْمٰنِ الرَّحِيْمِ

نَحْمَدُهٗ وَنُصَلِّيْ عَلٰى رَسُوْلِهِ الْكَرِيْمِ

ḤAJJ, THE FIFTH PILLAR OF ISLĀM:

To perform Ḥajj is the fifth pillar of Islām. It is obligatory for those Muslims who can afford the journey to Mecca once in a life-time. It is performed within the five days of the 2nd week of the 12th month, Dhul-Ḥijja of the Islāmic calendar.The lesser pilgrimage "'Umra" can be performed at any time of the year.

The history of the ceremonies of Ḥajj goes back to the beginning of time for man on Earth, and will go on till the end of time. It was first when Adam and Eve were asked to leave Paradise and descend to Earth, that they were asked to make a Shrine on Earth similar to the one in the Heavens. The Shrine in the Heavens is known as Bait-ul-Ma'mūr, and around it the angels circumambulate and worship Allāh, the Most Glorified, day and night.

The site chosen for the Shrine to be built on Earth was Mecca. This is clearly indicated in the Holy Qur'ān itself:

إِنَّ أَوَّلَ بَيْتٍ وُّضِعَ لِلنَّاسِ لَلَّذِىْ بِبَكَّةَ مُبٰرَكًا (آلِ عمران)

Thus was the first House of Allāh, the Ka'ba built by Adam with the help of the Angel Jibrīl, who brought a stone from Paradise and embedded it in the corner of the Holy Shrine. This stone was bright in the beginning, but with time it lost its lustre and now looks black, and is known as "The Black Stone", or Ḥajr-al-Aswad. The circumambulation of the Ka'ba is started by kissing this Black Stone.

When Adam finished building the House, Angel Jibrīl taught him the ceremonies, by the will of Allāh, of circumambulating the Ka'ba. This was to be in the most befitting manner to the Glory of Allāh.

The Ka'ba

Adam and Eve were separated in the beginning, but Allāh's Mercy was invoked by Adam's entreaties and Eve was made to join him at the top of a hill in the valley of 'Arafāt. This hill, since then, is known as Jabal-ur-Raḥma, the Mount of Mercy. Eve also joined in the ceremonies of Ḥajj of the Holy House. As Adam and Eve discovered and knew each other in the valley, it is called 'Arafāt meaning recognition or knowledge. To-day in the fashion of Adam, people stand in the same valley and invoke Allāh's Mercy, and it is the greatest Rukn or fundamental of Ḥajj. This valley is located about 15 miles to the East of Mecca.

Adam and Eve spent the whole day standing here in 'Arafāt, in a state of extreme humility, gratitude and awe and did nothing but worship their Creator. This is what is done to-day by the Pilgrims and is known as standing in 'Arafāt, or Waqūf-e-'Arafāt. Adam and Eve, then moved to Muzdalifa, the place between Minā and 'Arafāt, where they spent the night in remembrance of Allāh. Then they came to Minā and went to Mecca to perform the circumambulation of the House of the Almighty, to express their gratitude to Allāh. Later, the Ka'ba built by Adam was destroyed by the Storm of Noah, only a heap remained.

Prophet Ibrāhīm

Then came the time, when recognition of Allāh by the human intellect dawned upon mankind.

About two thousand B.C., Prophet Ibrāhīm was born. At that time the Babylonian Empire was on its zenith. The people had forgotten all about the Ka'ba and Allāh's unity and were worshipping their own man-made idols. Prophet Ibrāhīm started asking questions about the Deity. The eternal quest of the human intellect for the ultimate truth had begun. (See Qur'ān, 2:258-261 and 6:76-83). As a consequence he deviated from the path of the idolators and was guided to the straight path, the path which led to Allāh alone. He was known as "Musliman Haneefan" (The surrendered one, the deviated one). He was asked to migrate and came to Egypt. Here the King of Egypt gave his daughter Hagar (some authorities say she was a

The Holy Mosque with Mas'a in the Foreground

slave girl) to be brought up and taught in the good family of Prophet Ibrāhīm. His wife Sāra took the girl and looked after her. Sāra had no children, so on her insistence, Prophet Ibrāhīm married Hagar, to have an offspring.

Prophet Isma'il

On supplication by Ibrāhīm, Lady Hagar gave birth to a son named Ismā'īl. (Long after this Lady Sāra also gave birth to a son, Prophet Isḥāq). No one knows what went on, though some blame the first wife's envy, but we know that all acts of Prophet Ibrāhīm's were acts of faith. By the command of Allāh, Prophet Ibrāhīm was guided to go to Mecca with his son Ismā'īl and the wife and leave them there.

As he left the son and mother in the arid lands, he offered a supplication for their safety and departed.

> "O our Lord! I have made some of my offspring to dwell in a Valley without cultivation, by Thy Sacred House; in order, O Our Lord! that they may establish regular prayer. So fill the hearts of some among men with love towards them, and feed them with Fruits so that they may give thanks!" (Sūra Ibrāhīm: 37)

This was an act of great faith in his Creator, only He will be trusted, they all belong to Him.

Ṣafā and Marwa

After the departure of the father, mother and son were left alone in the arid land. Leaving the infant close to the heaped sign of the Holy House, the desperate mother went in search of water for him. She ran to the top of the hill, known as ṢAFĀ, beseeching and entreating Allāh's mercy on them. From the top of this hill she thought she saw a lake in the valley. She ran towards it with restless steps, only to find that it was a mirage. She then climbed atop the second neighbouring hill known as MARWA, to look around for water. But anxiety for her child brought her back to the valley. She ran between these two hills seven times in desperation, supplicating Allāh:

The Stairs to Zamzam Well With Pilgrims at Prayer

رَبِّ اغْفِرْ وَارْحَمْ وَاعْفُ وَتَكَرَّمْ وَتَجَاوَزْ عَمَّا تَعْلَمُ إِنَّكَ
تَعْلَمُ مَا لَا نَعْلَمُ أَنْتَ اللهُ الْأَعَزُّ الْأَكْرَمُ۔

O Lord, forgive, have mercy, ignore our sins, of course Thou knowest what we know not - Only Thou art the Holy, Merciful"

This is the origin of Sa'ī, "the struggle", reminding us of a mother's struggle in search of Allāh's mercy, and bounty. Again this act of trust in Allāh, by a desperate, lonely woman, is so loved by Allāh that it has to be revived by thousands of Pilgrims every year, and what a revival!

Well of Zamzam

The supplications of the mother were accepted, when she was looking around from the top for the seventh time. She saw water oozing out of a hole in the ground near her child. Seeing the precious water escaping into the surrounding sand, she cried "Zumi, yā Mubāraka!" Stop there, O blessed water of Divine Providence". A pool formed as she approached it, and this was ZAMZAM's beginning. This indeed was to be "Mubāraka" the blessed water for all to come and drink it, and thus cause an arid land to be inhabited and to bear fruits. The supplication of a parent was answered with the beginning of Mubāraka the ZAMZAM. Since then, people, wandering tribes came and seeing water settled and thrived, finding the answer to their own struggles. The Pilgrims to-day from far and near drink from this blessed well of ZAMZAM, which never ceased to flow!

The Building of the Ka'ba by Prophet Ibrāhīm

The infant Ismāīl grew into manhood, married and settled and was loved and cherished by his people. One day the father, Prophet Ibrāhīm, came back, and found that his prayers had been answered. But the reason he had come back was to fulfil

the command of His Creator to build the House again. Only this time, the ceremonies of worship will be taught never to be forgotten. The people will come, for the mellinia to come, "from far and near and on lean animals", and perform these ceremonies taught in the guided manner.

وَإِذْ بَوَّأْنَا لِإِبْرَاهِيمَ مَكَانَ الْبَيْتِ أَنْ لَا تُشْرِكْ بِي شَيْئًا
وَطَهِّرْ بَيْتِيَ لِلطَّائِفِينَ وَالْقَائِمِينَ وَالرُّكَّعِ السُّجُودِ وَأَذِّنْ
فِي النَّاسِ بِالْحَجِّ يَأْتُوكَ رِجَالًا وَعَلَىٰ كُلِّ ضَامِرٍ يَأْتِينَ
مِنْ كُلِّ فَجٍّ عَمِيقٍ، لِيَشْهَدُوا مَنَافِعَ لَهُمْ وَيَذْكُرُوا اسْمَ اللَّهِ
فِي أَيَّامٍ مَعْلُومَاتٍ عَلَىٰ مَا رَزَقَهُمْ مِنْ بَهِيمَةِ الْأَنْعَامِ. فَكُلُوا
مِنْهَا وَأَطْعِمُوا الْبَائِسَ الْفَقِيرَ. ثُمَّ لْيَقْضُوا تَفَثَهُمْ وَلْيُوفُوا
نُذُورَهُمْ وَلْيَطَّوَّفُوا بِالْبَيْتِ الْعَتِيقِ (الحج ٢٧-٢٩)

"Behold! when we gave the Site to Abraham of the (sacred) House. Associate not anything (in worship) with Me and Sanctify My House for those who compass it round, or stand up, or bow, or prostrate themselves (in prayer). And proclaim the Pilgrimage among men; they will come to thee on foot, and (mounted) on every kind of camels (animals), lean on account of Journeys through deep and distant mountain highways: that they may witness the benefits (provided) for them, and celebrate the name of Allāh--------- Let them complete the ceremonies prescribed for them, perform their vows, and circumbulate the "Ancient House". (Holy Qur'ān 22:27-29).

Thus, it was to be one of the obligations in surrendering man's will to Allāh's. Only He was to be worshipped. These ordained ceremonies were never to be confused. Every step was clearly taught. These ceremonies were repeated in the perfect manner of the guided ones, by the Seal of the Prophets, Prophet

Abraham's Shrine in the Holy Mosque of Mecca

Muḥammad (peace be upon him), only fourteen centuries ago. Every detail of the etiquette of the worship was thus safeguarded with faith and truth.

Maqām—e—Ibrāhīm

As the Ka'ba was being built, the builder, Prophet Ibrāhīm, stood on a standing place, and raised the foundations helped by his son, Prophet Ismā'īl. This was a landmark not only on the standing place, of a footprint of the builder, but a landmark in history. From now on only Allāh's sovereignty will prevail. The place of Ibrāhīm where he stood, can still be seen near the Ka'ba and is known as Maqām-e-Ibrāhīm. While the walls were being raised, so was the spirit of mankind, for there came the words in supplication from the depth of the human soul, for the benefit of the human race. The son and the father prayed to their Creator.

وَإِذْ يَرْفَعُ إِبْرَاهِيمُ الْقَوَاعِدَ مِنَ الْبَيْتِ وَإِسْمٰعِيلُ ط رَبَّنَا
تَقَبَّلْ مِنَّا ط إِنَّكَ أَنْتَ السَّمِيعُ الْعَلِيمُ ط رَبَّنَا وَاجْعَلْنَا مُسْلِمَيْنِ لَكَ
وَمِنْ ذُرِّيَّتِنَا أُمَّةً مُسْلِمَةً لَكَ ط وَأَرِنَا مَنَاسِكَنَا وَتُبْ عَلَيْنَا
إِنَّكَ أَنْتَ التَّوَّابُ الرَّحِيمُ ط رَبَّنَا وَابْعَثْ فِيهِمْ رَسُولًا مِنْهُمْ
يَتْلُوا عَلَيْهِمْ آيٰتِكَ وَيُعَلِّمُهُمُ الْكِتٰبَ وَالْحِكْمَةَ وَيُزَكِّيهِمْ
إِنَّكَ أَنْتَ الْعَزِيزُ الْحَكِيمُ ط (البقرة ١٢٧ - ١٢٩)

"And remember when Ibrāhīm and Ismā'īl raised The foundations of the House (with this prayer): "Our Lord accept from us (this service), for Thou art the All-Hearing, The All-Knowing".

Our Lord make us surrender bowing to Thy will And of our progeny, an Umma (of faith) Muslims, bowing to Thy will. And show us our places for the celebrations of (due) ceremonies, and

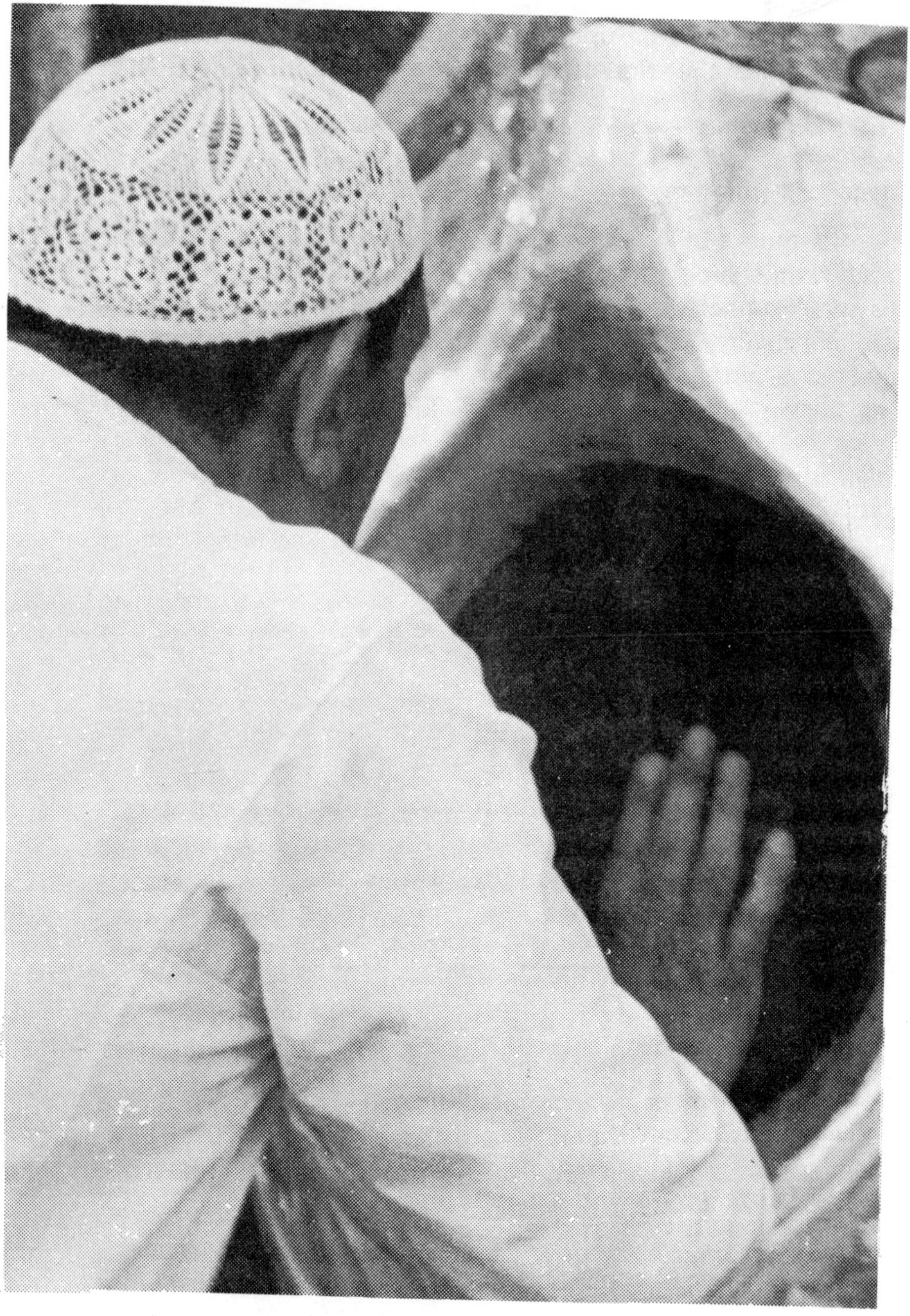

Hajar-al-Aswad (The Black Stone)

turn unto us (in Mercy). For Thou art the Oft-Returning Most Merciful.

"Our Lord! Send among these people (the Muslims) an Apostle of their own, who shall rehearse Thy Signs to them and instruct them, in Scripture and Wisdom, And sanctify them, for Thou art the Exalted-in Might, The Wise."

(Qur'ān: 2:127-129)

This was granted in the time to come, and fourteen centuries ago, there emerged these people, "the Umma", who took the responsibility to maintain that Allāh is the only Ultimate Truth.

To maintain equality of man and justice, and Discernment between right and wrong there came our Prophet (peace be upon him) who initiated this "Umma". This Umma is not a particular tribe, race, colour or creed but are those people, of any colour tribe and race, from all over the surface of the Earth, who submit their will to Allāh alone, and follow His guidance. As is clearly indicated in the above Ayas, the Manasik or the ceremonies of Pilgrimage were clearly taught to Ibrāhim and Ismā'īl.

Thus the ceremonies which the Pilgrims perform to-day are the same as those guided by Allāh to the Prophets. This is an immense experience in faith and serenity. The real test of Prophet Ibrāhīm's faith was yet to come. The father, this time, was asked to offer to Allāh a sacrifice, of that he loved the most.

This was the test of submission, of intellectual faith in the Ultimate Sovereignty and Truth of the Creator. Fortunately the human intellect did not fail. "The deviated one, The Ḥanīf," knew it had to be his son. And what a son, who surrendered to the Divine wish without a moment's hesitation; such was the perfection of their faith; such was the dignity of total submission. The son was brought to Minā to be offered as a sacrifice. It was here, that the devil came to tempt, in the name of paternal love, to tempt to disobey. This was only to know that the man's love for his Creator was greater. It was at this stage of human submission to Almighty Allāh that Ibrāhīm (peace be

Bab Multazim

upon him) took pebbles and cast them at the Devil, with the words:

بِسْمِ اللهِ اَللهُ اَكْبَرُ ۔ رَغْمَ الِلشَّيْطَانِ

"In the name ofAllāh, Allāh is Great. This casting is to condemn Shaiṭān."
This was to choose between Allāh and Evil.

This act of faith is part of the ceremonies of Pilgrimage today, and is called Ramī-al-Jamarāt. (To cast pebbles at Shaiṭān).

This story of complete submission and sacrifice is told in the Holy Qur'ān: (37:104-111).

Thus, all those, who visit the House of Allāh repeat these acts of faith, to commemorate the conquest of truth, in the name of Allāh. Of course "The Truth has (now) arrived and Falsehood perished, for Falsehood is the fleeing thing."

This is the Ḥajj and this is the story of Ḥajj.

The Holy Prophet's Pilgrimage
"Ḥajj-at–al–Wadā' "

In the 10th year of Hijra, Prophet Muḥammad (peace be upon him) decided to go for Pilgrimage to Mecca. The news travelled fast and soon a huge number of people, poured in to join him. On 26th of Dhul-Qa'da, on a Monday, the Prophet, offered Zuhr prayer in Medīna. Before the Prayer, in a Khuṭba (sermon) he expounded and explained to people the ceremonies of Pilgrimage. After the prayer, he set forth for the journey to Mecca, (between Ẓuhr and 'Aṣr prayers). When he arrived at Dhul-Ḥulaifa, he offered shortened prayer and spent the night there. Here he completed five prayers. In the morning he took a bath, and adopted Iḥrām, with two linen sheets. He then mounted his camel and recited for the first time, the Talbiya:

لَبَّيْكَ ۔ اَللّٰهُمَّ لَبَّيْكَ ط لَا شَرِيْكَ لَكَ لَبَّيْكَ ط

اِنَّ الْحَمْدَ وَالنِّعْمَةَ لَكَ وَالْمُلْكَ ط لَا شَرِيْكَ لَكَ

Here I come, O Allāh!
Here I come,
Here I am, Thou art without partner,
Here I am,
Praise and blessings are Thine, and the kingdom (of Heaven and Earth)
Thou art without Partner

Labbaik Allāhumma Labbaik,
Labbaik lā sharīka laka labbaik,
Inn-al-ḥamda wan-ni'mata laka wal-mulk,
Lā sharīka lak.

He then recited Talbiya many times, till he reached Mecca. Here he stayed in the valley of "Ṭuā". This was the 3rd of Dhul-Ḥijja. Next morning after Fajr prayer, he took a bath, and entered Mecca, with Pilgrims. As he first glanced at the Ka'ba, he pronounced Takbīr, "Allāh-u-Akbar" اَللّٰهُ اَكْبَرُ and recited:

اَللّٰهُمَّ اَنْتَ السَّلَامُ وَمِنْكَ السَّلَامُ وَاِلَيْكَ يَرْجِعُ السَّلَامُ فَحَيِّنَا
رَبَّنَا بِالسَّلَامِ وَاَدْخِلْنَا دَارَ السَّلَامِ ط تَبَارَكْتَ رَبَّنَا وَتَعَالَيْتَ
يَا ذَا الْجَلَالِ وَالْاِكْرَامِ ط اَللّٰهُمَّ زِدْ بَيْتَكَ هٰذَا تَعْظِيْمًا وَّتَشْرِيْفًا
وَزِدْ مِنْ تَعْظِيْمِهٖ وَتَشْرِيْفِهٖ مِنْ حَجَّتِهٖ وَعُمْرَتِهٖ ط

O Allāh! Thou art the peace and from Thee cometh peace, and to Thee returneth peace. Let us live, our Lord, in peace! and let us enter the Paradise. O Our Lord! you are the Blessed and the High, the Lord of Glory and Honour. O Allāh! Increase this Thy House in honour and dignity and increase its honour and dignity more with its Ḥajj and its'Umra

Allāhumma ant-as-salāmu wa mink-as-salāmu wa ilaika yarja'is-salāmu, fa-ḥayyinā Rabbanā bis-salāmi wa adkhilnā dar-as- salāmi tabārakta Rabbanā wa ta'ālaita yā dhal-Jalāl-i-wal-Ikrām. Allāhumma zid baitaka hādha ta'ẓīman wwa tashrīfan wwa zid min ta'ẓīmihī wa tastrīfihī min Hajjatihī wa 'Umratihī.

He then entered the mosque and went in front of Ḥajr-al-Aswad. After Istilām, he started circumambulating the Ka'ba in broad day light. In the first three circuits of the House, he walked swiftly, with short steps and shaking his shoulders like a soldier in a battlefield. (This is known as Ramal). He had his top sheet, such that it covered only his left shoulder and, went under the right arm. The rest of the circuits were completed at a slow gait. He had a stick in his hand and used to touch Ḥajr-al-Aswad with it sometimes when he came near it. Sometimes he kissed the Black stone.

After the completion of Ṭawāf, he came to Maqām-e-Ibrāhīm, and offered two Rak'at prayer. In the first Rak'a, he recited "Sūra Alkāfirūn" and in the second one "Sūra Ikhlāṣ". After the prayer of Ṭawāf, he went back to the Black Stone for Istilām.

He then went to perform Sa'ī between Ṣafā and Marwa.

On the 8th of Dhul-Ḥijja, the Prophet (peace be upon him) proceeded to Minā and stayed there that day and night. He offered five prayers in Minā from Ẓuhr of 8th to Fajr of the 9th day of Dhul-Ḥijja. He spent the night of the 9th of Dhul-Ḥijja, at Minā, on the way to 'Arafāt. It was here in Minā, that the Holy Prophet had first been acknowledged publicly, by twelve persons and in the following year by twenty.

On the morning of the 9th day of Dhul-Ḥijja, after sunrise he departed from Minā and continued on his way. At the entrance to the valley of 'Arafāt, (between Minā and 'Arafāt), he dismounted in the place called Namira. Here he took a bath before noon, and went to 'Arafāt. The whole valley of 'Arafāt was filled with throngs of people. Every one was busy reciting. Talbiya, Takbīr and Tahlil. There was a crowd of twenty-four thousand people according to some writers. Rasūl-Allāh, then mounted a camel and delivered his Khuṭba (the sermon of this Khutba established and emphasized the fundamental teachings of the Holy Qur'ān, and is well remembered for its beauty of eloquence, speech and its appeal.)

"O people! I believe that you may not gather like this again with me in this place. O people! your blood, your possessions, and your honour, is forbidden (ḥarām) on each other, like on this day, this city, this month is forbidden to you (for these matters). You will soon be in the presence of the Creator, and He will ask you about your actions. Be warned, do not deviate from the right path, after me, that you start cutting each other's throat. People, every bit of Ignorance, I trample here below my feet. I sweep away all quarrels, bloodshed, done in the days of Ignorance. The first bloodshed of my family, I forgive, of Ibn-Rabī'a. I destroy the habit of taking Ribā (the interest) of Ignorance. My clan's first Ribā has here been forfeited, that was of 'Abbās-bin-'Abdul Muttalib.

O people! Have fear of Allāh regarding your wives. You have made them your wives in the name of Allāh and the responsibility He bestowed on you regarding them. With the words of Allāh, their bodies have been made Ḥalāl to you. Your right on them is this that they will not permit another man to their bed. Their rights on you are that you feed and support them well.

O people! I am leaving one thing among you that if you hold it well, you will not be led astray - that is the Book of Allāh, the Holy Qur'ān

O people! There will not come any Prophet after me nor any other Umma will be raised. Listen carefully, that worship only Allāh, and offer prayers five times a day, keep fast for a month annually. Pay Zakāt wholeheartedly and cheerfully. Perform Pilgrimage to the House of Allāh, and obey those who are rulers among you. The reward of all this is that you will enter Paradise.

O people! On the Judgment Day, if you were asked about me, what will you say.?

The people proclaimed "We witness that you have conveyed His Message to us, and fulfilled your obligations as a Messenger, and told us the difference between Right and Wrong"

At this he raised his first finger of Shahāda and said "O Allah ! Listen to this and be a witness." Then he asked those who were near to him to repeat these words to those who were not present here."

As soon as he finished his sermon, the last Aya was revealed to him, there in the valley of 'Arafāt, "Today I have completed your Dīn (religion) for you and bestowed on you (the Umma) all my favours, and chose for you Islām as your Din (religion)."

After this, the Holy Prophet dismounted the camel and the distinguished companion, Bilāl, called the Ādhān. The Ẓuhr and 'Aṣr prayers were then offered together. He then climbed on his camel and on Jabal-ar-Raḥma, facing the Ka'ba offered supplications and entreaties to Allāh. In 'Arafāt he raised his hands upto his chest, and cried and begged to Allāh like a destitute person.

After sunset, he started for Muzdalifa, and kept the rope of the camel so tight that it walked very slow. He said to the people, "Walk slowly and humbly, as running and hurrying is impolite in front of Allāh." Talbiya was continuously recited.

When the Holy Prophet arrived in Muzdalifa, Ādhān was again pronounced and Maghrib was offered before dismantling the caravans. After Maghrib, the animals were unloaded, and with a second Iqāma, the prayer of 'Ishā was offered. There was no call of Ādhān for 'Ishā. No Nafl prayers were offered between Maghrib and 'Ishā. In the early hours of the morning before dawn, the Holy Prophet came near Mash'ar-al-Ḥarām and kept busy in invocations, Takbīr and Tasbīh. Near sunrise, he asked one of the Companions to pick up some pebbles, and cleansed them himself, saying "keep pebbles for throwing (at the devil) and avoid useless pursuits in life, other nations were destroyed because of their useless pursuits."

When he arrived in Minā, he stood near Jamrat-ul-'Aqaba for Ramī (to throw pebbles at the place where the devil tempted Prophet Ibrāhīm). He threw pebbles one by one sitting on the back of the camel. With the first throw he discontinued reciting Talbiya, and recited Takbīr with each throw. At this moment, Bilāl (Allāh be pleased with him) was holding the rope of the camel and 'Uthmān bin Zaid was making shade over the Holy Prophet with an umbrella. Here he gave another Khuṭba (sermon) in which he explained the ceremony of Naḥr (sacrifice). His voice was heard in every tent around him. This was one of his miracles. He then taught them Arkān or Ceremonies of Ḥajj, emphasizing to the people to follow the Qur'ān, and earn from him, in case he may not be with them any more.

He then collected the Emigrants and Anṣār together and warned them not to turn away from Islām, and to avoid killing each other.

He came to the place of sacrifice. After the sacrifice, he asked his cousin 'Alī (may Allāh be pleased with him) to distribute meat, skin etc., among the poor.

"All Mina is Manḥar, and all highways from Mecca are all Manhar", thus specifying the places of sacrifice.

After that, Mamer bin 'Abdullāh came and shaved his head. His nails were then trimmed. Before Zawāl time, the Prophet went to Mecca for Ṭawāf-e-Ziyāra, the second most important Rukn of Ḥajj. Here, too, he performed this Tawāf on the back of his camel.

He then came to the well of ZAMZAM. 'Abbas was drawing water from the well, on which he said "If there was no crowd of people, he would have drawn the water himself." He drank the water, standing so that people can see (and learn). He then returned to Minā where he spent the night. Next day, before Ẓuhr prayer, he went to Jamrat-al-Ū'lā, near Masjid-e-Khaif, and threw seven pebbles at it. Reciting Takbīr, he stepped aside and went forward to a place called "Sahl". Facing the Ka'ba, he kept busy in invocations, for a time equal to the recital of the second sūra. Then he went to the middle Jamra and performed Ramī. Again he stepped aside and prayed for a while. Then he went to Jamrat-al-'Aqaba, and performed Ramī at it. At this place the Holy Prophet (peace be upon him) did not stay, but immediately after Ramī went to his tent in Minā. He stayed in Minā, three days. The fourth day after Ẓuhr, Ramī was performed, and he proceeded to Mecca, pausing a little in the valley of Moḥassab. In Mecca he performed the Farewell Ṭawāf, but did not observe Ramal. After the ceremonies of Ḥajj were over, he entered the Bait-Allāh. He offered Fajr prayer in the Ka'ba and recited Sūra "Wattīn" in it. Then he left for al-Madīna-al-Munawwara.

With this introduction, I am presenting this guide for Ḥajj and 'Umra to our brothers and sisters who intend to come to the Holy Land, hoping that it will provide them with all the information necessary to undertake this Sacred Journey and complete all the ceremonies according to the tradition of Prophet Muhammad (peace be upon him).

I pray that Allāh may accept our humble efforts in His way, Āmeen.

آنِيْس دَاوُد مَيتهيُوسْ

August, 1977

Anis Daud Mathews

Pilgrims in Ihram Disembarking at Jedda

CHAPTER THREE

THE PERFORMANCE OF HAJJ

I. **To prepare oneself for the Pilgrimage:**

بِسْمِ اللّٰهِ الرَّحْمٰنِ الرَّحِيْمِ

إِنَّ أَوَّلَ بَيْتٍ وُّضِعَ لِلنَّاسِ لَلَّذِيْ بِبَكَّةَ مُبٰرَكًا وَّهُدًى لِّلْعٰلَمِيْنَ

فِيْهِ اٰيٰتٌ بَيِّنٰتٌ مَّقَامُ إِبْرٰهِيْمَ ۚ وَمَنْ دَخَلَهٗ كَانَ اٰمِنًا ۚ

وَلِلّٰهِ عَلَى النَّاسِ حِجُّ الْبَيْتِ مَنِ اسْتَطَاعَ إِلَيْهِ سَبِيْلًا ۚ وَمَنْ

كَفَرَ فَإِنَّ اللّٰهَ غَنِيٌّ عَنِ الْعٰلَمِيْنَ (اٰل عمران ٩٦ - ٩٧)

'The first House of Worship appointed for mankind was that at Becca (Makkah) – Full of Blessings, and a guidance to all worlds.

In it are signs manifest; (for example the standing-place of Ibrāhīm); whosoever enters it attains security. And Pilgrimage there to (the House of Allāh, the Ka'ba) is a duty men owe to Allāh – Those who can afford the journey thither. As for him who disbelieves, (let him know) that Allāh is above the needs of (all His) creatures."

(Holy Qur'ān 3:96,97)

The above Āyas in the Qur'ān manifest that Pilgrimage to the House of Allāh is obligatory for those believers who can afford the journey, once in a life-time.

A state of mental, material and spiritual preparation is required. One tries to present oneself in the best possible state of purification in front of the Creator during this Holy journey. It is advised that the following deeds should be performed or justified before taking up the blessed journey, so that Allāh's

Pilgrims Arriving at Jedda Airport

blessings and His mercy may be bestowed for the fulfillment of this sacred duty to Him.

1. Begin with repenting and asking forgiveness for your sins and fulfill all human and spiritual obligations. As the Holy Qur'ān says: "O believer, repent in front of Allāh all (of you) together so that you may find salvation."

   The conditions for repentance and its acceptance are:

   (i) To abandon sins
   (ii) To regret sincerely the previous sins
   (iii) To firmly determine to abstain from sins

   The true repentance depends very much on the above conditions, especially on the firm intention never to repeat it.

2. If a creditor is deceased, pay out his claim to his inheritors. If the inheritors are unknown then give it away as a charity or to his lawful relatives. To restore the belongings to the rightful owners is also advisable. Ask forgiveness for inflicting injustice of any kind on a fellow being. If the person is deceased then pray for Allāh's forgiveness for him.

3. The money required to spend on the formalities of Ḥajj should be earned by lawful (Ḥalāl) means. Ḥajj performed with unlawful money is not accepted. The Holy Prophet said "Allāh is Ṭayyab and does not accept anything other than Ṭayyab."

4. One should arrange for the needs and sustenance of one's dependents before departure. Ḥajj is not accepted at the cost of a family member's suffering.

5. One should start on this journey with the exclusive passion to carry out the commands of Allāh and to seek His guidance and pleasure. The sincerity of intention should not be tainted with pretentions. Every action, (even the thoughts) should be performed for Allāh's pleasure and His will. No sense of pride, ostentation, etc. should take away the purity, and humility of the servant to present oneself in front of the Owner of the Worlds.

Pilgrims arriving by Buses

6. Choose pious and learned companions for the journey, so no time is wasted in useless talks. Controlling one's anger and practicising the best possible manners are recommended. Most of one's time should be spent in the mention of Allāh, and prayers. Engaging in light trade for sustenance during the journey is not discouraged.

Since a Pilgrim offers himself before Allāh as a beggar (a servant), his attitude should be that of utmost humility. He is not permitted to comb his hair, or use perfume or decorate himself during Ḥajj. One sees dignitaries, and the poor all garbed in the same simple and humble dress known as 'Iḥrām'. Everyone is the same in the eyes of Allāh, king and slave alike. Only their good deeds and fear of Allāh raises them in His sight.

7. It is not permitted to marry or to propose marriage or assist anyone in this respect during the Ḥajj season. Hunting, and killing is strictly forbidden within the boundary of the Ḥaram, the Holy Qur'ān says:

"O ye who believe, kill not game, while in the sacred precincts, or in pilgrim garb. If any one of you doeth this intentionally, the compensation is an offering brought to the Ka'ba, of a domestic animal, equivalent to the one he killed, as judged by two just men among you: or by way of atonement the feeding of the indigent, or its equivalent in fasts, that he may taste of the penalty of his deeds."

(Al-Mai'da; 98)

According to the Holy Prophet: "There are five creatures which can be killed in the sacred territory of Mecca, and in Iḥram. They are rats, crows, eagles, scorpions or snakes and an attacking dog, or an attacking beast."

8 It is also prohibited to pluck flowers, cut trees and grass or lift any lost thing, unless the intention is to declare so that its owner can be found.

9 Sin in any form, quarrels, disputes, talks on obscene subjects and sexual intercourse are strictly prohibited during the Ḥajj time.

About those who, though having the means, do no perform Ḥajj, the Prophet said: "A person who has the means to meet the expenses and transport by which he could reach the house of Allāh, and even then he does not perform the Ḥajj, then his death under these circumstances is like the death of a Jew or a Christian."

(Bukhāri)

Regarding the reward of Ḥajj, the Prophet said: "The reward of a pious Ḥajj is nothing but Heaven ('Janna') or paradise". (Bukharı & Muslim). By "pious Ḥajj", it is meant that it is free from all kinds of shortcomings. A Ḥajj performed with sincerity according to the injunctions, free from shortcomings, will be accepted by Allāh, the Merciful.

II. THE JOURNEY TO THE SACRED GOAL

Departure from Home:

The prerequisites for Ḥajj, are the following conditions without which Ḥajj cannot be performed. (1) For the intending pilgrim to be a Muslim. (2) To be in the state of Iḥrām. (3) To perform Ḥajj in the same year in which the Iḥrām has been adopted. (4) To perform Ḥajj in the days of Ḥajj. (5) To perform each ceremony in its correct place and in its correct way. (6) The pilgrim should be a sane person. (7) To perform the ceremony himself or herself. (8) To abstain from doing those things which are prohibited while in the state of Ihram. (9) To be an adult.

At the time of leaving the house, you are to offer two Raka't Nafl, if it is not a Makrūh time. In the first Rak'a, recite, after Sūra Fātiḥa, (the opening page of the Holy Qur'ān), Sūra Kāfirūn i.e. "Qul Yā Ayyuhal Kāfirun" and in the second Rak'a recite Sūra Ikhlāṣ "Qul Huwa Allāhu Aḥad". After finishing the prayer, recite Āyat-ul-Kursī and then "Le-ilāf-i-Quraishin". It is better if you entertain the needy or the poor before departure, and give alms.

Pray to Almighty Allāh for help and comfort in the journey and recite the following prayer:

اَللّٰهُمَّ اَنْتَ الصَّاحِبُ فِى السَّفَرِ وَالْخَلِيْفَةُ فِى الْاَهْلِ وَالْمَالِ
اَللّٰهُمَّ اِنَّا نَسْأَلُكَ فِىْ مَسِيْرِنَا هٰذَا الْبِرَّ وَالتَّقْوٰى وَمِنَ الْعَمَلِ
مَا تُحِبُّ وَتَرْضٰى ط اَللّٰهُمَّ اِنَّا نَسْأَلُكَ اَنْ تَطْوِىَ لَنَا الْاَرْضَ
وَتُهَوِّنَ عَلَيْنَا السَّفَرَ وَارْزُقْنَا فِىْ سَفَرِنَا هٰذَا السَّلَامَةَ فِى الْعَقْلِ
وَالدِّيْنِ وَالْبَدَنِ وَالْمَالِ وَالْوَلَدِ ط وَ بَلِّغْنَا حَجَّ بَيْتِكَ
الْحَرَامِ وَزِيَارَةَ نَبِيِّكَ عَلَيْهِ اَفْضَلُ الصَّلٰوةِ وَالسَّلَامِ ط
اَللّٰهُمَّ اِنِّىْ لَمْ اَخْرُجْ اَشَرًا وَّلَا بَطَرًا وَّلَا رِيَاءً وَّلَا سُمْعَةً
بَلْ خَرَجْتُ اِتِّقَاءَ سَخَطِكَ وَابْتِغَاءَ مَرْضَاتِكَ وَقَضَاءً لِفَرْضِكَ
وَاتِّبَاعًا لِسُنَّةِ نَبِيِّكَ مُحَمَّدٍ صَلَّى اللّٰهُ عَلَيْهِ وَسَلَّمَ ط وَشَوْقًا
اِلٰى لِقَائِكَ ط اَللّٰهُمَّ فَتَقَبَّلْ ذَالِكَ وَصَلِّ عَلٰى اَشْرَفِ عِبَادِكَ
سَيِّدِنَا مُحَمَّدٍ وَّاٰلِهٖ وَصَحْبِهٖ اَجْمَعِيْنَ ط

"O Allāh! Thou alone is the Companion in the journey and Thou alone is the Inheritor of my family and property. O Allāh! We seek in this journey from Thee goodness and such action on our part which is dear and acceptable to Thee.

Allāhumma antaṣ-ṣāhibu fis-safar, walkhalīfatu fil-ahli wal-māl. Allāhumma inna nas'aluka fī masīrinā hādhal-birra wat-taqwā wa minal-a'mali mā tuḥibbu wa tarḍā.

O Allāh! We beseech Thee that the distances of earth are reduced for us and make easy the

Allāhumma inna nas'aluka an-taṭ-wiya la-nal-arḍa wa tuhaw-wina 'alaina-ssafara warzuqnā fī safarinā hādh-as-salāmata fil-

journey for us; and grant us in this journey the sustenance of wisdom, faith, body, property and the protection of the children and bring us in safety to Thy Blessed House and to the tomb of Thy Holy Prophet May Allāh's blessings be on him.

'aqli waddīni wal badani wal-māli wal-walad, wa tuballighanā Ḥajja Baitikal Ḥarāmī wa ziārata nabiyyika'alaihi afḍal-uṣ-ṣalawāti wassalām.

O Allāh! I have not taken this journey for pride and arrogance, neither have I started for show or popularity but to save myself from Thy displeasure, to seek Thy delight, to perform that which Thou hast enjoined, to follow the Sunna of Thy Prophet and with the desire to meet Thee. O Allāh, therefore, accept this prayer and salutation to the best of the creation, Your Prophet Muḥammad and his offspring and all of his companions.

Allāhumma innī lam akhruj asharan-wwa lā baṭaran-wwa lā riyā'an-wwa lā suma'ta. Bal kharajtu ittiqā'a sakhaṭika wa-btighā'a marḍātika wa qadā'an lifarḍika wa ittibā'an li sunnati nabiyyika Muḥammad. Ṣallallāhu 'alaihi wa sallam wa shawqan ilā liqā'ika, Allāhumma fataqabbal dhālika wa ṣalli 'alā ashraf 'ibādika sayyidinā Muḥammad wa ālihī wa ṣaḥbihī ajma'īn.

After leaving the prayer mat, recite the following:

اَللّٰهُمَّ بِكَ انْتَشَرْتُ وَاِلَيْكَ تَوَجَّهْتُ وَبِكَ اعْتَصَمْتُ وَعَلَيْكَ

تَوَكَّلْتُ ط اَللّٰهُمَّ اَنْتَ ثِقَتِيْ وَاَنْتَ رِجَائِيْ ط اَللّٰهُمَّ اكْفِنِيْ

مَا اَهَمَّنِيْ وَمَا لَا اَهْتَمُّ بِهٖ وَمَا اَنْتَ اَعْلَمُ بِهٖ مِنِّيْ عَزَّ جَارُكَ

وَلَا اِلٰهَ غَيْرُكَ ط اَللّٰهُمَّ زَوِّدْنِي التَّقْوٰى وَاغْفِرْ لِيْ ذُنُوْبِيْ

وَوَجِّهْنِيْ اِلَى الْخَيْرِ اَيْنَمَا تَوَجَّهْتُ ط اَللّٰهُمَّ اِنِّيْ اَعُوْذُ بِكَ

مِنْ وَعْثَاءِ السَّفَرِ وَكَاٰبَةِ الْمُنْقَلَبِ وَالْحَوْرِ بَعْدَ الْكَوْرِ

وَسُوْءِ الْمَنْظَرِ فِي الْاَهْلِ وَالْمَالِ ط

"O Allāh! I have undertaken this journey solely with Thy help and I have turned my face only towards Thee. Thee alone is my Protector and on Thee alone i depend. O Allāh! In Thee alone I have confidence and Thee alone is my help. O Allāh! Be sufficient for me in all my problems and in all such issues which Thou knowest better than me. One who comes under Thine protection is the one who succeeds. There is none to be adored except Thee. O Allāh! Bless me with the gift of piety and forgive sins; and in whichever direction I turn my face, Thou turneth me towards goodness. O Allāhl I seek Thy protection from the hardships of the journey, to and fro. O Allāh! I seek Thy protection from poverty after prosperity and seek Thy refuge against the calamity which my family and property may suffer."

Allāhumma bika antashartu wa ilaika tawajjahtu wa bika a'taṣamtu wa'alaika tawakkaltu Allāhumma anta thiqatī wa anta rijā'ī, Allāhumma'kfinī mā ahammanī wa mā lā ahtammu bihī wa mā anta a'lamu bihī minnī 'azzajāruka wa lā ilāha ghairuk, Allāhumma zawwidnittaqwā waghfirlī dhunūbī wa wajjihnī ilalkhairi ainamā tawajjahtu, Allāhumma innī a'ūdhu bika min wighthā'issafari wa kābat'il'munqalabi walḥauri ba'dalkauri wa sū'ilmanẓari fil ahli walmāl.

After reaching the door, recite Sūra "Innā anzalnāhu. . . .
When you come out of the house, recite:

بِسْمِ اللّٰهِ وَلَا حَوْلَ وَلَا قُوَّةَ اِلَّا بِاللّٰهِ الْعَلِيِّ الْعَظِيْمِ ط
تَوَكَّلْتُ عَلَى اللّٰهِ ط اَللّٰهُمَّ وَفِّقْنِىْ لِمَا تُحِبُّ وَ تَرْضٰى ط
وَاحْفَظْنِىْ مِنَ الشَّيْطَانِ الرَّجِيْمِ ط

"I come out in the name of Allāh. There is no power and strength except Allāh, the High, the Great. My trust is in Allāh, O Allāh! Favour me with the action with which Thou mayest be pleased and protect me from the accursed Devil."

Bismillāhi wa lā ḥawla wa lā quwwata illā billāh-il-'aliyyil-'Aẓīm. Tawakk-altu 'alAllāh, Allāhumma waffiqnī limā tuḥibbu wa tarḍā, waḥfiẓnī min-a sh-shaiṭān-ir-rajīm.

When you are on the road, recite:

اَللّٰهُمَّ اِنِّيْ اَعُوْذُ بِكَ مِنْ اَنْ اَضِلَّ اَوْ اُضَلَّ اَوْ اَظْلِمَ اَوْ اُظْلَمَ
اَوْ اَجْهَلَ اَوْ يُجْهَلَ عَلَيَّ ط بِسْمِ اللّٰهِ تَوَكَّلْتُ عَلَى اللّٰهِ ط
لَاحَوْلَ وَلَا قُوَّةَ اِلَّا بِاللّٰهِ الْعَلِيِّ الْعَظِيْمِ ط اَللّٰهُمَّ وَفِّقْنِيْ لِمَا
تُحِبُّ وَتَرْضٰى وَاعْصِمْنِيْ مِنَ الشَّيْطَانِ الرَّجِيْمِ

"O Allāh! I seek Thy refuge from going astray or being led astray or turning oppressor or being oppressed, or showing ignorance or being fooled. I start in the name of Allāh. There is neither power nor strength except Allāh, the Mighty, the Great. O Allāh! Favour me with the deed with which Thou mayest be pleased and protect me from accursed devil."

Allāhumma innī a'ūdhu bika min an aḍilla aw uḍalla aw aẓlima aw uẓlama aw ajhala aw yujhala 'alayya, Bismillāhi tawakkaltu 'alAllāhi lā ḥawla wa lā quwwata illā billāhil 'aliyyil'Aẓīm. Allāhumma waffiqnī limā tuḥibbu wa tarḍā wa'ṣimnī min ash-shaiṭān-ir-rajīm.

When bidding farewell to relatives, shake hands and recite:

اَسْتَوْدِعُ اللّٰهَ دِيْنَكَ وَاَمَانَتَكَ وَخَوَاتِيْمَ عَمَلِكَ وَغَفَرَ

ذَنْبَكَ وَيَسَّرَ لَكَ الْخَيْرَ حَيْثُمَا كُنْتَ وَزَوَّدَكَ اللّٰهُ التَّقْوٰى
وَجَنَّبَكَ الرَّدٰى ط

I entrust to Allāh your faith and the end of your affairs. Allāh may forgive your sins and may make goodness accessible to you, where-ever you may be. Allāh may bestow on you the gift of piety and protect you from destruction.

Asta'udi – 'ullāha dīnaka wa amānataka wa khawātima 'amalika wa ghafara dhambika wa yassara lakal-khaira ḥait-humā kunta wa zawwadak-Allah-ut-taqwa wa jannabak ar-raḍā.

When you start the journey, recite BISMILLĀH and then recite:

اَلْحَمْدُ لِلّٰهِ الَّذِىْ سَخَّرَ لَنَا هٰذَا وَمَا كُنَّا
لَهٗ مُقْرِنِيْنَ وَاِنَّآ اِلٰى رَبِّنَا لَمُنْقَلِبُوْنَ ط

"Praise be to Allāh. He has made this (vehicle) subservient to us and we were not able to do it. And surely to our Lord we must return.
(Holy Qur'ān 43:13).

Alḥamdu lillāh-illadhī sakhk-hara lanā hādhā wa mā kunnā lahū muqrinīn, wa innā, ilā Rabbinā la-munqalibūn.

CHAPTER FOUR

MĪQĀT

Entry into the Holy Land:

As you are approaching Holy Mecca, there are boundaries within which you cannot enter without being dressed in the sacred garment 'Iḥrām'. These boundaries, all round Mecca, are called 'Mīqāt', or the boundaries of 'Ḥaram'. There are certain signs displayed at well arranged boundaries. These signs were first fixed by prophet Ibrāhīm. Then they were renewed by the Holy Prophet, and later maintained by the guided companions. On the way from Jedda, 10 miles from Mecca, a minaret displaying the sign of Ḥaram is standing adjacent to the place known as SHUMAISIYYA.

The boundaries of 'Mīqāt' are shown in map No. (1), fig. (1)

Coming from Medīna to Mecca at Dhul-Ḥulaifa or Tan'īm at a distance of 3 miles, and from Yemen to Mecca at 'Izzat-i-Laban at a distance of 7 miles, from South Irāq at a distance of 7 miles and towards Ja'rana at a distance of 9 miles and from Ṭā'if at a distance of 7 miles are the precincts of the Ḥaram. Within these boundaries, hunting, catching of animals, and cutting grass or trees is forbidden.

'Qurn-al-Manāzil' is the 'Mīqāt' boundary for people living in Najd, Saudi Arabia.

Yalamlam	:	for people coming from the Yemen.
Dhāt-Iraq	:	for people coming from Irāq.
Al-Juhfa	:	for people coming from Syria.

People coming with the intention of performing Ḥajj or 'Umra cannot enter these boundaries of 'Mīqāt' without adopting 'Iḥrām', whether they may be travelling by land or by air. In the plane or the ship, the boundaries of 'Mīqāt' are announced so that people put on their 'Iḥrām' before entering these boundaries. Those who do not intend to perform Ḥajj or 'Umra, for example residents, etc. do not have to be in the state of

LIMITS OF MIQĀT

(From where it is forbidden to enter Mecca Without Ihram)

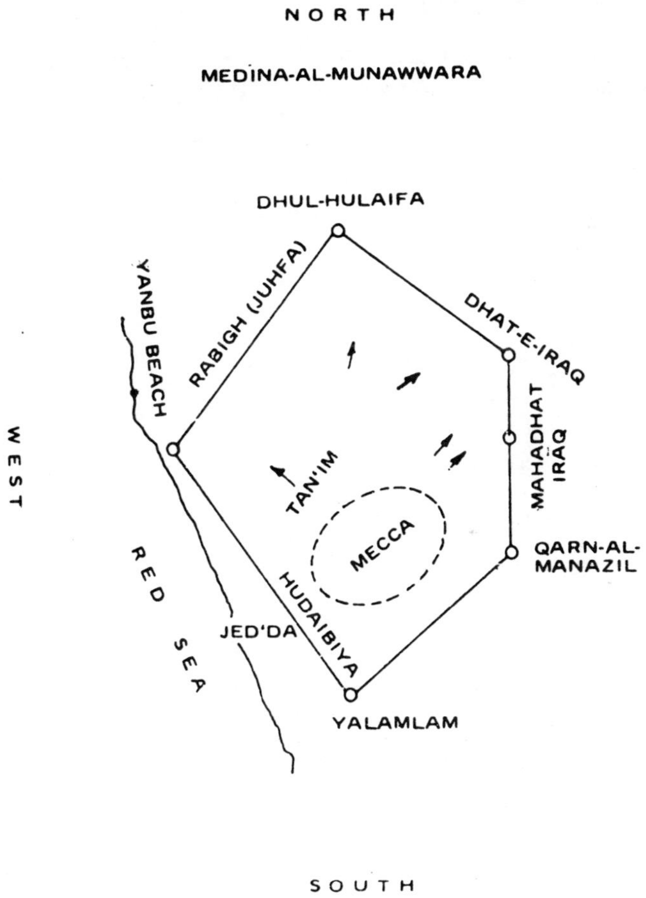

'Iḥrām' while they travel within these boundaries. Those who live in Mecca or within the boundaries of the Ḥaram, can adopt 'Iḥrām' for Ḥajj from their own houses, but for 'Umra, they have to go out to 'Ḥal', and adopt Iḥrām from there and then enter the boundaries of the Ḥaram. Those coming to Jedda by air or sea must adopt Iḥrām before entering the port.

The Holy Prayers: The five prayers of the day are to be shortened while travelling.

The Holy Prophet adopted his Iḥrām from Dhul-Ḥulaifa when he came for the Final Ḥajj, from al-Medīna.

CHAPTER FIVE

I. DUTIES OF ḤAJJ AND 'UMRA

The following is a brief account of the duties of Ḥajj and 'Umra which are to be performed by Pilgrims.

1. (i) The intention of Ḥajj or 'Umra or both.
   (ii) Adoption of the sacred garment, the 'Iḥrām'.
   (iii) Recitation of Talbiya.

The above three are done at the same time. For Ḥajj, the duties include:

2. The stay at 'Arafāt called Waqūf-e-'Arafāt. This is the greatest Rukn of Ḥajj. It is to stay at 'Arafāt from noon of the 9th of Dhul-Ḥijja to the sunset.
3. To throw pebbles at Jamarāt (to condemn Shaiṭān)
4. To offer sacrifice (option for Mufrid).
5. To shave the head, called Ḥalaq, or to trim the hair, called Qaṣr.
6. To perform Ṭawāf of the Ka'ba between 10th to 12th of Dhul-Ḥijja; 10th is preferred. This is called Ṭawāf-e-Ziyāra and is the second most important Rukn of Ḥajj.
7. To perform Sa'ī between Ṣafā and Marwa.
8. To perform the farewell Ṭawāf, called Ṭawāf-al-Wadā'.

DUTIES FOR 'UMRA

1. (i) Intention for 'Umra
   (ii) Adoption of Iḥrām
   (iii) Recital of Talbiya

2. Ṭawāf of the Ka'ba

3. Sa'ī between Ṣafā and Marwa

4. Shaving of the head or trimming of hair.

The modes of performing Ṭawāf and Sa'ī are the same both for Hajj and 'Umra, only the intentions differ.

In this chapter the conditions and obligations for adopting Iḥrām and the recitation of Talbiya will be discussed in detail.

II. IḤRĀM

Just as you enter the boundaries of 'Mīqāt', you have to perform two 'Manāsik' in the following order.

(1) Adopt 'Iḥrām' just before entering the 'Mīqāt'. Offer two Nafl Rak'at for 'Iḥrām'.

(2) After adopting 'Iḥrām', begin reciting Talbiya, "Labbaik, Allāhumma Labbaik".

These two 'Manāsik' are discussed in detail in this Chapter.

It is 'Mustaḥab' to take a bath on reaching 'Mīqāt'. The Holy Prophet took a bath, at 'Mīqāt'. If a bath is not possible, then ablution (Wuḍū) will suffice. It is also Sunna of the Holy Prophet to clip the nails, to trim the moustaches, so that they are shortened before the bath. The other unnecessary hair on the body should be removed. It is also 'Mustaḥab' to trim hair before adopting the 'Iḥrām'.

Iḥrām for Men:

Two clean seamless white linen, woolen or towel sheets are necessary. If they are not new, then washed ones can be used. Both sheets should be 2½ yards each. One of them should be used to wrap round the waist and above the navel, and the other one is used as a wrap round the left shoulder, the right shoulder and the head should be uncovered. The lower sheet should remain above the ankles. The stitched garment such as a shirt, pyjamas, undershirt, underwear, coat, sherwani, etc. is prohibited. If the sheet has been mended or stitched in between then there is no harm. These sheets, or two large white towels, are available for this purpose at all ports in Saudi Arabia.

Iḥrām for Women:

Women do not wear the 'Iḥrām' garments worn by men. They can wear their customary stitched garments, as well as, gloves, shawls, sweaters, silk, jewellery and socks. But they are not to veil their faces. The hair should be fully covered; for each hair falling during the pilgrimage there is a penalty of one sheep. Their garments should reach their ankles, and sleeves to their wrists and the neckline should be high. The women should avoid wearing perfume or the type of dress which attracts attention i.e. tight trousers and bright colours, or a dress which resembles men's dress. Female pilgrims who are menstruating at the time they take Iḥrām, or who menstruate the days they are in Iḥrām, should not perform any of the daily prayers or other ceremonial prayer until their menses have ceased, but they may read all other forms of prayers – except those requiring obeisances. They will not be able to perform Ṭawāf or Sa'ī during the menses.

Ladies are not to recite the Talbiya loudly.

Mubaḥāt of Iḥrām (things allowed in Iḥrām):

To take bath, to enter the house, to sit in the shade, to use umbrellas, to trim the broken nail, to see in the mirror, to clean the clothes, to dive, to bathe with cold or hot water, (but rubbing the body with soap or hand is prohibited), to tie a purse over or under the lower sheet, to be armed, to hide the other parts of the body except the head (for men) and the face to cover the beard below the chin, to bear a water bucket or a bedding on the head, to kill dangerous insects or animals, like snake, scorpion, beetles, etc. and to sacrifice the pet sheep and eat them.

Makrūhāt of Iḥrām (Things disallowed or discouraged in Iḥrām)

To touch perfume after wearing Iḥrām, to smell the

perfume intentionally, to tie the sheet round the neck in a knot, to knot the sheets or sew them together, to cover the chin and the nose with cloth, to comb the hair or the beard, to scratch the head and the hair wildly, to wash the hair, beard, or the body with soap to remove dirt, only to splash the body is necessary, avoid rubbing.

Mumnūāt of Iḥrām (the restrictions):

To wear stitched garments (for men), to wear shoes or sandals which hide the middle bone of the foot, to bandage the head and the face, to use perfume, or perfumed clothes, to cut hair, to trim nails, to hide the head (for men only) and the face, to quarrel, to kiss or pet, to hunt on the land, to tempt others to hunt, to help the hunter, to race the animals, and games on the land, to break the eggs of animals, to kill lice, to spread the clothes in the sun in order to kill the lice or insects, to have sexual intercourse, to murder, to disobey, to cut the grass or pluck plants.

The Holy Qur'ān says in this respect:

> "For Ḥajj are the months well known, if any one undertakes the duty therein, let there be no obscenity, nor wickedness, nor wrangling in the Ḥajj. And whatever good you do (be sure) Allāh knows it. And take provisions for the journey but the best of provisions is right conduct. So fear Me; O ye that are wise!" (Qur'ān 2:197)

> "It is not a crime in you, if you seek the bounty of your Lord during Ḥajj." (Qur'ān 2:198)

The Intention of Iḥrām:

Before entering the state of Iḥrām, each Pilgrim, male or female should trim the fingernails, and remove underarm and pubic hair. Women should wash the head, men should trim or shave the face and wash the head; for to trim nails, clip the hair or beard, or shave the face is not permissible until the ceremonies have been fulfilled. The Holy Qur'ān says in this respect:

> "And complete the Ḥajj or 'Umra in the service of Allāh. But if you are prevented, send an offering for sacrifice

such as you may find, and do not shave your heads until the offering reaches the place of sacrifice. And if any of you is ill, or has an ailment in his scalp (necessitating shaving during Ḥajj and 'Umra) in compensation either fast, or feed the poor, or offer sacrifice, and when you are in peaceful conditions (again). If any one wishes to continue 'Umra on to the Ḥajj, he must make an offering such as he can afford. But if he can not afford it, he should fast three days during the Ḥajj and seven days on his return, making ten days in all. This is for those whose household is not by the Sacred Mosque. And fear Allāh and know that Allāh is strict in punishment."

(Qur'ān 2:196)

When you have finished with the trimming of hair, nails etc. and taking bath, then you adopt the Iḥrām and offer two Rak'at of prayer. You should now make a declaration of intention of Ḥajj and/or 'Umra, as the case may be, as the Holy Prophet said, "The fulfillment of actions depends on the intention"

The Intention of 'Umra:

The Iḥrām of 'Umra is adopted with this declaration:

اَللّٰهُمَّ اِنِّىْٓ اُرِيْدُ الْعُمْرَةَ فَيَسِّرْهَا لِىْ وَ تَقَبَّلْهَا مِنِّىْ
نَوَيْتُ الْعُمْرَةَ وَ اَحْرَمْتُ بِهَا مُخْلِصًا لِلّٰهِ تَعَالٰى ۔

"O Allāh! I intend to perform 'Umra, therefore make it easy for me and accept it for me. I make the intention for 'Umra and enter into its state of Iḥrām purely for the sake of Allāh, the most High."

Allāhumma innī urīd-ul-'Umrata fa yassirhā lī wa taqabbalhā minnī, Nawait-ul-'Umrata wa Aḥramta bihā mukhlisan lillāhi ta'ālā.

The intention of Ḥajj is given in chapter 6.

Talbiya: The call, the acknowledgment:

As soon as you have adopted the Iḥrām and prayed two Rak'at, recite the following prayer known as Talbiya:

لَبَّيْكَ اَللّٰهُمَّ لَبَّيْكَ ، لَبَّيْكَ لَا شَرِيْكَ لَكَ لَبَّيْكَ

إِنَّ الْحَمْدَ وَالنِّعْمَةَ لَكَ وَالْمُلْكَ لَا شَرِيْكَ لَكَ ،

Here I am, O Allāh! Here I am! Here I am, there is no one who is Your partner, here I am!	Labbaik , Allāhumma labbaik, Labbaik , lā sharīka laka labbaik,
Surely, all praise and blessings are Yours, and dominion. You are without companion.	Innal-ḥamda wanni'mata laka-waḷ mulk, Lā sharīka lak.

Talbiya is the most frequently uttered of all the prayers of the Pilgrimage. Immediately after the declaration of intent, each Pilgrim should recite the above Talbiya. You must repeat this prayer countless times through the Pilgrimage. You must repeat it when travelling, when you turn to the right or to the left, when you start and when you stop. You recite Talbiya when ascending, or descending, when hearing other pilgrims utter these words, when awakening, before sleeping and before addressing anyone. If you come upon men disputing you must tell it to them. Along with this you must occasionally recite the Salutation i.e. Darūd-e-Ibrāhīmī on the Holy Prophet.

The recitation of Talbiya is an acknowledgement of the call of Allāh for the believers. When Prophet Ibrāhīm (may Allāh be pleased with him), was asked by Allāh to build a house for the worship of Allāh alone, he was asked to call people to the house of Allāh. Talbiya is an answer, an acknowledgment to this call.

"And we gave the site to Ibrāhīm of the Sacred House. Associate not anything (in worship) with Me, and sanctify My House for those who compass it around, or stand up, or bow, prostrate themselves (in prayers). And proclaim the Pilgrimage among men, they will come to three on foot, on every kind of camel lean on account of journeys through deep and distant mountain highways. That they witness the benefits (provided for them) and celebrate the name of Allāh, through the days appointed, over the cattle which He has provided for them, then eat you thereof and feed the distressed ones in need" (Qur'ān 22:26-28)

It is the reply to this proclamation for Ṭāyifīn, Rākiyīn in Sujūd, that pilgrims say "I am here, O Allāh! and there is no partner for you"). It is Sunna to pause in the four places, and to leave out any word from it is Makrūh. To recite the Talbiya loud for men is Mustaḥab, but do not shout, nor raise your voice as it would interrupt the worshippers. Whenever you say Talbiya, say it three times without speaking in between the recitals. After reciting Talbiya, recite Darūd and pray to Allāh. It is traditional to pray this.

اَللّٰهُمَّ اِنِّیْ اَسْأَلُكَ رِضَاكَ وَالْجَنَّةَ

وَاَعُوْذُبِكَ مِنْ غَضَبِكَ وَمِنَ النَّارِ

"O Allāh! I beseech Thee to grant me Thy pleasure and Paradise, and I seek Thy protection from Thy Wrath and Hell-fire."

Allāhumma inni as'aluka riḍāka wal- Jannata wa a'ūdhu bika min ghaḍabika wa min-an-nār.

From now on you are a Muḥrim i.e. in the state of Iḥrām and all obligations for this state are binding on you!

For Ladies:

A lady Pilgrim should not recite Talbiya loudly, and may not worship loudly. Nor is she to make the Pilgrimage unless she is accompanied by her husband, or if she is unwed, by two male members of her immediate family, both of whom must be of such close relationship as to preclude sexual interest or eventual marriage. No man is to approach his wife sexually or the woman to encourage it while wearing Ihram.

Following is the summary of functions to be performed.

ON/OR JUST BEFORE ENTERING MĪQĀT

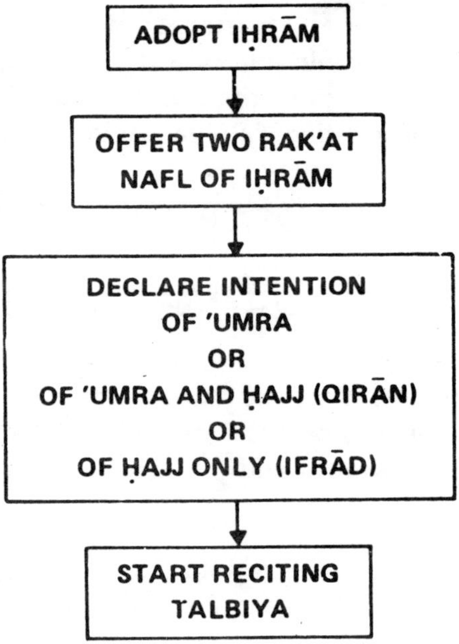

Figure 2

CHAPTER SIX

THREE KINDS OF ḤAJJ

There are three different ways of performing Ḥajj. Each requires different conditions depending on the facilities open to the Ḥājis, corresponding to their individual circumstances:

(1) **Ḥajj-e-Ifrād.** (حَجِّ اِفْرَاد) This is when a Pilgrim does not intend to perform 'Umra before Ḥajj but intends only to perform Ḥajj. (He may not have enough time or means or convenience to perform 'Umra and Ḥajj together). A Pilgrim who performs Ḥajj-e-Ifrād is called Mufrid. For this kind of Ḥajj when the Iḥrām is adopted from Mīqāt the intention of Iḥrām declares the intention of Ḥajj only.

The declaration of intention of Ḥajj-e-Ifrād is as follows:

"اَللّٰهُمَّ اِنِّىٓ اُرِيْدُ الْحَجَّ فَيَسِّرْهُ لِىْ وَتَقَبَّلْهُ مِنِّىْ"
نَوَيْتُ الْحَجَّ وَاَحْرَمْتُ بِهٖ مُخْلِصًا لِلّٰهِ تَعَالٰى

"O Allāh! I want to perform Ḥajj, so Thou make it easy for me and accept it on my behalf. I declare the intention for Ḥajj and enter into its state of Iḥrām for the sake of Allāh, the Most High.

Allāhumma innī urīd-ul-Ḥajja fa yassirhu lī wa taqabbalhu minnī, Nawait-ul-Ḥajja wa Aḥramtu bihī mukhlisan lillāhi ta'ālā.

(2) **Ḥajj-e-Tamattu'** (حَجِّ تَمَتُّع) :
The performance of Ḥajj & 'Umra together (The convenient way)

This combination of Ḥajj and 'Umra may be achieved by Pilgrims who arrive early for Ḥajj. This type of Ḥajj is called Tamattu' and the Pilgrim Mutamattī.' (Tamattu' in Arabic means to take advantage of a facility).

Iḥrām for Tamattu' is adopted from Mīqāt with the declaration of intention for 'Umra first. When 'Umra has been performed, the Iḥrām is taken off and all which was unlawful in the state of Iḥrām is now lawful until the first day of Ḥajj (i.e. 8th of Dhul-Ḥijja) arrives i.e. usual garments and normal activities are resumed. On this day the Iḥrām is again adopted with the intention of Ḥajj and the Manāsík of Ḥajj performed. So that in this type of Pilgrimage, a concession of taking off the Iḥrām is provided between the interim period of 'Umra and Ḥajj. Pilgrims availing themselves of this convenience should make a sacrifice. Those who cannot afford a blood sacrifice should fast three days during Ḥajj and another seven days after its completion i.e. in all ten days.

The declaration of intention for 'Umra:

اَللّٰهُمَّ اِنِّيْٓ اُرِيْدُ الْعُمْرَةَ فَيَسِّرْهَا لِيْ وَ تَقَبَّلْهَا مِنِّيْ ط

نَوَيْتُ الْعُمْرَةَ وَ اَحْرَمْتُ بِهَا مُخْلِصًا لِّلّٰهِ تَعَالٰى ط

"O Allāh, I intend to perform 'Umra, so make it easy for me. I make the intention of 'Umra and enter into its state of Iḥrām purely for Allāh, the most High.

Allāhumma innī urīd-ul-'Umrata fa yassirhā lī wa taqabbalhā minnī, Nawait-ul-'Umrata wa Aḥramtu bihā mukhliṣan lillāhi ta'ālā.

On the 8th of Dhul-Ḥijja the same Iḥrām is again adopted in the Holy Mosque of Ka'ba. The ceremonies of Ḥajj-e-Tamattu' are as follows:

There are two circumstances:

(i) If the Pilgrim has brought an animal of sacrifice with him, from the boundaries of Mīqāt, he will perform 'Umra and remain in the state of Iḥrām of 'Umra and without shaving his head till 8th of Dhul-Ḥijja. On this day he will renew his Iḥrām for Ḥajj with the declaration of Intention of Ḥajj and perform all the Manāsik.

(ii) If the Pilgrim has no animal of sacrifice brought from Mīqāt, he will perform 'Umra (with declaration of Intention of 'Umra only) and then remove the Iḥrām and wait until the 8th of Dhul-Ḥijja as a 'Muḥlil'. On the 8th of Dhul-Ḥijja he will resume his Iḥrām with the declaration of the Intention of Ḥajj and perform the Manāsik. On the 10th, or 11th or 12th of Dhul-Ḥijja he will offer a blood sacrifice and then shave his head. [Animals can be bought – (sacrifice for a Tamattu' is obligatory) at Minā]. In both these cases the declaration of the intention of Ḥajj is as given on the previous page, i.e. the same as for a Mufrid.

(3) Ḥajj-e-Qirān (حَجّ قِرَان)

This is the combination of 'Umra and Ḥajj in the month of Ḥajj. The Pilgrim adopts the Iḥrām from Mīqāt with the declaration of Intention of Ḥajj and 'Umra. Then on entering Mecca, he performs 'Umra and remains in the state of Iḥrām till he performs all the Manāsik of Ḥajj in the same state of Iḥrām. This is true for a Pilgrim who brings an animal of sacrifice along with him from Mīqāt.

In case a Pilgrim has no animal of sacrifice from Mīqāt he can perform Tamattu' but on the other hand if a Mutamattī' changes his mind to perform Ḥajj-i-Qirān (i.e. without abandoning Iḥrām after 'Umra for the interim period) he can do so before the 4th circuit of Ṭawāf of the Ka'ba during 'Umra. For travellers from abroad, who cannot bring animal of sacrifice with them, they can perform Ḥajj-i-Qirān, provided they buy the animal in Minā and offer sacrifice. The sacrifice for a Qārin is Wājib.

The declaration of intention of Ḥajj-e-Qirān is as follows:

اَللّٰهُمَّ اِنِّیْ اُرِیْدُ الْعُمْرَةَ وَالْحَجَّ فَیَسِّرْهُمَا لِیْ وَتَقَبَّلْهُمَا مِنِّیْ

نَوَیْتُ الْعُمْرَةَ وَالْحَجَّ وَاَحْرَمْتُ بِهِمَا مُخْلِصًا لِلّٰهِ تَعَالٰی ۔

"O Allāh! I prepare myself both for 'Umra and Ḥajj. Make both of them easy for me and accept both of them on my behalf. I declare the intention of 'Umra and Ḥajj and I enter the state of Iḥrām for both of them purely for Allāh, the Most High."

Allāhumma innī urīd-ul-'Umrata wal-Ḥajja fa yassirhumā lī wa taqabbalhumā minnī, Nawait-ul-'Umrata wal-Ḥajja wa Aḥramtu bihimā mukhliṣan lillāhi ta'ālā.

After the declaration of intention for the kind of Pilgrimage you intend to perform, offer two Rak'at for Iḥrām. Start reciting Talbiya and proceed for the greatest spiritual experience of this life.

The Holy Prophet performed a Qirān and had the animal of sacrifice brought with him. This is a harder kind of performance of Ḥajj and carries more Thawāb (reward), but may not be convenient for Pilgrims arriving early (say during the month of Ramaḍān) for Ḥajj.

The Summary of three kinds of Ḥajj is given in Figure Three (3).

SUMMARY OF 3 KINDS OF ḤAJJ

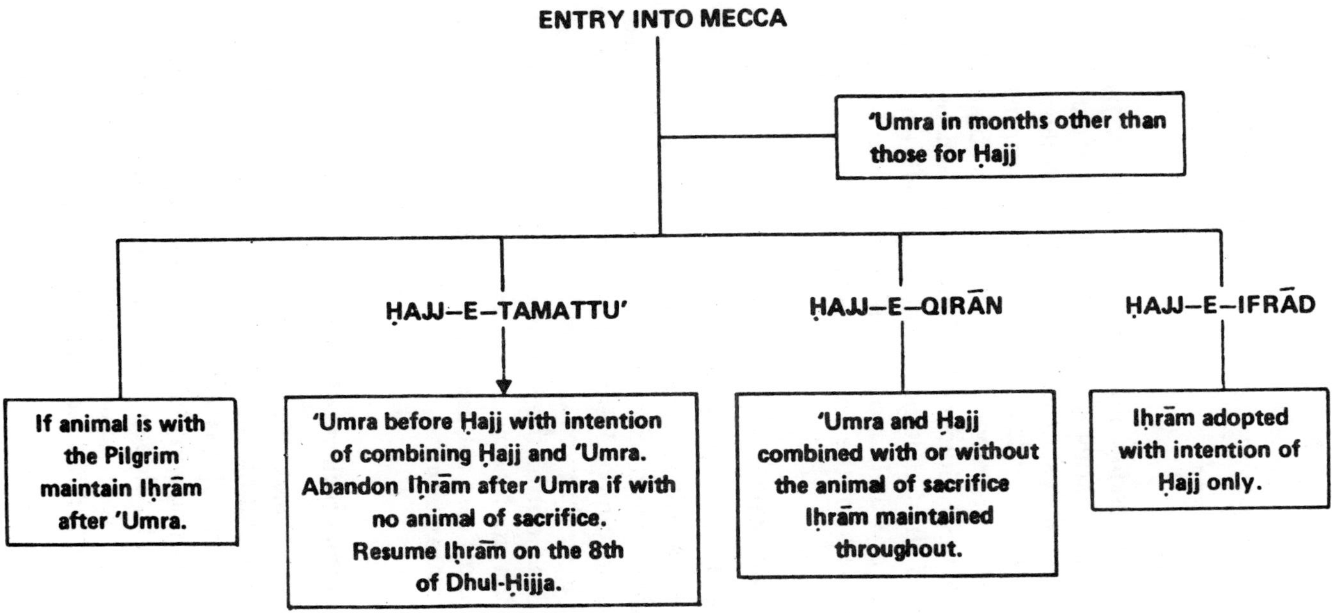

CHAPTER SEVEN

STAY IN THE HOLY LAND

Jedda:

The intending Pilgrim travelling either by sea or air first reaches Jedda. Having adopted the Iḥrām before reaching Jedda, pronounce Talbiya often and keep yourselves busy with the remembrance of Allāh. After clearing customs etc. you will inform the man responsible for Mu'allims about the name and address of your Guide (Mu'allim). You will be introduced to an agent of the Guide or the Guide himself. He will take you to your tent, or hotel, and he will arrange your journey and take care of the rest of the procedures during Ḥajj.

Mecca Mukarrama

It is 75 km from Jedda. You may stay in Mecca till the 8th of Dhul-Ḥijja if it is convenient and according to your Guide's instructions. Your tent or lodging may be arranged in Minā from the beginning. Here is a map of Minā, 'Arafāt, Muzdalifa and Mecca, so that you can see the relative distances, and places you will visit during the Ḥajj season. A taxi takes about an hour from Jedda to Mecca, and further means of transport, like trucks, buses, cars are provided by the Mu'allims if you have to travel to these places.

Entry into the precincts of Ḥaram

Around Mecca, the precincts of Ḥaram are already given in Fig. (1) Minā and Muzdalifa are within the boundaries of Ḥaram. All restrictions of the Ḥaram are applied within these lands. Hunting. catching and chasing animals, fighting, cutting grass and trees etc. are forbidden. After leaving Jedda, when you reach Shumaisiyya, from where Mecca is only 10 miles, a minaret will be visible, which indicates the precincts of the Ḥaram. To enter the precincts of the Ḥaram is to enter the presence of Rubbul 'Ālamīn, the Lord of the Worlds. A very fortunate privilege has been bestowed on you, hence extreme reverence, humility and devotion is required. At this moment you are in the state of Iḥrām so recite the following Du'ā at the time of entry into the Holy precincts of Mecca.

اَللّٰهُمَّ إِنَّ هٰذَا حَرَمُكَ وَحَرَمُ رَسُوْلِكَ فَحَرِّمْ لَحْمِيْ وَدَمِيْ
وَعَظْمِيْ عَلَى النَّارِ ، اَللّٰهُمَّ آمِنِّيْ مِنْ عَذَابِكَ يَوْمَ تَبْعَثُ
عِبَادَكَ ، وَاجْعَلْنِيْ مِنْ اَوْلِيَائِكَ وَاَهْلِ طَاعَتِكَ وَتُبْ عَلَيَّ
اِنَّكَ اَنْتَ التَّوَّابُ الرَّحِيْمُ ،

O Allāh! Of course this land is Your Ḥaram and Your Prophet's Ḥaram. So make my flesh and my blood and my bone Ḥaram (forbidden) to the fire of Jahannum. O Allāh! Shelter me from Your anger, on the day when You will resurrect Your servants. And make me from Your obedient friends and forgive me of course You are Merciful, Forgiving.

Allāhumma inna hādha ḥaramuka was ḥaramu Rasūlika faḥarrim laḥmī wa dammī wa 'aẓamī 'alannār, Allāhumma āminnī min 'adhābika yawma tab'athu 'ibādaka, waj'alnī min auliyā'ika wa ahli ṭā'atika wa tub 'alayya innaka ant-at-Tawwāb-ur-Raḥīm.

Entrance to Mecca Mukkarrama

Before reaching Mecca, you will reach a place called Mudaa', between the Great Mosque and Mu'alla cemetery, the prayers here are accepted. It is Mustahab to recite the following Du'ā:

رَبَّنَا آتِنَا فِي الدُّنْيَا حَسَنَةً وَّفِي الْآخِرَةِ حَسَنَةً وَّقِنَا
عَذَابَ النَّارِ ، اَللّٰهُمَّ اِنِّيْ اَسْأَلُكَ مِنْ خَيْرِ مَا سَأَلَكَ
نَبِيُّكَ مُحَمَّدٌ صَلَّى اللّٰهُ عَلَيْهِ وَسَلَّمَ ، وَاَعُوْذُبِكَ مِنْ شَرِّ
مَا اسْتَعَاذَكَ مِنْهُ نَبِيُّكَ مُحَمَّدٌ صَلَّى اللّٰهُ عَلَيْهِ وَسَلَّمَ ،

O Allāh! Grant us goodness in this world and goodness in the hereafter and save us from the chastisement of Hell-fire. O Allāh! I ask Thee for the goodness for which Thy Prophet Muḥammad (peace be upon him) prayed and I beseech Thee to save me from the evil for which Thy Prophet Muḥammad (peace be upon him) prayed.

Rabbanā ātinā fiddunyā ḥasanatan wwa fil ākhirati ḥasanatan wwa qinā 'adhāb-an-nār. Allāhumma innī as'aluka min khairi mā sa'aluka nabīyyuka Muḥammad ṣallallā-hu 'alaihi wa sallam, wa a'ūdhu bika min sharri masta'ādhaka minhu nabīyyuka Muḥammad ṣallallā-hu 'alaihi wa sallam.

Mecca Mukkarrama

At the first sight of the Holy city of Mecca recite:

اَللّٰهُمَّ اجْعَلْ لِّيْ بِهَا قَرَارًا وَّارْزُقْنِيْ بِهَا حَلَالًا ط اَللّٰهُمَّ
اَلْبَلَدُ بَلَدُكَ وَالْبَيْتُ بَيْتُكَ ط جِئْتُ اَطْلُبُ رَحْمَتَكَ وَ اَرُوْمُ
طَاعَتَكَ، مُتَّبِعًا لِاَمْرِكَ رَاضِيًا بِقَدَرِكَ مُسْلِمًا لِاَمْرِكَ ط وَاَسْاَلُكَ
مَسْاَلَةَ الْمُضْطَرِّ اِلَيْكَ ط اَلْمُشْفِقِ مِنْ عَذَابِكَ اَنْ تَسْتَقْبِلَنِيْ
بِعَفْوِكَ وَ اَنْ تُجَاوِزَ عَنِّيْ بِرَحْمَتِكَ وَ اَنْ تُدْخِلَنِيْ جَنَّتَكَ ط

O Allāh! Bless me with peace and tranquillity in its precincts and bestow on me the lawful sustenance in it. O Allāh This city is Thine city and this House is Thine House. I have presented myself in search of Thy mercy and with the intention of submission to Thee, following Thy commands willingly to Thy desires. I beseech Thee as the discomforted one who is afraid of Thy wrath. Accept my apology

Allāhumma-j'al li bihā qarāran wwarzuqnī bihā ḥalālan, Allāhummal-baladu baladuka wal-baitu baituka ji'tu aṭlabu raḥmataka wa arūmu tā'ataka muttabi'-an li-amrika rāḍiyan biqadrika, Musliman li-amrika, wa as'aluka -mas'ala-tal-muḍtarra ilaika, almushfiqi min 'adhābi-ka an tastaqbil-nī bi-'afwika

alongwith Thine forgiveness and pardon me alongwith Thine mercy, and enter me into Thine Paradise.	wa an tujāwaza 'annī bi-raḥ-matika wa an tudkhilnī jannatak.

As you approach Mecca and the Holy Mosque in it, make sure you are in the state of Iḥrām. You then enter the Great Mosque which encloses the Holiest of the Holy shrines, the BAITALLĀH, which is radiant with Mercy and Blessings of Allāh.

Here after entering, in the mannerism of presenting yourself to the Highest Authority of Heaven and Earth, humble yourself like a beggar at the doorsteps of the Almighty, the Highest. Here you perform all ceremonies in the manner befitting Allāh's Grandeur and His Jalla. The impact of the first sight of the Ka'ba is great, inexplicable and you will feel extremely humble and full of emotions of worship. Recite Talbiya as you enter the Mosque; enter it from Bāb-us-Salām if you can. The first thing you notice will be the Ka'ba itself!

The Holy Mosque

It is here that you perform circumambulation or Ṭawāf of the Holy Ka'ba. The description of the Holy Mosque from inside is given here for the Pilgrims. The Ka'ba itself is a cube-shaped structure, measuring approximately 33 feet in width and 50 feet in length, and 45 feet high. The four faces of the Ka'ba are covered with black brocaded drapery, with Qur'ānic verses on it. The Ka'ba is also known as the Most Ancient House (Baitul-'Atīq), the Sacred Mosque (al-Masjid-al-Harām) and the House of God (Bait-Allāh).

The Zam-zam well lies opposite the face which has the Door of Mercy. At the left corner of this face, is embedded the Black Stone known as Ḥajr-al-Aswad. The part of Bait-Allāh between Ḥajr-al-Aswad and Bab-ur-Raḥma is called Multazim. This place has special significance, as supplications, wishes, are

MASJID—AL—HARĀM
(Mecca Mukarrama)

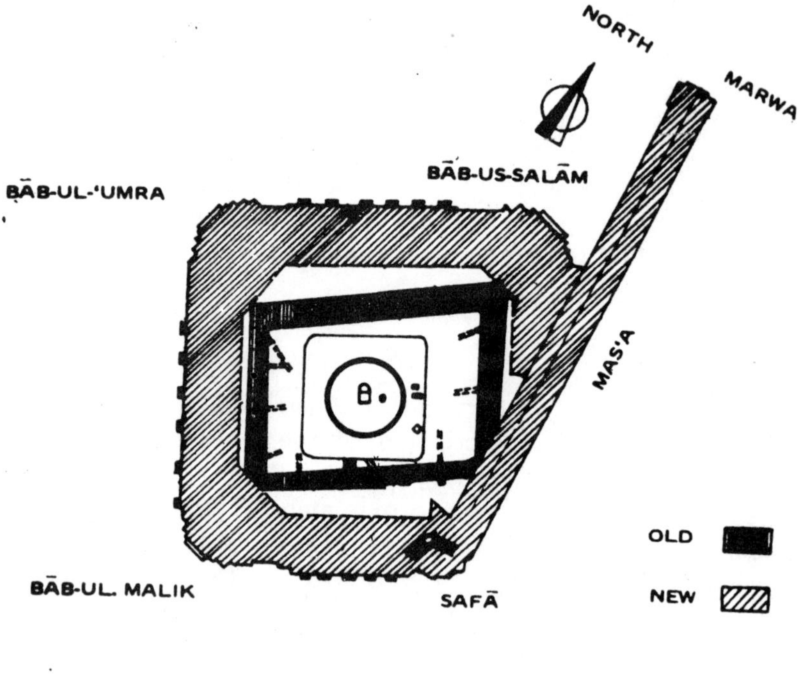

granted here at all times of day and night. The Ṭawāf is begun from Ḥajr-al-Aswad moving towards Bab-ur-Raḥma. The second face of the Ka'ba is surrounded by a shoulder high semicicrular wall called Ḥateem (حطيم). The space within Ḥaṭīm in part of the greater Ka'ba. It is Wajib to include Ḥaṭīm is the Ṭawāf. It is said that the floor inside the Ḥaṭīm has seventy Prophets buried under it, including Prophet Ismā'īl (peace be on him) and his mother Hager (may Allāh be pleased with her). The place of their burial inside the Ḥaṭīm is called al-Ḥijr. (الحجر)

It is said that Prophet Muhammad (peace be upon him) was asleep inside the Ḥaṭīm when Angel Jibrīl appeared to take him for ascension, (اَلْمِعْرَاجُ) al-Mi'rāj, to seven Heavens and to Allāh. This is where the ascent, the Mi'rāj started. Opposite the faces containing Bāb-ur-Raḥma lies Maqām-e-Ibrāhīm. This is the standing place of Prophet Ibrāhīm (peace be on him) when he used to stand here while building the Ka'ba with his son Prophet Ismā'īl.

This standing place is mentioned in the Holy Qur'ān:

وَاتَّخِذُوْا مِنْ مَّقَامِ اِبْرٰهِيْمَ مُصَلًّى (البقرہ ۱۲۵)

And take ye the Station of Ibrahim as a place of worship (prayer).

(Holy Qur'ān 2:125)

Wattakhidhū mimmaqāmi Ibrāhīma muṣallā.

It is Wājib to offer two Rak'at of Nafl here at Maqām-e-Ibrāhīm after completing the Ṭawāf of Bait-Allāh.

The Ṭawāf is continued in the direction of Bāb-ur-Raḥma, and ends at Ḥajr-al-Aswad again, circumambulating in this way all the four faces of the Ka'ba. The corner reached just before the corner with Ḥajr-al-Aswad is known as Rukn-al-Yamānī. It is Sunna to caress this Rukn by hand only, without actually kissing it during the Ṭawāf. When you enter the Holy Mosque, you have to perform some ceremonies, the etiquette of worship here are different than in any other mosque in the world.

You enter the mosque with the intention of performing

(1) 'Umra or
(2) Ḥajj-e-Qirān
or (3) Ḥajj-e-Ifrād.

The ceremonies you have to perform in order of preference are:

(1) Ṭawāf of the Holy Ka'ba. It means circumambulating the Ka'ba seven times.

(2) After the Ṭawāf, offer two Raka't of Tawāf at Maqām-e-Ibrāhīm.

(3) Then drink water of the well of Zam-zam.

(4) Perform the Sa'ī between the hills of Ṣafā and Marwa. It means running seven times between these hills in the fashion of Hagar, when she was looking for water and invoking Allāh's mercy.

(5) After the Sa'ī is over, cutting of hair (Qaṣr), or shaving the head (Ḥalaq) is done depending on the type of Pilgrimage you are performing.

(6) Offer two Rak'at of Nafl at the end of the ceremonies in Masjid-al-Ḥarām.

These constitute the main Manāsik (ceremonies) of 'Umra as well as the first of the main Manāsik of Ḥajj. Fig. (4)

The summary of functions you have to perform as you enter the Holy Mosque of the Ka'ba, for ceremonies of 'Umra.

CEREMONIES FOR 'UMRA

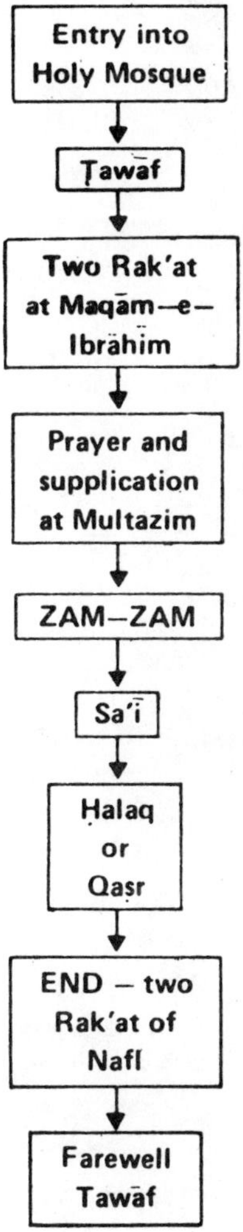

Fig. (4)

CHAPTER EIGHT

THE ṬAWĀF,
(For 'Umra or Ḥajj)

After reaching Mecca Mukarrama, perform ablution before entering the Holy Sanctuary. There, the first performance is to circumambulate the Ka'ba, the House of Allāh. This procedure is known as Ṭawāf. The Ṭawāf means seven circuits performed around the House of Allāh, the Ka'ba. Each circuit is called a SHAWṬ. Seven Shawāṭ make one Ṭawāf. This has to be performed by all Pilgrims, those coming for 'Umra and/or for Ḥajj. For Ṭawāf the intention is obligatory. Ṭawāf will remain unaccepted without intention no matter what number of Ṭawāf may be completed. For 'Umra the intention is for the Ṭawāf of 'Umra. For Ḥajj it is for the Ṭawāf of Ḥajj.

WĀJIBĀT–E–ṬAWĀF (obligatory)

(1) Declaration of Intention (Niyya) of Ṭawāf.

(2) Cleanliness of body and clothes, and the state of Wuḍū (ablution)

(3) Covering of women folk (up to wrists and ankles but not the face).

(4) It is Wājib to complete the Ṭawāf i.e. circumambulating the Ka'ba seven times, or completing the seven Shawāt.

(5) If there is no proper excuse, of illness or inability to walk on foot, it is Wājib to perform Ṭawāf on foot. In case of inability to do so, chairs are available for the Pilgrims, to be carried by bearers, for completing the seven Shawāṭ.

(6) To start the circuits, it is Wājib that you start walking towards your right in the direction of the door of the Ka'ba in such a way that the Ka'ba remains opposite your left shoulder. The entire Ḥajr-al-Aswad (Black Stone) remains on your right.

(7) It is Wājib that the Tawaf is always started from Ḥajr-al-

Aswad, kissing it, if possible; if not, saluting is acceptable. If it has not been started from Ḥajr-al-Aswad, you will have to repeat the Ṭawāf while you are in Mecca, and if you return home without completing the Ṭawāf, then you are liable for a claim at home i.e., slaughtering a goat or a sheep becomes Wājib.

(8) It is also Wajib to encircle the Ḥaṭīm while performing Ṭawāf. Do not pass in between it or else you will have to repeat the Ṭawāf.

(9) After completing the Ṭawāf, it is Wājib to offer two Rak'at Prayers at the standing place of Ibrāhīm or "Maqām—e—Ibrāhīm"

RULES OF ACTION CONCERNING ṬAWĀF

(1) You can perform the Ṭawāf provided you do not omit an obligatory prayer or a Jamā'at at Wiṭr or a Sunnat—e—Mu'-akkida, for these will have to be performed first and then commence the Ṭawāf.

(2) It should be remembered that neither here nor anywhere else in Ḥajj or 'Umra a specific Du'ā (invocation) is prescribed for a particular occasion. Recite such prayers where the mind and the soul are easily absorbed and readily concentrated. You may pray in whatever words or language you feel easy. A particular text of invocations, which has been published, have been narrated from the Messenger of Allāh (peace be upon him). But there are not specifically meant for Ṭawāf. If one can pronounce them understandably then they are good, otherwise, carrying pamphlets and reciting them in a blind fashion without understanding their meaning may impair the sincerity of the appeal.

(3) During Ṭawāf, no eating, drinking or talking is accepted. Remembrance of Allāh, prayers to Him alone and salutations to the Holy Prophet are preferable. It is performed in the manner of offering Ṣalāt. This is the best form of wor-

ship and can be achieved only here of all the places in this Universe.

(4) It should also be remembered that pushing, hurting, or any unkind gesture is prohibited. If you cannot reach Ḥajr–al–Aswad easily then you can start the Ṭawāf fro.n far by gesturing a kiss at it by hand, without causing discomfort to other Muslims. It is Ḥarām to cause discomfort and push Muslims, while it is only a Sunna to kiss the Ḥajr–al–Aswad.

AL–ISTILĀM (اَلْإِسْتِلَامُ)

The Ṭawāf is started by kissing Ḥajr–al–Aswad. Kissing Ḥajr–al–Aswad in any manner described below is known as Istilām.

After declaring the intention of Ṭawāf, place both your palms on Ḥajr–al–Aswad. Placing your mouth in between the palms, kiss noiselessly, placing your head over it. Repeating the kiss three times is Mustaḥab , if time and place allow it.

If Istilām becomes impossible due to the rush of Pilgrims, it should be abandoned, for it is Wājib to refrain from harming others while kissing is Sunna.

On such occasions, be content by merely placing your hands on Ḥajr–al–Aswad and kissing your hands. If this also is impossible, then place only your right hand and kiss it. If that too is impossible then touch it with a long stick and kiss the stick. If even this is impossible which is most likely, then just RAISE BOTH HANDS AS FAR AS THE EARS, facing the palms toward Ḥajr–al–Aswad, assuming you have placed them on it, then recite Takbīr, and Tahlīl and kiss your hands.

TAKBĪR AND TAHLĪL:

بِسْمِ اللّٰهِ اَللّٰهُ اَكْبَرُ ۔ لَآ اِلٰهَ اِلَّا اللّٰهُ وَلِلّٰهِ الْحَمْدُ

In the name of Allāh, Allāh is Great, there is no one worthy of worship except Allāh and all praise is due to Allāh alone.

Bismillāhi Allāh-u-Akbar, Lā ilāha illallāhu wa lillāh-il-ḥamd

Istilām of Ḥajr—al—Aswad for the first Shawṭ as well as for the last Shawt is accepted to be as Sunnat-e—Mu'akkida. In between the two it is not much emphasized.

(5) RAMAL AND IḌṬIBĀ': The Ṭawāf after which you have to observe Sa'ī between Ṣafā and Marwa requires you to perform Ramal and Iḍṭibā'.

Ramal: The way of performing Ramal is to walk hurriedly with forceful and narrow paces while shaking the shoulders like a brave soldier going to the battlefield. It is Sunna to do Ramal in the first three circuits of Ṭawāf.

Iḍṭibā': You are to put the upper sheet of Iḥrām on your left shoulder taking it under your right armpit. In Ṭawāf followed by Sa'ī, Iḍṭibā' is Sunna only for male Pilgrims from the beginning to the end. But at the time of offering two rak'at of prayers at the end of Ṭawāf, the two shoulders are to be covered as usual.

Iḍṭibā' and Ramal are Sunna for men only. Women are exempted.

KIND OF ṬAWĀF

The intention of the kind of Ṭawāf depends on the kind of Pilgrimage you intend to perform.

(1) Ṭawāf for 'Umra

(2) Ṭawāf for Ḥajj—e—Ifrād

(3) Ṭawāf for Ḥajj—e—Qirān

(4) Nafl Ṭawāf

(1) Ṭawāf for 'Umra will be with the intention of 'Umra only. It is also performed by a Pilgrim performing Ḥajj—e—Tamattu'. This Ṭawāf is followed by a Sa'ī, which is Wājib, therefore, in the first three circuits of the Ṭawāf, Ramal and Iḍṭibā' are required.

(2) For Mufrid: The first Ṭawāf of Bait—Allāh is called Ṭawāf-e—Qadūm which is Sunna and not Wājib. Sa'ī is not

followed by it, therefore, Ramal and Idtibā' are not Wājib in this Ṭawāf for a Mufrid.

(3) For a Qārin: He will first perform Ṭawāf of 'Umra with Ramal and Iḍṭibā' in first three Shawāṭ followed by Sa'ī, which is Wājib. Then he will perform Ṭawāf—e—Qadūm on the 8th of Dhul—Ḥijja as the first Ṭawāf for Ḥajj followed by Sa'ī, which is again Wājib. Therefore, Ramal and Iḍṭibā' are to be performed in the first three Shawāt of both Tawāfs.

(4) Nafl Ṭawāf is performed at any other time during your stay in Mecca, which is not to be followed by Sa'ī.

(5) Ṭawāf—e—Ziyāra: This is one of the Rukn of Ḥajj and is obligatory for all kinds of Pilgrimage. This is performed upto the 12th of Dhul—Ḥijja. Sa'ī is Wājib for Mufrid, Qārin and Mutamattī' after this.

(6) Ṭawāf—e—Ṣadr or Wadā': It is Wājib for an Āfāqī when leaving Mecca for home, to perform a farewell Ṭawāf. It is Wājib for all Pilgrims.

THE CONDITIONS FOR ṬAWĀF

(1) To declare the Intention of Ṭawāf

(2) To perform Ṭawāf inside the Masjid—al—Ḥarām.

(3) For Ṭawāf—al—Ḥajj, to perform it at prescribed times, to have Iḥrām and Waqūf—e—'Arafāt.

(4) To stop saying Talbiya at the commencement of Ṭawāf by Istilām.

MUSTAḤABĀTS OF ṬAWĀF (Recommended, Likeable)

(1) It is Mustaḥab to touch Rukn—al—Yamānī (with palms only) when passing near it during Ṭawāf.

(2) Save these two places, viz: Ḥajr—al—Aswad and Rukn—al—Yamānī it is Makrūh to touch or kiss any other corner or wall of the Ka'ba during Ṭawāf.

(3) To recite prescribed prayers.

(4) To avoid any action which breaks the concentration.

(5) To do Ṭawāf near the Ka'ba for men during the day, but for women to do it at night.

(6) If Ṭawāf is interrupted or started in a Makrūh way, to restart the Ṭawāf is Mustaḥab.

(7) To start every Shawṭ by Istilām of Ḥajr—al—Aswad.

If the prescribed prayer cannot be remembered, any prayers in any language will do and your entreaties should be placed before your Creator in a way which humbles you most and they would, Inshā Allāh, be heard.

ṬAWĀF—UL—'UMRA AND ḤAJJ.

Perform ablution and enter the Holy Sanctuary through Bāb-us-Salām, if possible, or through Bāb—ul—'Umra, for those who want to perform 'Umra.

Recite Talbiya as you enter, placing the right foot first, recite:

بِسْمِ اللهِ وَالْحَمْدُ لِلّٰهِ وَالصَّلٰوةُ عَلٰى رَسُوْلِ اللهِ
اَللّٰهُمَّ اغْفِرْ لِيْ ذُنُوْبِيْ وَافْتَحْ لِيْ اَبْوَابَ رَحْمَتِكَ

In the name of Allāh, all praises are due to Him, and salutations on the Messenger of Allāh, O Allāh! Forgive my sins and open for me the gates of Thy mercy.

Bismillāhi wal-ḥam-du lillāhi waṣṣalātu 'alā Rasūl-Allāh, Allāhummaghfir lī dhunūbī waftaḥ lī abwāba raḥmatika.

Any prayer is accepted at the moment when you first glance at the Ka'ba. You may recite the following supplication in the manner of the Messenger of Allāh (peace be upon him) who used to recite it when he first glanced at the Ka'ba.

اَللّٰهُ اَكْبَرُ لَآ اِلٰهَ اِلَّا اللّٰهُ وَاللّٰهُ اَكْبَرُ

Allāh is Great None has the right to be worshipped but Allāh and He is Great.

Allāh-u-Akbar, Lā ilāha illallāhu wallāh-u-Akbar.

With your first glance at the Ka'ba, recite in the manner of the Prophet, (peace be upon him):

اَعُوْذُ بِرَبِّ الْبَيْتِ مِنَ الْكُفْرِ وَالْفَقْرِ
وَمِنْ ضِيْقِ الصَّدْرِ وَعَذَابِ الْقَبْرِ

I seek protection from the Lord of this House from Kufr, from destitution, from narrowness of heart and also from the torture of the grave.

A'ūdhu bi-Rabbil-bait-i min-al-kufri walfaqri wa min ḍīq-iṣ-ṣadri wa 'adhāb-il-qabr.

Even looking at the Ka'ba is an act of worship. This is the only place in the world which has such a privilege and is so blessed.

Approaching the corner of the Ka'ba which holds Ḥajr—al—Aswad, raise your hands in supplication as it is the Sunna of the Holy Prophet, and recite :

اَللّٰهُمَّ اَنْتَ السَّلَامُ وَمِنْكَ السَّلَامُ فَحَيِّنَا رَبَّنَا بِالسَّلَامِ
اَللّٰهُمَّ زِدْ بَيْتَكَ هٰذَا تَشْرِيْفًا وَّتَعْظِيْمًا وَّتَكْرِيْمًا وَّمَهَابَةً
وَّزِدْ مَنْ حَجَّهُ اَوِ اعْتَمَرَ تَشْرِيْفًا وَّتَكْرِيْمًا وَّتَعْظِيْمًا وَّبِرًّا

"O Allāh! Thou art the peace and from Thee cometh peace. So keep us alive, O our Lord, in peace! O Allāh! Increase

Allāhumma ant-as-salāmu wa mink-as-salāmu, fa-ḥayyinā Rabbanā bis-salām. Allāhumma zid baitaka hādhā tashrīfan

this Thy House in dignity honour, nobleness and sacredness and its awe. And increase those who perform the Pilgrimage in honour, nobleness and righteousness."

wwa ta'ẓīman wwa takrīman wwa maḥabatan wwa zid man Ḥajjahu awi'tamara tashrīfan wwa takrīman wwa ta'ẓīman wwa birran.

Now proceed to perform the Ṭawāf.

THE MODE OF PERFORMING ṬAWĀF

Entering the Maṭāf through Bāb—us—Salām, to recite the following prayers from the Holy Qur'ān, is Sunna:

وَقُل رَّبِّ أَدْخِلْنِي مُدْخَلَ صِدْقٍ وَأَخْرِجْنِي مُخْرَجَ صِدْقٍ
وَاجْعَل لِّي مِن لَّدُنكَ سُلْطَانًا نَّصِيرًا ۝ وَقُلْ جَاءَ الْحَقُّ
وَزَهَقَ الْبَاطِلُ ۚ إِنَّ الْبَاطِلَ كَانَ زَهُوقًا (بنی اسرائیل ۸۰-۸۱)

And say, "O my Lord! Let my entry be by the Gate of Truth and my exit by the Gate of Truth: and grant me aid from Thy presence and authority to help (me). And say: Truth has arrived, and falsehood has fled. Verily falsehood was a fleeting thing." (Hold Qur'ān 17:80-81).

Wa qul Rabbi adkhilnī mudkhala ṣidqin wwa akhrijnī mukhraja ṣidqin wwaj'allī milladunka sulṭānan naṣīrā. Wa qul jā-'al-ḥaqqu wa zahaq-al-bāṭilu, innal bāṭila kāna zahuqā.

Now go near to the Black Stone and stand in front of it, or a portion thereof, moving the whole body in front of it is Mustaḥab. Then declare the intention of performing Ṭawāf. It is OBLIGATORY.

INTENTION FOR ṬAWĀF

اَللّٰهُمَّ إِنِّي أُرِيدُ طَوَافَ بَيْتِكَ الْحَرَامِ فَيَسِّرْهُ لِي

وَتَقَبَّلْهُ مِنِّيْ سَبْعَةَ اَشْوَاطٍ لِلّٰهِ تَعَالٰى عَزَّ وَجَلَّ

O Allāh! I desire to perform Ṭawāf of Your Sacred House. So make it easy for me, and receive from me the seven circuits, for your sake Allāh, the most High.

Allāhumma innī urīdu Ṭawāfa baitik-al-ḥarāmi fa-yassirhu lī wa taqabbalhu minnī sab'ata ashwāṭin lillāhi Ta'āla 'azza wa jall.

Concluding, declare whether this Ṭawāf is that of 'Umra or Ḥajj or Tamattu'

For each shawt of the Ṭawāf, remember:

(1) Begin with Istilām of Ḥajr–al–Aswad, When kissing is impossible, this is done by raising your hands, palms facing Ḥajr–al–Aswad and pronouncing Takbīr and Ḥamd viz.

بِسْمِ اللّٰهِ اَللّٰهُ اَكْبَرُ وَلِلّٰهِ الْحَمْدُ

In the name of Allāh, Allāh is Great, and all praise is due to Allāh alone.

Bismillāhi Allāh-u-Akbar, wa lillāh-il-ḥamd.

Memorize the above formula of Takbīr and Ḥamd, if you can.

(2) Drop your hands after pronouncing the Takbīr and Ḥamd.

(3) Proceed (in the direction of Bāb–ul–Ka'ba) and recite the prescribed Du'ā for each Shawṭ, and your own invocations.

(4) At Rukn–al–Yamānī, (the last corner before you reach Ḥajr–al–Aswad again) do Istilām, say Takbīr and Ḥamd and then always recite the following Du'ā:

رَبَّنَا آتِنَا فِي الدُّنْيَا حَسَنَةً وَّفِي الْاٰخِرَةِ حَسَنَةً وَّقِنَا عَذَابَ النَّارِ وَاَدْخِلْنَا الْجَنَّةَ مَعَ الْاَبْرَارِ يَا عَزِيْزُ يَا غَفَّارُ يَا رَبَّ الْعَالَمِيْنَ

Our Lord! Give us goodness in this world and goodness hereafter, and save us from the chastisement of Fire and enter us in Paradise along-with the righteous ones, O Powerful, O Forgiving, O Lord of the Worlds.

Rabbanā ātinā fiddunyā ḥasanatan wwa fil-ākhirati ḥasanatan wwa qinā 'adhāban- nār, wa adkhilnal-jannata ma'al abrār, yā 'A-zīzu yā Ghaffāru yā Rabbul 'alamīn.

Memorise the above prayers, if you can, you will need them at the end of every Shawṭ. It is Sunna of the Holy Prophet to recite this Du'ā at the end of each Shawṭ. You reach Ḥajr—al-Aswad as you finish the Shawṭ. After the first Shawṭ hands should not be raised to ears, but a little lower. Following are the prescribed Du'ās for each Shawṭ. If you prefer to pray in your own style and language you may do so during each Shawṭ.

THE FIRST SHAWṬ

Kiss or raise hands for Istilām of Ḥajr—al—Aswad, recite:

بِسْمِ اللّٰهِ اَللّٰهُ اَكْبَرُ وَلِلّٰهِ الْحَمْدُ

In the name of Allāh, Allāh is Great, and All praise is due to Allāh alone.

Bismillāhi Allāh-u-Akbar wa lillāh-il-ḥamd.

Drop hands, and proceed reciting Du'ā for first Shawṭ of Ṭawāf:

سُبْحَانَ اللّٰهِ وَالْحَمْدُ لِلّٰهِ وَلَا إِلٰهَ إِلَّا اللّٰهُ . وَاللّٰهُ اَكْبَرُ
وَلَا حَوْلَ وَلَا قُوَّةَ إِلَّا بِاللّٰهِ الْعَلِيِّ الْعَظِيْمِ ط وَالصَّلٰوةُ
وَالسَّلَامُ عَلٰى رَسُوْلِ اللّٰهِ صَلَّى اللّٰهُ عَلَيْهِ وَسَلَّمَ ط اَللّٰهُمَّ
إِيْمَانًا بِكَ وَتَصْدِيْقًا بِكَلِمَاتِكَ وَوَفَاءً عَهْدِكَ وَإِتِّبَاعًا
لِسُنَّةِ نَبِيِّكَ وَحَبِيْبِكَ مُحَمَّدٍ صَلَّى اللّٰهُ عَلَيْهِ وَسَلَّمَ ط اَللّٰهُمَّ
إِنِّيْ اَسْأَلُكَ الْعَفْوَ وَالْعَافِيَةَ وَالْمُعَافَاةَ الدَّائِمَةَ فِي الدِّيْنِ

وَالدُّنْيَا وَالْآخِرَةِ وَالْفَوْزَ بِالْجَنَّةِ وَالنَّجَاةَ مِنَ النَّارِ ؕ

Allāh is Holy; All praise is to Allāh; there is nobody worthy to be adored except Allāh, Allāh is Great; There is no power or strength except Allāh, the Great, the Powerful. Peace and salutation be on the Apostle of Allāh. O Allāh! (I start the ṬAWĀF) having faith in Thee, obeying Thy commands, fulfilling the promise made to Thee and fo'lowing the Sunna of Thy Prophet and Thy beloved Muḥammad (peace be upon him). O Allāh! I beseech Thee for the forgiveness of my sins and protection from every evil and eternal safety from every calamity, to be rewarded in this world and the next and render us immune from the Hell-fire."

Subḥān-ə lāhi wal-ḥamdu lillāhi wa lā ilāha illallāhu wall-āhu Akbar wa lā ḥawla wa lā quwwata illā billāh-il- 'Aliyyil 'Aẓīm, waṣ-ṣalātu was-salāmu 'alā rasūl-illāhi ṣallallāhu 'alaihi wa sallam, Allāhumma īmānan bika wa taṣdīqan bikalimātika wa wafā'an bi-'ahdika wa ittibā'an li-sunnatin nabiyyika wa ḥabībika Muḥammad ṣallal-lāhu 'alaihi wa sallam, Allā-humma innī as'alukal-'afwa wal-'āfiyata wal-mu'āfātaddā'i-mata fiddīni waddunyā wal-ākhirati, wal-fauza bil-jannati wan-najāta min-an-nār.

At Rukn—e—Yamānī, do Istilām, say Takbir and Hamd and

رَبَّنَا آتِنَا فِي الدُّنْيَا حَسَنَةً وَّفِي الْآخِرَةِ حَسَنَةً وَّقِنَا عَذَابَ النَّارِ وَأَدْخِلْنَا الْجَنَّةَ مَعَ الْأَبْرَارِ يَا عَزِيزُ يَا غَفَّارُ يَا رَبَّ الْعَالَمِينَ ؕ

Our Lord! Give us goodness in this world and goodness hereafter and save us from the chastisement of the Fire, and enter us in Paradise along-with the righteous ones, O Powerful, O Forgiving, O Lord of the worlds.

Rabbanā ātinā fiddunyā ḥasan-atan wwa fil-ākhirati ḥasana-tan wwa qinā ʿadhāb-an-nār, wa adkhilnal-jannata ma'al-abrār, yā 'Azīzu yā Ghaffāru yā Rabbul 'ālamīn.

Here you have reached Ḥajr—al -Aswad. For every other Shaw now, just raise your palms slightly not up to the ears, for Istilām. If you are following your Mu'allim, then recite prayers after him.

THE SECOND SHAWṬ

Kiss or raise hands for Istilām and recite:

بِسْمِ اللّٰهِ اَللّٰهُ اَكْبَرُ وَلِلّٰهِ الْحَمْدُ

In the name of Allāh, Allāh is Great, and all praise is due to Allāh alone.

'Bismillāhi Allāh-u-Akbar, wa lillāh-il-ḥamd.

Drop hands, and proceed reciting Du'ā for second Shawṭ of

اَللّٰهُمَّ اِنَّ هٰذَا الْبَيْتَ بَيْتُكَ وَالْحَرَمَ حَرَمُكَ وَالْاَمْنَ اَمْنُكَ
وَالْعَبْدُ عَبْدُكَ وَاَنَا عَبْدُكَ وَابْنُ عَبْدِكَ وَهٰذَا مَقَامُ الْعَائِذِ بِكَ
مِنَ النَّارِ ط فَحَرِّمْ لُحُوْمَنَا وَ بَشَرَتَنَا عَلَى النَّارِ ط اَللّٰهُمَّ حَبِّبْ
اِلَيْنَا الْاِيْمَانَ وَ زَيِّنْهُ فِىْ قُلُوْبِنَا وَكَرِّهْ اِلَيْنَا الْكُفْرَ وَ الْفُسُوْقَ
وَالْعِصْيَانَ وَاجْعَلْنَا مِنَ الرَّاشِدِيْنَ ط اَللّٰهُمَّ قِنِىْ عَذَابَكَ
يَوْمَ تَبْعَثُ عِبَادَكَ ط اَللّٰهُمَّ ارْزُقْنِىَ الْجَنَّةَ بِغَيْرِ حِسَابٍ ط

"O Allāh! Verily this House is Thine House and this Ḥaram is Thine Ḥaram and the peace and tranquility which prevails here is from Thine bounties. And every servant is Thy servant and I am also Thy servant and this is the place of those who seek Thine refuge from the Hell-fire. So Thou should make our flesh and our

Allāhumma inna hādhal-baita baituka wal-ḥarama ḥaramuka wal-amna amnuka wal-'abdu 'abduka wa anā 'abduka wab-nu 'abdika wa hādhā maqāmul-'ā'idhi bika min-an-nār, fa-ḥarrim luḥūmanā wa bashar-tanā 'al-an-nār, Allāhumma ḥabbib ilainal-īmāna wa zayyinhu fī qulūbinā wa karrih ilain—al-kufra wal

blood ḤARAM (forbidden) to Hell-fire. O Allāh! Make faith our passion and create its love in our hearts and make infidelity and corruption and disobedience distasteful for us and include us in the category of those who obtained guidance. O Allāh! on the Day when Thee resurrects all, spare me from Thy punishment. O Allāh! Reward me with the Paradise without any interrogation."

fusūqa wal-'iṣyāna waj'alnā min-ar-rāshidīn, Allāhumma qinī 'adhābaka yauma tab'athu 'ibādaka, Allāhumma arzuqnil-jannata bighairi ḥisāb.

At Rukn—al—Yamānī, do Istilām, say Takbīr and Ḥamd and recite:

رَبَّنَا آتِنَا فِي الدُّنْيَا حَسَنَةً وَّفِي الْآخِرَةِ حَسَنَةً وَّقِنَا
عَذَابَ النَّارِ وَ اَدْخِلْنَا الْجَنَّةَ مَعَ الْاَبْرَارِ يَا عَزِيْزُ
يَا غَفَّارُ يَا رَبَّ الْعٰلَمِيْنَ ط

Our Lord! Give us goodness in this world and goodness hereafter, and save us from the chastisement of Fire and enter us in Paradise along-with the righteous ones, O Powerful, O Forgiving, O lord of the worlds.

Rabbanā ātinā fiddunyā ḥasanatan wwa fil-ākhirati ḥasanatan wwa qinā 'adhāban- nār, wa adkhilnal-jannata ma'al-abrār, yā 'Azīzu yā Ghaffāru yā Rabbul 'ālamīn.

The end of the second Shawṭ, and you are at Ḥajr—al—Aswad again.

THE THIRD SHAWṬ

Kiss and raise hands for Istilām of Ḥajr—al—Aswad, and recite:

بِسْمِ اللهِ اَللهُ اَكْبَرُ وَ لِلّٰهِ الْحَمْدُ

In the name of Allāh, Allāh is Great; and All praise is due to Allāh alone.

Bismillāhi Allāh-u-Akbar wa lillāh-il-ḥamd.

Drop hands, proceed reciting Du'ā for third Shawṭ of Ṭawāf:

اَللّٰهُمَّ إِنِّيْ اَعُوْذُبِكَ مِنَ الشَّكِّ وَالشِّرْكِ وَالشِّقَاقِ وَالنِّفَاقِ
وَسُوْءِ الْاَخْلَاقِ وَسُوْءِ الْمَنْظَرِ وَ الْمُنْقَلَبِ فِي الْمَالِ وَالْاَهْلِ
وَالْوَلَدِ ط اَللّٰهُمَّ إِنِّيْ اَسْئَلُكَ رِضَاكَ وَالْجَنَّةَ وَ اَعُوْذُبِكَ مِنْ
سَخَطِكَ وَالنَّارِ ط اَللّٰهُمَّ إِنِّيْ اَعُوْذُبِكَ مِنْ فِتْنَةِ الْقَبْرِ
وَاَعُوْذُبِكَ مِنْ فِتْنَةِ الْمَحْيَا وَالْمَمَاتِ ط

"O Allāh! I want to come under Thine shelter from doubt from associating Thee with any other thing, shelter from differences, dissensions, immorality, adverse state and ultimate end. I pray for Thine blessings for my property and family. I pray for Paradise and shelter from Thine wrath and Hell-fire. I pray for the shelter from the agony of the grave. O Allāh! Protect me from every misfortune of life and death."

Allāhumma inni a'ūdhu bika min-ash-shakki wash-shirki wash-shiqāqi wannifāqi wa sū'il-akhlāqi wa sū'il manẓari wal-munqalibi fil-māli walahli wal-walad, Allāhumma innī as'aluka riḍāka wal-jannata wa a'ūdhu bika min sakhaṭika wan-nār, Allā-humma innī a'ūdhu bika min fitnatil qabri wa a'ūdhu bika min fitnatil-maḥyā wal-mamāt.

At Rukn—al—Yamānī, do Istilām, say Takbīr and Ḥamd and

رَبَّنَا آتِنَا فِي الدُّنْيَا حَسَنَةً وَّ فِي الْاٰخِرَةِ حَسَنَةً وَّقِنَا
عَذَابَ النَّارِ وَ اَدْخِلْنَا الْجَنَّةَ مَعَ الْاَبْرَارِ يَا عَزِيْزُ
يَا غَفَّارُ يَا رَبَّ الْعَالَمِيْنَ ط

Our Lord! Give us goodness in this world and goodness hereafter and save us from the chastisement of Fire, and enter us in Paradise along with the righteous ones, O Powerful, O Forgiving, O Lord of the worlds.

Rabbanā ātinā fiddunyā ḥasanatan wwa fil-ākhirati ḥasanatan wwa qinā 'adhab-an-nār, wa adkhilnal-jannata ma'al-abrār, yā 'Azīzu yā Ghaffāru yā Rabbul 'Ālamīn.

The end of the 3rd Shawṭ, and you are at Ḥajr—al—Aswad again.

THE FOURTH SHAWṬ

Kiss, or raise hands for Istilām and recite:

بِسْمِ اللّٰهِ اَللّٰهُ اَكْبَرُ وَلِلّٰهِ الْحَمْدُ

In the name of Allāh, Allāh is Great, and all praise is due to Allāh alone.

Bismillāhi Allah-u-Akbar, wa lillāh-il-ḥamd.

Drop hands, proceed reciting Du'ā for fourth Shawṭ of Ṭawāf:

اَللّٰهُمَّ اجْعَلْهُ حَجًّا مَّبْرُوْرًا وَّسَعْيًا مَّشْكُوْرًا وَّذَنْبًا مَّغْفُوْرًا ط وَّعَمَلًا صَالِحًا مَّقْبُوْلًا وَّتِجَارَةً لَّنْ تَبُوْرَ ط يَا عَالِمَ مَا فِى الصُّدُوْرِ ط اَخْرِجْنِىْ يَا اَللّٰهُ مِنَ الظُّلُمَاتِ اِلَى النُّوْرِ ط اَللّٰهُمَّ اِنِّىْ اَسْأَلُكَ مُوْجِبَاتِ رَحْمَتِكَ وَعَزَائِمَ مَغْفِرَتِكَ وَالسَّلَامَةَ مِنْ كُلِّ اِثْمٍ وَّالْغَنِيْمَةَ مِنْ كُلِّ بِرٍّ وَّالْفَوْزَ بِالْجَنَّةِ وَالنَّجَاةَ مِنَ النَّارِ ط رَبِّ قَنِّعْنِىْ بِمَا رَزَقْتَنِىْ وَبَارِكْ لِىْ فِيْمَا اَعْطَيْتَنِىْ وَاخْلُفْ عَلٰى كُلِّ غَائِبَةٍ لِّىْ مِنْكَ بِخَيْرٍ ط

"O Allāh! Render this Pilgrimage of mine acceptable and successful and a means of forgiveness of my sins. Bless me with honest dealings and a business where there is no loss. O Knower of the state of hearts! Drag me out of the darkness of sins into the light of good deeds. O Allāh! I pray for the safe escape from every sin and make me virtuous and enable me to reap its advantages. Make me worthy of Paradise and protect me from Hell-fire. O Allāh! Grant me contentment for all Thou hast blessed me with; BARAKĀT (auspiciousness) for all that Thou hast conferred on me. O Allāh! Compensate me for every sin of mine."

Allāhumma—j'alhu Ḥajjam-mabrūran wwa sa'yam-mashkūran wwa dhambam-maghfūr-an wwa 'amalan ṣāliḥam-maqbūlan wwa tijāratallan-tabūra, yā 'ālima mā fiṣ-ṣudūri akhrijnī yā Allāhu min-aẓ-ẓulumāti il-an-nūr, Allāhumma innī as'aluka mūjibāti raḥmatika wa 'azā-'ima maghfiratika was-salāmata min kulli ithmin wwal-ghanīmata min kulli birrin wwal-fauza bil-jannata wannajāta min-an-nār. Rabbi qanni'nī bimā razaqtanī wa bārik lī fīma a'taitanī wakhluf 'alā kulli ghā'ib-atillī minka bi-khair.

At Rukn—al—Yamānī, do Istilām, say Takbīr and Ḥamd and recite:

رَبَّنَا آتِنَا فِي الدُّنْيَا حَسَنَةً وَّفِي الْآخِرَةِ حَسَنَةً وَّقِنَا
عَذَابَ النَّارِ وَ اَدْخِلْنَا الْجَنَّةَ مَعَ الْاَبْرَارِ يَا عَزِيْزُ
يَا غَفَّارُ يَا رَبَّ الْعَالَمِيْنَ ط

Our Lord! Give us goodness in this world and goodness hereafter, and save us from the chastisement of Fire and enter us in Paradise alongwith the righteous ones, O Powerful, O Forgiving, O Lord of the worlds!

Rabbanā ātinā fiddunyā ḥasanatan wwa fil-ākhirati ḥasanatan wwa qinā 'Adhāban- nār wa adkhil-nal-jannata ma'al abrār, yā 'Azīzu yā Ghaffāru yā Rabbul 'ālamīn.

The end of fourth Shawt, and you are Ḥajr—al—Aswad again.

THE FIFTH SHAWṬ

Kiss or raise hands for Istilām and recite:

بِسْمِ اللّٰهِ اَللّٰهُ اَكْبَرُ وَلِلّٰهِ الْحَمْدُ

In the name of Allāh, Allāh is the Great, and All praise is due to Allāh alone.

Bismillāhi Allāh-u-Akbar wa lillāh-il-ḥamd.

Drop hands, proceed reciting Du'ā for fifth Shawṭ of Tawāf:

اَللّٰهُمَّ اَظِلَّنِيْ تَحْتَ ظِلِّ عَرْشِكَ يَوْمَ لَا ظِلَّ اِلَّا ظِلَّ عَرْشِكَ
وَلَا بَاقِيَ اِلَّا وَجْهَكَ وَاسْقِنِيْ مِنْ حَوْضِ نَبِيِّكَ سَيِّدِنَا مُحَمَّدٍ
صَلَّى اللّٰهُ عَلَيْهِ وَسَلَّمَ شَرْبَةً هَنِيْئَةً مَّرِيْئَةً لَّا نَظْمَأُ
بَعْدَهَا اَبَدًا ۔ اَللّٰهُمَّ اِنِّيْ اَسْاَلُكَ مِنْ خَيْرِ مَا سَاَلَكَ مِنْهُ
نَبِيُّكَ سَيِّدُنَا مُحَمَّدٌ صَلَّى اللّٰهُ عَلَيْهِ وَسَلَّمَ ۔ وَاَعُوْذُبِكَ مِنْ شَرِّ
مَا اسْتَعَاذَكَ مِنْهُ نَبِيُّكَ سَيِّدُنَا مُحَمَّدٌ صَلَّى اللّٰهُ عَلَيْهِ وَسَلَّمَ ۔
اَللّٰهُمَّ اِنِّيْ اَسْاَلُكَ الْجَنَّةَ وَنَعِيْمَهَا وَمَا يُقَرِّبُنِيْ اِلَيْهَا
مِنْ قَوْلٍ اَوْ فِعْلٍ اَوْ عَمَلٍ وَاَعُوْذُبِكَ مِنَ النَّارِ وَمَا يُقَرِّبُنِيْ
اِلَيْهَا مِنْ قَوْلٍ اَوْ فِعْلٍ اَوْ عَمَلٍ ۔

"O Allāh! Give me peace beneath Thy canopy on the Day when there will be no shelter except Thine and there will be no being except Thyself. O Allāh! Provide a pleasant and delicious draught from the Hauḍ-i-Kauthar (the Reservoir of Plenty) of Your Prophet

Allāhumma aẓillanī taḥta ẓilli 'arshika yauma lā ẓilla illā ẓilla 'arshika wa lā bāqiya illā wajhaka wasqinī min ḥauḍi nabiyyika sayyidinā Muḥammad ṣallallāhu 'alaihi wa sallam sharbatan hanī'atan marī'at-al-lā naẓma'u ba'da-hā abadā, Allāhumma innī as'aluka min khairi

(peace be upon him), that thereafter I feel no thirst whatsoever. O Allāh! I request Thee for the blessings of all those things which the Prophet Muḥammad (peace be upon him) asked and beg Thy protection against all those vices from which the Prophet Muḥammad (peace be upon him) sought your protection. O Allāh! I invoke Thy blessings for Paradise and its blissful possessions and for every word and act which could draw me closer to Paradise. I seek Thy protection from Hell-fire and for every word and act which could draw me closer to Hell-fire.

ma sa'alaka minhu nabīyyuka sayyidunā Muḥammad ṣallall-āhu 'alaihi wa sallam, wa a'ūdhu bika min sharri masta'-ādha bika minhu nabīyyuka sayyidunā Muhammad ṣallall-āhu 'alaihi wa sallam, Allā-humma innī as'aluk-al-jannata wa na'īma-hā wa mā yuqarri-bunī ilaihā min qaulin au fi'-lin au 'amalin wa a'ūdhu bika min-an-nāri wa mā yuqarri-bunī ilaihā min qaulin au fi'-lin au 'amal.

At Rukn—al—Yamānī, do Istilām, say Takbīr and Ḥamd and recite:

رَبَّنَا آتِنَا فِي الدُّنْيَا حَسَنَةً وَّ فِي الْآخِرَةِ حَسَنَةً وَّ قِنَا عَذَابَ النَّارِ وَ أَدْخِلْنَا الْجَنَّةَ مَعَ الْأَبْرَارِ يَا عَزِيزُ يَا غَفَّارُ يَا رَبَّ الْعَالَمِينَ

Our Lord! Give us gooaness in this world and goodness here-after and save us from the chastisement of Fire, and enter us in Paradise along with the righteous ones O Powerful, O Lord of the worlds.

Rabbanā ātinā fiddunyā ḥasanatan wwa fil-ākhirati ḥasanatan wwa qinā 'adhāb-an-nār, wa adkhilnal-jannata ma 'al-abrār, yā 'Azīzu yā Ghaffāru yā Rabbul 'ālamīn.

The end of the fifth Shawṭ, and you are at Ḥajr—al—Aswad again

THE SIXTH SHAWṬ

Kiss or raise hands for Istilām and recite:

بِسْمِ اللهِ اَللهُ اَكْبَرُ وَلِلّٰهِ الْحَمْدُ

In the name of Allāh, Allāh is Great, and all praise is due to Allāh alone.

Bismillāhi Allāh-u-Akbar, wa lillāh-il-ḥamd.

Drop hands, proceed reciting Ḍu'a for sixth Shawṭ of Tawāf:

اَللّٰهُمَّ اِنَّ لَكَ عَلَيَّ حُقُوْقًا كَثِيْرَةً فِيْمَا بَيْنِيْ وَبَيْنَكَ وَحُقُوْقًا
كَثِيْرَةً فِيْمَا بَيْنِيْ وَبَيْنَ خَلْقِكَ ۔ اَللّٰهُمَّ مَا كَانَ لَكَ مِنْهَا
فَاغْفِرْهُ لِيْ وَمَا كَانَ لِخَلْقِكَ فَتَحَمَّلْهُ عَنِّيْ وَاَغْنِنِيْ بِحَلَالِكَ
عَنْ حَرَامِكَ وَبِطَاعَتِكَ عَنْ مَّعْصِيَتِكَ وَبِفَضْلِكَ عَنْ مَّنْ
سِوَاكَ يَا وَاسِعَ الْمَغْفِرَةِ ۔ اَللّٰهُمَّ اِنَّ بَيْتَكَ عَظِيْمٌ وَّوَجْهَكَ
كَرِيْمٌ وَّاَنْتَ يَا اَللهُ حَلِيْمٌ كَرِيْمٌ عَظِيْمٌ تُحِبُّ الْعَفْوَ فَاعْفُ عَنِّيْ ۔

"O Allāh! There are many rights of Thine which devolve on me and there are many rights which subsist between me and Thine creatures. Forgive me for all my trespasses and, for my shortcomings in my relationship with Thine creatures and be my guarantor for the forgiveness. O Allāh! Provide me lawful subsistence as against the unlawful, instil in myself faithfulness and provide me with Thy favours and render me independent of the favours of others except the ones originating from Thee, O

Allāhumma inna laka 'alayya huqūqan kathīratan fīmā bainī wa bainaka wa huqūqan kathīratan fīmā bainī wa baina khalqika, Allāhumma mā kāna laka minhā faghfirhu lī wa mā kāna li-hkalqika fa-taḥammal-hu 'annī wa aghninī bi-ḥalālaka 'an ḥarāmaka wa bi-ṭā'atika 'am-ma'ṣivatika wa bi-faḍlika 'amman sawāka yā wāsi-'al-maghfirati, Allā humma inna baitika 'aẓımun wwa wajhika karīmun wwa anta yā Allāhu Ḥalīmun Karīmun tuḥibb-ul-'afwa fa'fu 'annī.

Allāh! The Beneficent and Merciful, Forgiver, verily Thy House is the abode of great height and Thyself is of Great Honour. O Allāh! Thine is the Majesty, Compassion and Glory. Thee liketh to forgive, so be kind and forgive me of my sins and errors."

At Rukn—al—Yamānī, do Istilām, say Takbīr and Ḥamd and recite:

رَبَّنَا آتِنَا فِى الدُّنْيَا حَسَنَةً وَّفِى الْآخِرَةِ حَسَنَةً ۔ وَّقِنَا
عَذَابَ النَّارِ وَ اَدْخِلْنَا الْجَنَّةَ مَعَ الْاَبْرَارِ يَاعَزِيْزُ
يَاغَفَّارُ يَا رَبَّ الْعَالَمِيْنَ ،

Our Lord! Give us goodness in this world and goodness hereafter, and save us from the chastisement of Fire and enter us in Paradise along-with the righteous ones, O Powerful, O Forgiving, O Lord of the worlds.

Rabbanā ātinā fiddunyā ḥasanatan wwa fil-ākhirati ḥasanatan wwa qinā 'adhāban-nār wa adkhilnal-jannata ma'al abrār, ya 'Azīzu yā Ghaffāru yā Rabbul 'ālamīn.

The end of sixth Shawṭ, and you are at Ḥajr—al—Aswad aqain.

THE SEVENTH SHAWṬ

Kiss or raise hands for Istilām, and recite:

بِسْمِ اللّٰهِ اَللّٰهُ اَكْبَرُ وَلِلّٰهِ الْحَمْدُ

In the name of Allāh, Allāh is Great, and All praise is due to Allāh alone.

Bismillāhi Allāh-u-Akbar wa lillāh-il-ḥamd.

Drop your hands, proceed to complete the final Shawṭ, reciting Du'ā for seventh shawṭ of Ṭawāf.

اَللّٰهُمَّ اِنِّىْٓ اَسْأَلُكَ اِيْمَانًا كَامِلًا وَّ يَقِيْنًا صَادِقًا وَّ رِزْقًا
وَّاسِعًا وَّ قَلْبًا خَاشِعًا وَّ لِسَانًا ذَاكِرًا وَّ رِزْقًا حَلَالًا طَيِّبًا
وَّ تَوْبَةً نَّصُوْحَةً وَّ تَوْبَةً قَبْلَ الْمَوْتِ وَ رَاحَةً عِنْدَ الْمَوْتِ
وَ مَغْفِرَةً وَّ رَاحَةً بَعْدَ الْمَوْتِ وَ الْعَفْوَ عِنْدَ الْحِسَابِ وَ الْفَوْزَ
بِالْجَنَّةِ وَ النَّجَاةَ مِنَ النَّارِ بِرَحْمَتِكَ يَا عَزِيْزُ يَا غَفَّارُ ؕ
رَبِّ زِدْنِىْ عِلْمًا وَّ اَلْحِقْنِىْ بِالصّٰلِحِيْنَ ؕ

"O Allāh! I pray for perfect faith, true belief, plentiful provisions, humble heart, and a tongue that speaks about Thee. I pray for lawful and pure food, repentance of truthful heart, repentance before death, comfort at the time of death, forgiveness and blessings after death and Paradise without interrogation and protection from Hell-fire. All this I pray by invoking Thine blessing, O The Highly Honourable, the Forgiver! O the Creator! Increase my knowledge (of faith) and include me among the faithful people."

Allāhumma innī as'aluka īmānan kāmilan wwa yaqīnan ṣādiqan wwa rizqan wwāsi'an wwa qalban khāshian wwa lisānan dhākiran wwa rizqan ṭayyiban wwa taubatan-naṣū-ḥatan wwa taubatan qabl-al-mauti wa rāḥatan 'indal-mauti wa maghfiratan wwa rāḥatan ba'dal-mauti wal-'afwa 'indal ḥisābi wal-fauzi bil-jannati wan-nijāta min-an-nāri, bi-raḥmatika yā 'Azīzu yā Ghaf-fār, Rabbi zidnī 'ilman wwal-ḥiqnī biṣ-ṣāliḥīn.

At Rukn—al—Yamānī, do Istilām, say Takbīr and Ḥamd and recite:

رَبَّنَا آتِنَا فِى الدُّنْيَا حَسَنَةً وَّ فِى الْاٰخِرَةِ حَسَنَةً وَّ قِنَا
عَذَابَ النَّارِ وَ اَدْخِلْنَا الْجَنَّةَ مَعَ الْاَبْرَارِ يَا عَزِيْزُ

يَا غَفَّارُ يَا رَبَّ الْعَالَمِينَ ۔

Our Lord! Give us goodness in this world and save us from the chastisement of Fire, and enter us in Paradise along with the righteous ones, O Powerful O Forgiving, O Lord of the worlds.

Rabbanā ātinā fiddunyā ḥasanatan wwa fil-ākhirati ḥasanatan wwa qinā 'adhāb-an-nār, wa adkhilnal-jannata ma'al-abrār, yā 'Azīzu yā Ghaffāru yā Rabb-ul-'ālamīn.

At the end of the seventh Shawṭ come to the Black Stone, kiss it if possible, for Istilām, reciting:

بِسْمِ اللّٰهِ اَللّٰهُ اَكْبَرُ وَلِلّٰهِ الْحَمْدُ

In the name of Allāh, Allāh is Great, and all praise is due to Allāh alone.

Bismillāhi Allāh-u-Akbar, wa lillāh-il-ḥamd.

If you prefer to pray in your own language and feel that the prescribed Du'ās above, were not communicating (meaning to you and your supplications) then pray in your own heart by all means. This is the chance of your life. All good prayers, are accepted during Ṭawāf if appealed with sincerity. Pray for your parents, children, family and friends. Pray especially for your faith, and the rest of the Muslim world.

After the Istilām of Ḥajr—al—Aswad for the 8th time, proceed to Multazim. This is the place between Ḥajr—al—Aswad and the door of the Ka'ba.

Remember Multazim has a special blessing for the efficacy of prayers. It is Sunna of the Prophet that after completing Ṭawāf you reach Multazim, and stand upright facing the portion of the wall. Raise your hands above your head and, touch Multazim with your chest and put your cheek on Multazim and invoke the Mercy and blessing of Allāh. Prayers are always and all the time (day and night) accepted here. Recite:

DU'Ā AT MULTAZIM:

اَللّٰهُمَّ يَا رَبَّ الْبَيْتِ الْعَتِيْقِ اَعْتِقْ رِقَابَنَا وَ رِقَابَ
آبَائِنَا وَ اُمَّهَاتِنَا وَ اِخْوَانِنَا وَ اَوْلَادِنَا مِنَ النَّارِ ط
يَا ذَا الْجُوْدِ وَالْكَرَمِ وَالْفَضْلِ وَالْمَنِّ وَالْعَطَاءِ وَالْاِحْسَانِ ط
اَللّٰهُمَّ اَحْسِنْ عَاقِبَتَنَا فِي الْاُمُوْرِ كُلِّهَا وَ اَجِرْنَا مِنْ خِزْيِ الدُّنْيَا
وَعَذَابِ الْآخِرَةِ ط اَللّٰهُمَّ اِنِّيْ عَبْدُكَ وَابْنُ عَبْدِكَ
وَاقِفٌ تَحْتَ بَابِكَ مُلْتَزِمٌ بِاَعْتَابِكَ مُتَذَلِّلٌ بَيْنَ يَدَيْكَ
اَرْجُوْ رَحْمَتَكَ وَاَخْشٰى عَذَابَكَ مِنَ النَّارِ يَا قَدِيْمَ الْاِحْسَانِ ط
اَللّٰهُمَّ اِنِّيْ اَسْأَلُكَ اَنْ تَرْفَعَ ذِكْرِيْ وَتَضَعَ وِزْرِيْ وَتُصْلِحَ
اَمْرِيْ وَ تُطَهِّرَ قَلْبِيْ وَ تُنَوِّرَ لِيْ فِيْ قَبْرِيْ وَ تَغْفِرَ لِيْ ذَنْبِيْ ط
وَ اَسْأَلُكَ الدَّرَجَاتِ الْعُلٰى مِنَ الْجَنَّةِ آمِيْنَ ط

"O Allāh, O Lord of this old House! Save our necks and those of our forefathers, mothers, brothers, and children from the Hell-fire. O The Forgiver, The Merciful, The Bountiful and the Benefactor! Aquit us well in all our dealings and save us from a bad name in this world and the wrath in our life after death. O Allah! I am Thy slave and the son of Thy slave. I am standing beneath the Gate of Thine House, I am begging in front of Thee and seek Thy blessings. I am afraid of the Hell-fire and seek salvation. O

Allāhuma yā Rabb-al-bait-il-'atīqi a'tiq riqābanā wa riqāba ābā'inā wa ummahātinā wa ikhwāninā wa aulādinā min-an nār. Yā dhal-jūdi wal-karami wal-faḍli wal-manni wal-'aṭā'i wal-iḥsān, Allāhumma aḥsin 'āqibatanā fil-umūri kullihā wa ajarna min khiz yiddynya wa adhabil-akhirati, Alla humma in ni 'abduka wabnu 'abdika wa-qifun taḥta bābika Multazi-mun bi-a'tābika mutazallilun baina yadaika arjū raḥmataka wa akhshā 'adhābaka min-an-nār Yā-Qadīm-aliḥsān. Allā-humma innī as'aluka an tarfa'a dhikrī wa taḍa's wizarī wa-

The Ever Bountiful! Shower now as ever, Thy bounties. O Allāh! I pray Thee that my prayers may reach Thee. O Allāh! Lessen the weight of my sins and correct me. Cleanse my heart and provide light in my grave and forgive my sins. I beg Thee for the high places in Thine Paradise."

tuṣliha amrī wa tuṭahhira qalbī wa tunawwwira lī fī qabrī wa taghfiralī dhanbī wa as'aluka-ddarajāt-i-l'ūlā min-al-janna, Āmīn.

Pray to Allah besides the above Du'ā, for whatever you wish, for your parents etc. People cry and sob here like children lost and found by loving parents. Remember if your guide is waiting for you, make your prayers short. If the crowdsof people are keen to get close to the Multazim, give them a chance too.

PRAYER AT MAQĀM—E—IBRĀHĪM:

When you finish praying at the Multazim, move to Maqām—e—Ibrāhīm. Offer two Nafl rak'at of Wājib—ut—Ṭawāf at Maqām—e—Ibrāhīm or in its vicinity (due to the crowd). It is Sunna to recite Sūra Al—Kāfirūn in the first rak'a and Sūra Ikhlās in the second.

After the Ṣalāt, raise your hands in supplication with humility and lowliness and pray in your own language. Then recite the following Du'ā:

اللّٰهُمَّ إِنَّكَ تَعْلَمُ سِرِّي وَعَلَانِيَتِي فَاقْبَلْ مَعْذِرَتِي وَتَعْلَمُ
حَاجَتِي فَأَعْطِنِي سُؤَالِي وَتَعْلَمُ مَا فِي نَفْسِي فَاغْفِرْ لِي ذُنُوبِي ط
اللّٰهُمَّ إِنِّي أَسْأَلُكَ إِيمَانًا يُبَاشِرُ قَلْبِي وَيَقِينًا صَادِقًا حَتّٰى
أَعْلَمَ أَنَّهُ لَا يُصِيبُنِي إِلَّا مَا كَتَبْتَ لِي وَرِضًا مِّنْكَ بِمَا قَسَمْتَ
لِي ط أَنْتَ وَلِيِّي فِي الدُّنْيَا وَالْآخِرَةِ تَوَفَّنِي مُسْلِمًا وَّأَلْحِقْنِي
بِالصَّالِحِينَ ط اللّٰهُمَّ لَا تَدَعْ لَنَا فِي مَقَامِنَا هٰذَا ذَنْبًا إِلَّا

غَفَرْتَهُ وَلَا هَمًّا إِلَّا فَرَّجْتَهُ وَلَا حَاجَةً إِلَّا قَضَيْتَهَا وَيَسَّرْتَهَا
فَيَسِّرْ أُمُورَنَا وَاشْرَحْ صُدُورَنَا وَنَوِّرْ قُلُوبَنَا وَاخْتِمْ
بِالصَّالِحَاتِ أَعْمَالَنَا ، اَللّٰهُمَّ تَوَفَّنَا مُسْلِمِينَ وَأَلْحِقْنَا
بِالصَّالِحِينَ غَيْرَ خَزَايَا وَلَا مَفْتُونِينَ آمِينَ يَا رَبَّ الْعٰلَمِينَ ط

"O Allāh! Thou knoweth my affairs be they hidden or open. So pardon me. Thou knoweth what I need, So concede my desire. Thou knoweth what is there in my heart. So pardon me of my sins. I pray, O Allāh! for a faith with which my heart should be filled and the true belief so that I may know I will receive all that Thou hast ordained for me. Thou ist my Helper in this world and in the life Hereafter. May I die only in the faith of Islām and be included among the faithfuls. O Allāh! Spare me not from forgiveness, for my trespasses, on the occasion of my Pilgrimage to this Holy Place; give me riddance of all the worries; solve all my problems; lessen the weight of my task; open our hearts and illuminate them and make our deeds pious. O Allāh! Give us death only in the Faith of Islām and include us among the faithful. Neither should we earn a bad name nor be subjected to trials. Āmeen, O Allāh, Creator of the worlds.

Allāhumma innaka ta'lam'u sirrī wa 'alāniyatī faqbal ma'-dhiratī wa ta'lamu ḥājatī fa'tinī sū'li wa ta'lam-u mā fī nafsī faghfir lī dhunūbī, Allāhumma innī as'aluka īmānan-yyubāshir qalbī wa yaqīnan ṣādiqan ḥattā a'lamu annahū lā yuṣībunī illā mā katabta lī wa riḍamminka bimā qasamta lī anta waliyyī fiddunyā wal-ākhirati tawaff-anī Musliman-wwa-alḥiqnī biṣ-ṣāliḥīn. Allāhumma lā tada' lanā fī maqāminā hādhā dhan-ban illā ghafarta-hū wa lā hamman illā farrajtahū wa lā ḥājatan qadaitahā wa yassar-tahā fa-yassir umūranā wash-raḥ ṣudūranā wa naw-wir qulūbanā wakhtim biṣ-ṣāl-iḥāti a'mālana, Allāhumma tawaffa-nā Muslimīna wa al-ḥiqnā biṣ-ṣāliḥīna ghaira khaz-āya wa lā maftūnina, Āmīn, Yā Rabb-al-'ālamīn.

This is the end of Ṭawāf.

AT THE WELL OF ZAM—ZAM:

After the prayers at Maqām—e—Ibrāhīm come to the Zam-zam well. Facing towards the Ka'ba recite Bismillāh three times, and drink in plenty its water in three draughts. Recite the following Du'ā, in the Sunna of the Prophet.

اَللّٰهُمَّ اِنِّیْ اَسْأَلُكَ رِزْقًا وَّاسِعًا
وَّعِلْمًا نَّافِعًا وَّشِفَاءً مِّنْ كُلِّ دَاءٍ

I beseech Thee, O Allāh! Bestow on me generous subsistence, advantageous knowledge and cure from all ailments.

Allāhumma innī as'aluka rizqan wwasi'an wwa' 'ilman nāfi'an wwa shifā' - am-min kulli dā'in.

RULE OF ACTION

The first Ṭawāf performed by a Qārin or a Mutamattī' will be treated as Ṭawāf of 'Umra, whereafter Sa'ī of 'Umra becomes obligatory. As such, Ramal and Idṭibā' are necessary for both of them. For a Mufrid, his first Ṭawāf of Baitallāh will be Ṭawāf—e—Qadūm, whereafter Sa'ī for Ḥajj is not necessary to be observed at that time. He has the choice to perform Sa'ī at this time or after Ṭawāf—e—ziyāra on the 10th of Duhl—Ḥijja. If he chooses to perform Sa'ī after Ṭawāf—e—Qadūm, he will have to observe the Sunna of Ramal and Idṭibā'. It is preferable to perform Sa'ī of Ḥajj for a Mufrid after Ṭawāf—e—Ziyāra.

CHAPTER NINE

SA'Ī BETWEEN ṢAFĀ AND MARWA:

Description:

The next step towards the ceremony of 'Umra and/or Ḥajj is the performance of Sa'ī between the two hills ṢAFĀ and MARWA. These are the two hills in the neighbourhood of Masjid–al–Ḥarām. The literal meaning of Sa'ī is "struggle". This ceremony reminds one of the struggle a mother had in a desolate arid place when searching for water for her infant, the Prophet Ismā'īl. It is observed as a memorial of the struggle Hagar had when she ran between the two hills looking for water and entreating Almighty Allāh for His mercy and blessing "Innaka ta'lamu mā lā na' lam" ["Of course You are the One Who Knows (of the future and the unseen), we are the ignorant ones."]

Her prayers invoking Allāh's mercy on her and her forsaken child in the desert are repeated, reviving the most blessed struggle in human history, when she found the water sprouting at the feet of the child. This struggle is also one of the ceremonies of the Ḥajj. This ceremony is called "Sa'ī". The two places between which she ran faster is known as Meelain Akhḍarain.

The Rules and Conditions of SA'Ī:

1) The Sa'ī should always be performed after Ṭawāf. It is Sunna to perform Sa'ī soon after Ṭawāf, though a little pause due to fatigue or thirst is allowed.

2) Sa'ī should be performed on foot unless there is a valid reason for hiring a wheel chair, available at Mas'ā (the place where Sa'ī is performed). If it is performed on a chair without any valid excuse, a Damm will become obligatory.

3) Declaration of the Intention to perform Sa'ī is preferable.

4) Iḥrām is a condition for Sa'ī for a pilgrim performing 'Umra or Ḥajj—e—Tamattu'

5) Iḥrām is also a condition for Sa'ī for a Qārin and a Mufrid when he/she is performing Ṭawāf—e—Qadūm before Waqūf—e—'Arafāt i.e. the first Ṭawāf or Ḥajj.

6) If Sa'ī was not performed by a Mufrid after Ṭawāf—e—Qadūṃ, it must be performed within Ayyām—e—Naḥr, i.e. on the 10th, 11th and 12th of Dhul-Ḥijja. It is Makrūh to delay Sa'ī after the days of Naḥr.

7) Sa'ī is Wājib for a Qārin after Ṭawāf—e—Qadūm before the stay at 'Arafāt, where Iḥrām is a condition, and after Ṭawāf—e—Ziyāra, where Iḥrām is not a condition.

8) For a Pilgrim performing only 'Umra, Sa'ī is Wājib after performing Tawāf.

THE MASNŪN METHOD OF SA'Ī

After the completion of Ṭawāf, prayers at Maqām-e-Ibrāhīm and drinking Zam-Zam water, one proceeds for the ninth Istilām of Ḥajr-al-Aswad, if time and your guide permit. Otherwise, proceed towards the Ṣafā Hill. According to the tradition of the Prophet, it is Mustaḥab to exit from Bab-us-Safa, if possible. If not, proceed or follow your guide to mount Safā, reciting the following verses from the Holy Qur'ān:

إِنَّ الصَّفَا وَالْمَرْوَةَ مِنْ شَعَآئِرِ اللّٰهِ ۚ فَمَنْ حَجَّ الْبَيْتَ أَوِ اعْتَمَرَ فَلَا جُنَاحَ عَلَيْهِ أَنْ يَّطَّوَّفَ بِهِمَا ۚ وَمَنْ تَطَوَّعَ خَيْرًا فَإِنَّ اللّٰهَ شَاكِرٌ عَلِيْمٌ ۚ

"Behold! Ṣafā and Marwa are among the symbols of Allāh. So if those who visit the House (of Allāh) in the season, or at other times, should encompass these hills, and if anyone obeys

Inn-aṣ-Ṣafā wal-Marwata min sha'ā'irillāh, faman Ḥajj-al-baita awi'tamara falā junāḥa 'alaihi an-yyaṭṭawwafa bihimā, wa man taṭawwa'a khairan fa-innallāha Shākirun 'Alīm.

his own impulse to do good, be sure that Allāh is He Who appreciates and knows."

As you approach mount Ṣafā, male Pilgrims climb up to the top, till Bait—Allāh is visible while females may stay at the bottom due to the crowds of men at the top. When the Ka'ba is visible, facing it, make the intention of performing Sa'ī. Recite the intention:

اَللّٰهُمَّ إِنِّيْ أُرِيْدُ السَّعْيَ بَيْنَ الصَّفَا وَالْمَرْوَةِ سَبْعَةَ
أَشْوَاطٍ لِوَجْهِكَ الْكَرِيْمِ ط فَيَسِّرْهُ لِيْ وَتَقَبَّلْهُ مِنِّيْ ط

O Allah! I intend the Sa'i of seven Shawāṭ between Ṣafā and Marwa solely for Thine pleasure. Make it easy for me and accept it.

Allāhumma inni uridu as-Sa'ya bain-aṣ-Ṣafā wal-Marwata sab-'ata ashwāṭin li-wajhikal Karīm, fa-yassirhu lī wa taqabbalhu minnī.

To feel the intention at heart is sufficient, but to pronounce it is better.

The hands should now be raised as in supplication, and not as in Takbīr (at prayer).

Then pronounce Takbīr and Tahlīl and salutation on Prophet Muḥammad (peace be upon him), with a tender voice, and pray to Allāh humbly and submissively. Pray for the rest of the Muslim world and oneself and praise Allāh, recite Kalima-i-Tawḥīd and Tamjīd. This mount is a place where prayers are accepted and it attracts Allāh's approbation. This is where your struggles may be accepted by the Grace of Allāh.

The Du'ā at this place narrated from the Messenger of Allāh (peace be upon him), is preferable and is as follows:

اَللّٰهُ أَكْبَرُ اَللّٰهُ أَكْبَرُ وَلِلّٰهِ الْحَمْدُ ط اَلْحَمْدُ
لِلّٰهِ عَلٰى مَا هَدَانَا اَلْحَمْدُ لِلّٰهِ عَلٰى مَا أَوْلَانَا ط اَلْحَمْدُ
لِلّٰهِ عَلٰى مَا أَلْهَمَنَا ط اَلْحَمْدُ لِلّٰهِ الَّذِيْ هَدَانَا وَمَا كُنَّا

لِنَهْتَدِيَ لَوْلَا اَنْ هَدَانَا اللّٰهُ لَا اِلٰهَ اِلَّا اللّٰهُ وَحْدَهٗ لَا
شَرِيْكَ لَهٗ لَهُ الْمُلْكُ وَلَهُ الْحَمْدُ يُحْيِيْ وَيُمِيْتُ وَهُوَ حَيٌّ لَّا
يَمُوْتُ بِيَدِهِ الْخَيْرُ وَهُوَ عَلٰى كُلِّ شَيْءٍ قَدِيْرٌ ط لَا اِلٰهَ اِلَّا اللّٰهُ
وَحْدَهٗ وَصَدَقَ وَعْدَهٗ وَنَصَرَ عَبْدَهٗ وَاَعَزَّ جُنْدَهٗ وَهَزَمَ الْاَحْزَابَ
وَحْدَهٗ ط لَا اِلٰهَ اِلَّا اللّٰهُ وَلَا نَعْبُدُ اِلَّا اِيَّاهُ مُخْلِصِيْنَ
لَهُ الدِّيْنَ وَلَوْ كَرِهَ الْكَافِرُوْنَ ط اَللّٰهُمَّ اِنَّكَ قُلْتَ
وَقَوْلُكَ الْحَقُّ اُدْعُوْنِيْ اَسْتَجِبْ لَكُمْ وَاِنَّكَ لَا تُخْلِفُ الْمِيْعَادَ
وَاِنِّيْ اَسْأَلُكَ كَمَا هَدَيْتَنِيْ لِلْاِسْلَامِ اَنْ لَّا تَنْزِعَهٗ مِنِّيْ حَتّٰى
تَوَفَّانِيْ وَاَنَا مُسْلِمٌ ط سُبْحَانَ اللّٰهِ وَالْحَمْدُ لِلّٰهِ وَلَا اِلٰهَ
اِلَّا اللّٰهُ وَاللّٰهُ اَكْبَرُ وَلَا حَوْلَ وَلَا قُوَّةَ اِلَّا بِاللّٰهِ الْعَلِيِّ
الْعَظِيْمِ ط اَللّٰهُمَّ صَلِّ وَسَلِّمْ عَلٰى سَيِّدِنَا مُحَمَّدٍ وَّعَلٰى آلِهٖ
وَصَحْبِهٖ وَاَتْبَاعِهٖ اِلٰى يَوْمِ الدِّيْنِ ط اَللّٰهُمَّ اغْفِرْ لِيْ وَلِوَالِدَيَّ
وَلِمَشَائِخِيْ وَلِلْمُسْلِمِيْنَ اَجْمَعِيْنَ وَالسَّلَامُ عَلَى الْمُرْسَلِيْنَ
وَالْحَمْدُ لِلّٰهِ رَبِّ الْعٰلَمِيْنَ ط

Allah is Great, Allāh is Great, Allāh is Great, and all praise is due to Allāh. All praise is due to Allāh for He showed us the guidance, All praise is due to Allāh who blessed us, All praise is due to Allāh who inspired us All praise is to Allāh who showed us the right path and

Allāh-u-Akbar Allāh-u-Akbar Allāh-u-Akbar wa lillāh-il-ḥamd, Al-ḥamd-u-lillāhi 'alā mā hadānā al-ḥamd-u-li--llāhi 'alā ma aulānā, al-ḥamd-u-lil-lāhi 'alā mā alhamanā, al-ḥamd -u-lillāh-il-ladhī hadānā wa mā kunnā li-nahtadiya lau lā an hadānallāhu lā ilāha illallā-

if He had not guided us, we would not have been guided. None has the right to be worshipped but Allāh, He is one, without companion. For Him is the Kingdom of heaven and earth, and all praise. He makes to live and to die; and He Himself lives, but never dies. And in His Hand is goodness, and He is All-Powerful. None has the right to be worshipped but Allāh, Allāh is true to His promise, He helped His servant and gave strength to his troops and routed the Confederates by Himself. None has the right to be worshipped but Allāh and we offer sincere worship unto none but Him. O Allāh! Verily Thou hast said, and Your saying is True, that if you call upon Me, I will harken unto you, verily Thou wilt not fail Thy promise. And I beseech Thee not to tear off from me the (faith of) Islām as Thou hast guided me unto it, till Thou causest me to die a Muslim. Glory be to Allāh and All praise is due to Allāh and none has the right to be worshipped but Allāh and He is Great, and there is neither power nor strength except Allāh, the Mighty, the Great. O Allāh! Peace and blessings be on our Chief Muḥammad and his family and his Com-

hu waḥdahū lā sharīka lahū lah-ul-mulku wa lah -ul-ḥamdu yuḥyī wa yumītu wa huwa ḥayhun - llā yamūtu bi-yadihil-khairi wa huwa 'alā kulli shai'-in Qadīr, lā ilāha illallā- hu waḥdahū wa ṣadaqa wa'dahū wa naṣara 'abdahū wa a'azza jundahū wa hazam-al-aḥzaba waḥdahū lā ilāha illallāhu wa lā na'budu illā iyyāhu mukhil-iṣīna lah-ud-dīn wa lau karih-al -kāfirūn, Allāhumma innaka qulta wa qauluk-al-ḥaqqu ud'-ūni astajib lakum wa innaka lā tukhlif-ul mī'ād, wa innī as'-aluka kamā hadaitanī lil-Islāmi an lā tanzi'ahū minnī ḥattā tawaffanī wa ana Muslim, sub-ḥān-al-lāhi wal-ḥamdu lillāhi wa lā ilāha illallāhu wallāhu Akbar, wa lā ḥawla wa lā quwwata illā billāh-il 'Aliyy-il-'Aẓīm, Allāhumma ṣalli wa sallim 'alā sayyidinā Muḥammad wa 'alā ālihī wa ṣaḥbihī wa atbā'ihī ilā yaum-id-dīn, Allāhumma-ghfir lī wa li-wālidayya wa li-mashā'ikhī wa lil-Muslimīna ajma'īna was-salāmu 'al-al-Mur-salīna wal-ḥamdu lillāhi Rabb-il-'ālamīn.

panions and his followers till the day of Judgement, O Allāh! Forgive me and my parents and my elders and all Muslims and blessings be on all Prophets and all praise is due to Allah, the sustainer of the worlds.

This is the start of your Sa'ī: You start the first Shawṭ of Sa'ī from Ṣafā and end it at Marwa. As you descend from Ṣafā and proceed to Marwa, you will pass betweem two green pillars in the dip of the valley. These pillars indicate Meelain-Akhḍarain. Between these, the male Pilgrims are to run, as it is Sunna of the Prophet (peace be upon him). If a man is on a carriage, it should be borne at a fast pace between these two pillars. You are to invoke whatever blessings you desire.

Female Pilgrims are not supposed to run between Meelain—Akhḍarain.

(1) THE FIRST SHAWṬ OF SA'Ī

While descending from Safā, recite:

اَللّٰهُ اَكْبَرُ اَللّٰهُ اَكْبَرُ اَللّٰهُ اَكْبَرُ وَالْحَمْدُ لِلّٰهِ كَثِيْرًا
وَّسُبْحَانَ اللّٰهِ الْعَظِيْمِ وَبِحَمْدِهِ الْكَرِيْمِ بُكْرَةً وَّاَصِيْلًا
وَّمِنَ اللَّيْلِ فَاسْجُدْ لَهٗ وَسَبِّحْهُ لَيْلًا طَوِيْلًا ؕ
لَا اِلٰهَ اِلَّا اللّٰهُ وَحْدَهٗ اَنْجَزَ وَعْدَهٗ وَنَصَرَ عَبْدَهٗ وَهَزَمَ
الْاَحْزَابَ وَحْدَهٗ ؕ لَا شَيْءَ قَبْلَهٗ وَلَا بَعْدَهٗ ؕ يُحْيِيْ وَيُمِيْتُ
وَهُوَ حَيٌّ دَائِمًا لَا يَمُوْتُ وَلَا يَفُوْتُ اَبَدًا ؕ بِيَدِهِ الْخَيْرُ
وَاِلَيْهِ الْمَصِيْرُ وَهُوَ عَلٰى كُلِّ شَيْءٍ قَدِيْرٌ ؕ رَبِّ اغْفِرْ وَارْحَمْ
وَاعْفُ وَتَكَرَّمْ ؕ وَتَجَاوَزْ عَمَّا تَعْلَمُ ؕ اِنَّكَ تَعْلَمُ مَا لَا نَعْلَمُ

إِنَّكَ أَنْتَ اللّٰهُ الْأَعَزُّ الْأَكْرَمُ ، رَبَّنَا نَجِّنَا مِنَ النَّارِ سَالِمِيْنَ

غَانِمِيْنَ فَرِحِيْنَ مُسْتَبْشِرِيْنَ مَعَ عِبَادِكَ الصَّالِحِيْنَ الَّذِيْنَ مَنَّ

أَنْعَمَ اللّٰهُ عَلَيْهِمْ مِّنَ النَّبِيِّيْنَ وَالصِّدِّيْقِيْنَ وَالشُّهَدَاءِ

وَالصَّالِحِيْنَ وَحَسُنَ أُولٰٓئِكَ رَفِيْقًا ط ذٰلِكَ الْفَضْلُ مِنَ اللّٰهِ

وَكَفٰى بِاللّٰهِ عَلِيْمًا ط لَآ إِلٰهَ إِلَّا اللّٰهُ حَقًّا حَقًّا ط لَآ إِلٰهَ

إِلَّا اللّٰهُ تَعَبُّدًا وَّرِقًّا ط لَآ إِلٰهَ إِلَّا اللّٰهُ وَلَا نَعْبُدُ إِلَّا

إِيَّاهُ مُخْلِصِيْنَ لَهُ الدِّيْنَ وَلَوْ كَرِهَ الْكَافِرُوْنَ ، إِنَّ الصَّفَا

وَالْمَرْوَةَ مِنْ شَعَآئِرِ اللّٰهِ فَمَنْ حَجَّ الْبَيْتَ أَوِ اعْتَمَرَ فَلَا جُنَاحَ

عَلَيْهِ أَنْ يَّطَّوَّفَ بِهِمَا وَمَنْ تَطَوَّعَ خَيْرًا فَإِنَّ اللّٰهَ شَاكِرٌ عَلِيْمٌ ط

Allāh is Great, Allāh is Great, Allāh is Great and Immense praise is due to Allāh, Allāh the Great is free from all imperfection, and with praise unto Him who is Noble, in the morning and in the evening. And (during some part) of the night worship Him and glorify Him in the livelong night. None is worthy of worship but Allāh alone He fulfilled His promise, helped His servant, and routed the confederates by Himself. Nothing existed before Him nor shall anything survive Him. He

Allāh-u-Akbar, Allāh-u-Akbar, Allāh-u-Akbar wal ḥamdu lillāhi kathīran wwa subhān-allāh-il-'Aẓīm, wa bi-ḥamdih-il-Karīmu bukratan wwa aṣīlan wwa min-al-laili fas-judhu lahū wa sabbiḥ-hu lailan ṭawīlā, lā ilāha illallahu waḥdahū anjaza wa'dahu wa naṣara 'abdahū wa hazam-al-aḥzāba waḥdahū lā shai'a qablahū wa lā ba'dahū yuḥyī wa yumītu wahuwa ḥayyun dā'imun llā yamūtu wa lā yafūtu abadan bi-yadih-il-khairu, wa ilaihil-maṣīr, wa huwa 'alā kulli shai'in Qadīr,

giveth life: He putteth to Death. He is Living, Eternal and is never to die. In His hand is good, and to Him shall come back (everything at the last). He hath power over all things.

[O my Lord forgive me and have mercy (on me). pardon and do good unto me. Pass off (my sins) of which Thou art aware. Thou art Allah. Thou knowest what we know not. Thou art indeed the Most Powerful, the Most Noble.]

O my Lord; deliver us from (the torment of) Fire, as perfectly safe, succeeding (without trouble) as happy and greeted along with Thy righteous servants, and with those of the Prophets, of the Sincere of the Martyrs and and of the Righteous, unto whom Allāh hath been gracious These are the most excellent company. This is the bounty from Allah, and in knowledge doth Allāh suffice. There is none worthy of worship except Allah, indeed, indeed. There is none worthy of worship but Allāh (in respect of His) servant and slave. There is certainly none worthy of worship except Allah and we offer sincere worship unto none but Him, though infidels abhor it.

(Rabbighfir warḥam wa'fu wa takarram wa tajāwaz 'ammā ta'lamu innaka ta'lamu ma lā na'lamu innaka antallāh-ul-A'azzul-Akram.)

Rabbanā najjinā min-an-nāri sālimīna ghānimīna fariḥina mustabshirīna ma'a 'ibādik-aṣ-ṣalihīn-al-ladhīna an'am-allāhu 'alaihim min-an-nabiyyīna waṣ-ṣiddīqina wash-shuhadā'i waṣ-ṣāliḥīna, wa hasuna ulā'ika rafīqā, dhālik-al-faḍlu min-allāhi wa kafā billāhi 'Alīmā, lā ilāha illallāhu ḥaqqan haqqā, lā ilāha illallāhu ta'abbu-dan wwariqā, lā ilāha illallāhu wa lā na'budu illā iyyāhu mukhliṣīna lah-ud-dīna wa lau karih-al-kāfirun.

(Inn-aṣ-Ṣafā wal Marwata min sha'ā.irillāh faman Ḥajj-al-baita awi'tamara falā junāḥa 'alaihi an-yyaṭṭawwafa bihimā wa man taṭawwa'a khairan fa-innallāha Shākirun 'Alīm.)

(Verily Ṣafā and Marwa are two of the chief signs of Allāh. Whosoever therefore goeth to the Pilgrimage of the House or visiteth it, shall not be to blame if he compass them both. And for him who voluntarily performeth a good deed, Allah is Grateful and Knowing.)

Between Meelain—Akhḍarain, recite:

رَبِّ اغْفِرْ وَارْحَمْ وَاعْفُ تَكَرَّمْ وَ تَجَاوَزْ . . . .

Approaching Marwa, recite again:

إِنَّ الصَّفَا وَالْمَرْوَةَ مِنْ شَعَائِرِ اللهِ . . . . . .

(Note: The last two Du'ās are given above in parenthesis).

(2) THE SECOND SHAWṬ OF SA'Ī

Again climb up to the heights of Marwa, from where you can see the Ka'ba and facing it raise your hands and recite Takbīr and Tahḷīl, and then pray as you did on Ṣafā. This is the end of your first Shawṭ of the Sa'ī. As you begin your journey to Safā again, start the second Shawṭ of Sa'ī. Recite the following Du'ā for the second Shawṭ or repeat after your guide (which will most probably be the case), or pray in your own language.

اَللّٰهُ اَكْبَرُ اَللّٰهُ اَكْبَرُ اَللّٰهُ اَكْبَرُ وَلِلّٰهِ الْحَمْدُ لَآ اِلٰهَ
اِلَّا اللّٰهُ الْوَاحِدُ الْفَرْدُ الصَّمَدُ الَّذِىْ لَمْ يَتَّخِذْ صَاحِبَةً
وَّلَا وَلَدًا وَّلَمْ يَكُنْ لَّهٗ شَرِيْكٌ فِى الْمُلْكِ وَلَمْ يَكُنْ لَّهٗ وَلِىٌّ
مِّنَ الذُّلِّ وَكَبِّرْهُ تَكْبِيْرًا ط اَللّٰهُمَّ اِنَّكَ قُلْتَ فِىْ كِتَابِكَ

الْمُنَزَّلِ ادْعُوْنِيْ أَسْتَجِبْ لَكُمْ ط دَعَوْنَاكَ رَبَّنَا فَاغْفِرْ لَنَا كَمَا
اَمَرْتَنَا اِنَّكَ لَا تُخْلِفُ الْمِيْعَادَ ط رَبَّنَا اِنَّنَا سَمِعْنَا مُنَادِيًا
يُّنَادِيْ لِلْاِيْمَانِ أَنْ آمِنُوْا بِرَبِّكُمْ فَآمَنَّا ط رَبَّنَا فَاغْفِرْ لَنَا
ذُنُوْبَنَا وَكَفِّرْ عَنَّا سَيِّئَاتِنَا وَتَوَفَّنَا مَعَ الْاَبْرَارِ ط رَبَّنَا
وَآتِنَا مَا وَعَدْتَّنَا عَلٰى رُسُلِكَ وَلَا تُخْزِنَا يَوْمَ الْقِيَامَةِ اِنَّكَ
لَا تُخْلِفُ الْمِيْعَادَ ط رَبَّنَا عَلَيْكَ تَوَكَّلْنَا وَاِلَيْكَ أَنَبْنَا
وَاِلَيْكَ الْمَصِيْرُ ط رَبَّنَا اغْفِرْ لَنَا وَلِاِخْوَانِنَا الَّذِيْنَ سَبَقُوْنَا
بِالْاِيْمَانِ وَلَا تَجْعَلْ فِيْ قُلُوْبِنَا غِلًّا لِّلَّذِيْنَ آمَنُوْا رَبَّنَا اِنَّكَ
رَؤُوْفٌ الرَّحِيْمُ رَبِّ اغْفِرْ وَارْحَمْ وَاعْفُ وَتَكَرَّمْ وَتَجَاوَزْ عَمَّا
تَعْلَمُ اِنَّكَ تَعْلَمُ مَا لَا نَعْلَمُ اِنَّكَ اَنْتَ اللّٰهُ الْاَعَزُّ الْاَكْرَمُ)
(اِنَّ الصَّفَا وَالْمَرْوَةَ مِنْ شَعَائِرِ اللّٰهِ فَمَنْ حَجَّ الْبَيْتَ
أَوِ اعْتَمَرَ فَلَا جُنَاحَ عَلَيْهِ أَنْ يَّطَّوَّفَ بِهِمَا وَمَنْ تَطَوَّعَ
خَيْرًا فَاِنَّ اللّٰهَ شَاكِرٌ عَلِيْمٌ)

Allāh is Great, Allāh is Great, Allāh is Great, and all praise is due to Allāh. There is none worthy of worship but Allāh, the Solitary, the One the Single, the eternally besought of all, who hath taken no spouse, nor hath he begotten any offspring, who hath no partner in the kingdom (of

Allāh-u-Akbar, Allāh-u-Akbar, Allāh-u-Akbar, wa lillāh-il-ḥamd, Lā ilāha illallāh ul-wāḥid-ul-fard-uṣ-ṣamad-ullad-hī lam yattakhidh ṣahibatan wwa lā waladan wwa lam yak-ullahu sharīkun filmulki walam yakullahū waliyyu minadh-dhulli wa kabbirhu takbira Allāhumma innaka qulta fī

heaven and earth), nor does He need any friend to protect Him, or Magnify Him by pronouncing His greatness. O Allāh! Verily Thou hast said in Thy Revealed Book: Call upon me — I will harken unto you. We call upon Thee. O our Lord! Forgive us then, as Thou hast commanded us. Verily Thou will not fail Thy promise. O Our Lord! We have indeed, heard of a preacher inviting (us) to the faith — 'Believe in your Lord' — and we have believed. Therefore, our Lord, forgive us our sins and expiate our evil deeds from us and cause us to die with the righteous. O our Lord! Give us also (the reward) which Thou hast promised us by Thine Apostles and put us not to shame on the Day of Resurrection., for Thou art not contrary to the promise. O our Lord! Forgive us, and our brothers, those who preceded us in Faith and leave not in our hearts malice to those who are with Faith. Verily Thou art Kind the Merciful. (O my Lord! Forgive me and have mercy on me, pardon and do good unto me. Pass off my sins of which Thou art aware. Thou art Allah. Thou knowest what we know not. Thou art indeed the

kitābikal munazzali ud-'ūnī astajib lakum, da'aunaka Rabbanā faghfir lanā kamā 'amratanā innaka lā tukhlif-ul-mī'ad. Rabbanā innanā sami'nā munādiyan-yunādī lil-īmāni an āminū bi-Rabbikum fa-āmannā, Rabbanā fafghirlanā dhunūbanā wa kaffir 'annā sayyi'ātinā wa tawaffanā ma'al-abrār. Rabbanā wa ātinā mā wa'adtanā 'alā rusūlika wa lā tukhiznā yaum-al-qiyāma, innaka lā tukhlif-ul-mi'ād. Rabbanā 'alaika tawakkalnā wa ilaika 'anabnā wa ilaik-al-maṣīr. Rabbanaghfir lanā wa li-ikhwānin-al-ladhīna sabaqūnā bil-īmāni wa lā taj'al fī qulūbinā ghil-al-ladhīna āmanū, Rabbanā innaka Ra'ūf-ur-Raḥīm. (Rabbighfir warḥam wa'fu wa takarram wa tajāwaz 'ammā ta'lamu innaka ta'lamu mā lā na'lamu innaka antallāh-A'azz-ul-Akram). (Inn-as-Ṣafā wal-Marwata min sha'ā'ir-illāh, faman Ḥajj-al-baita awi'tamara falā junāḥa 'alaihi an-yyaṭṭawwafa bihimā wa man taṭawwa-'a khairan fa-innallāha Shākirun 'Alīm.)

most Powerful the Most Noble.)

(Verily Ṣafā and Marwa are two of the chief signs of Allāh. Whosoever therefore goeth to the Pilgrimage of the House or visiteth it, shall not be to blame if he compass them both. And for him who voluntarily performeth a good deed, Allāh is Grateful and Knowing.)

Remembering that Mīlain-Akhḍarain now are the pillars on your right, you recite between them again:

رَبِّ اغْفِرْ وَارْحَمْ وَاعْفُ وَتَكَرَّمْ وَتَجَاوَزْ ......

Approaching Marwa recite again:

اِنَّ الصَّفَا وَالْمَرْوَةَ مِنْ شَعَائِرِ اللّٰهِ ....

(Note: These two prayers are given above in parenthesis).

While invoking prayers, again run between the green lights (or pillars) till you reach Ṣafā again. As you climb, recite or repeat after your guide the prayer recited between Marwa and Ṣafā, and back. You complete seven Ashwāṭ in this manner. The Du'ā for each Shawṭ is given below. Recite approaching Ṣafā:

3. Du'ā for Third Shawṭ of Ṣafā to Marwa):

اَللّٰهُ اَكْبَرُ اَللّٰهُ اَكْبَرُ وَلِلّٰهِ الْحَمْدُ ط رَبَّنَا
اَتْمِمْ لَنَا نُوْرَنَا وَاغْفِرْ لَنَا اِنَّكَ عَلٰى كُلِّ شَيْءٍ قَدِيْرٌ ط
اَللّٰهُمَّ اِنِّيْ اَسْاَلُكَ الْخَيْرَ كُلَّهُ عَاجِلَهُ وَآجِلَهُ وَاَسْتَغْفِرُكَ
لِذَنْبِيْ وَاَسْاَلُكَ رَحْمَتَكَ يَا اَرْحَمَ الرَّاحِمِيْنَ رَبِّ اغْفِرْ وَارْحَمْ

وَاعْفُ وَتَكَرَّمْ وَ تَجَاوَزْ عَمَّا تَعْلَمُ إِنَّكَ تَعْلَمُ مَا لَا نَعْلَمُ إِنَّكَ
أَنْتَ اللّٰهُ الْأَعَزُّ الْأَكْرَمُ) رَبِّ زِدْنِي عِلْمًا وَّ لَا تُزِغْ قَلْبِي بَعْدَ
إِذْ هَدَيْتَنِي ط وَ هَبْ لِي مِنْ لَّدُنْكَ رَحْمَةً إِنَّكَ أَنْتَ الْوَهَّابُ
اَللّٰهُمَّ عَافِنِي فِي سَمْعِي وَ بَصَرِي لَا إِلٰهَ إِلَّا أَنْتَ ط اَللّٰهُمَّ إِنِّي
أَعُوذُبِكَ مِنْ عَذَابِ الْقَبْرِ ط لَا إِلٰهَ إِلَّا أَنْتَ سُبْحَانَكَ إِنِّي كُنْتُ
مِنَ الظَّالِمِينَ ط اَللّٰهُمَّ إِنِّي أَعُوذُبِكَ مِنَ الْكُفْرِ وَالْفَقْرِ ط
اَللّٰهُمَّ إِنِّي أَعُوذُ بِرِضَاكَ مِنْ سَخَطِكَ وَ بِمُعَافَاتِكَ مِنْ عُقُوبَتِكَ
وَأَعُوذُبِكَ مِنْكَ لَا أُحْصِي ثَنَاءً عَلَيْكَ أَنْتَ كَمَا أَثْنَيْتَ عَلَى
نَفْسِكَ فَلَكَ الْحَمْدُ حَتّٰى تَرْضٰى (إِنَّ الصَّفَا وَالْمَرْوَةَ مِنْ شَعَائِرِ
اللّٰهِ فَمَنْ حَجَّ الْبَيْتَ أَوِ اعْتَمَرَ فَلَا جُنَاحَ عَلَيْهِ أَنْ يَطَّوَّفَ بِهِمَا
وَمَنْ تَطَوَّعَ خَيْرًا فَإِنَّ اللّٰهَ شَاكِرٌ عَلِيمٌ)

Allāh is Great, Allāh is Great, Allāh is Great and all praise is due to Allāh. O our Lord! Make our light perfect and forgive us, for Thou hast power over all things. O Allāh! I beg of Thee all good, (that may come) soon or late. I also seek Thy refuge from all (types of) evil, (that may come) soon or late. I also seek Thy forgiveness of my sin, and I beseech Thy mercy. (O Lord! Forgive me and have mercy on me:

Allāh-u-Akbar, Allāh-u-Akbar, Allāh-u-Akbar, wa lillāh-il-ḥamd. Rabbanā atmim lanā nūranā waghfir lanā innaka 'alā kulli shai'in Qadīr. Allāhumma innī as- 'aluk-al-khaira kullahū 'ajilahu wa ajilahu was-taghfiruka li-dhanbi wa as'aluka raḥmataka yā Arḥam-ar-Rāḥimīn. (Rabbighbir war-ḥam wa'fu wa takarram wa tajāwaz 'ammā ta'lam innaka ta'lamu mā lā na'lamu innaka antAllāh-ul-A'azz-al-Akram.)

pardon and do good unto me. Pass off my sins of which Thou art aware. Thou art Allāh. Thou knowest what we know not. Thou art indeed the Most Powerful, the Most Noble.

Rabbi zidnī 'ilman wwa lā tuzigh qalbī ba'da idh hadaitanī wa hab lī milla-dunka raḥmatan innaka ant-al-wahhāb. Allāhumma 'āfinī fī sam'ī wa baṣarī lā ilāha illā anta.

O my Lord! Increase knowledge unto me. O Allāh, my Lord! Suffer not my heart to go astray after Thou hast once guided me, and grant me mercy from before Thee, for verily Thou art He who giveth. O Allāh! Preserve me in respect of my hearing and seeing. There is none worthy of worship except Thee. O Allāh! I seek Thy refuge from the torment of the grave. There is none worthy of worship but Thee. O Allāh! Glory be unto Thee. Verily I have been one of the evil doers. O Allāh! I seek Thy refuge from infidelity and destitution. O Allāh! I seek the refuge of Thy pleasure from Thy anger. (I also seek the refuge of) Thy forgiveness from Thy torment. I also seek Thy refuge from (anything unpleasant that cometh from) Thee. I cannot take account of Thy praises as Thou hast praised Thyself. All praise is due unto Thee so that Thou art pleased (with me).

Allāhumma innī a'ūdhu bika min 'adhāb-il-qabri, lā ilāha illā anta subḥānaka innī kuntu min-aẓ-ẓālimīn. Allāhumma innī a'ūdhu bika min-al-kufri wal-faqri, Allāhumma innī a'ūdhu bi-riḍāka min sakhaṭika wa bi-mu'ā-fātika min' 'uqūbatika wa a'ūdu bika minka lā uḥṣī thanā'an 'alaika anta kamā athnaita 'alā nafsika falak-al-ḥamdu ḥattā tarḍā,

(Verily Ṣafā and Marwa are two of the chief symbols of

(Inn-aṣ-Ṣafā wal-Marwata min sha'-ā'ir-illāh faman Ḥajj-al-baita awi'tamara falā junāḥa 'alaihi an-yyaṭṭawwafa bihimā wa man taṭawwa'a khairan, fa-innallāha Shākirun 'Alīm.)

Allāh. Whosoever therefore goeth on Pilgrimage to the House or visiteth it shall not be to blame if he compass them both. And for him who voluntarily performeth a good deed — Allāh is Grateful and Knowing).

4. Du'ā for fourth Shawṭ of Sa'ī (from Marwa to Ṣafā).

اَللّٰهُ اَكْبَرُ اَللّٰهُ اَكْبَرُ اَللّٰهُ اَكْبَرُ وَ لِلّٰهِ الْحَمْدُ ط اَللّٰهُمَّ
اِنِّیْ اَسْأَلُكَ مِنْ خَيْرِ مَا تَعْلَمُ وَ اَعُوْذُ بِكَ مِنْ شَرِّ مَا تَعْلَمُ
وَاَسْتَغْفِرُكَ مِنْ كُلِّ مَا تَعْلَمُ اِنَّكَ اَنْتَ عَلَّامُ الْغُيُوْبِ ط لَآ اِلٰهَ
اِلَّا اللّٰهُ الْمَلِكُ الْحَقُّ الْمُبِيْنُ مُحَمَّدٌ رَّسُوْلُ اللّٰهِ الصَّادِقُ
الْوَعْدِ الْاَمِيْنِ ط اَللّٰهُمَّ اِنِّیْ اَسْأَلُكَ كَمَا هَدَيْتَنِیْ لِلْاِسْلَامِ
اَنْ لَّا تَنْزِعَهُ مِنِّیْ حَتّٰی تَتَوَفَّانِیْ وَ اَنَا مُسْلِمٌ ط اَللّٰهُمَّ اجْعَلْ
فِیْ قَلْبِیْ نُوْرًا وَّ فِیْ سَمْعِیْ نُوْرًا وَّ فِیْ بَصَرِیْ نُوْرًا ط اَللّٰهُمَّ
اشْرَحْ لِیْ صَدْرِیْ وَ يَسِّرْ لِیْ اَمْرِیْ وَ اَعُوْذُ بِكَ مِنْ شَرِّ وَسَاوِسِ
الصَّدْرِ وَ شَتَاتِ الْاَمْرِ وَ فِتْنَةِ الْقَبْرِ ط اَللّٰهُمَّ اِنِّیْ اَعُوْذُ بِكَ
مِنْ شَرِّ مَا يَلِجُ فِی اللَّيْلِ وَ شَرِّ مَا يَلِجُ فِی النَّهَارِ وَ مِنْ
شَرِّ مَا تَهُبُّ بِهِ الرِّيَاحُ يَا اَرْحَمَ الرَّاحِمِيْنَ ط سُبْحَانَكَ مَا
عَبَدْنَاكَ حَقَّ عِبَادَتِكَ يَا اَللّٰهُ ط سُبْحَانَكَ مَا ذَكَرْنَاكَ حَقَّ ذِكْرِكَ
يَا اَللّٰهُ (رَبِّ اغْفِرْ وَارْحَمْ وَ اعْفُ وَتَكَرَّمْ وَ تَجَاوَزْ عَمَّا تَعْلَمُ

إِنَّكَ تَعْلَمُ مَا لَا نَعْلَمُ إِنَّكَ أَنْتَ اللّٰهُ الْأَعَزُّ الْأَكْرَمُ) إِنَّ
الصَّفَا وَالْمَرْوَةَ مِنْ شَعَائِرِ اللّٰهِ فَمَنْ حَجَّ الْبَيْتَ أَوِ اعْتَمَرَ
فَلَا جُنَاحَ عَلَيْهِ أَنْ يَطَّوَّفَ بِهِمَا وَمَنْ تَطَوَّعَ خَيْرًا فَإِنَّ اللّٰهَ
شَاكِرٌ عَلِيمٌ)-

Allāh is Great, Allāh is Great, Allāh is Great and all praise is due to Allāh. O Allāh! I beg Thee of good that Thou knowest, and ask Thee to forgive me every (slip or sin) that Thou knowest, for verily Thou art the best knower of the secrets. There is none worthy of worship but Allāh, the King, the Perspicuous Truth — (and) Muḥammad is the Messenger of Allāh, (who was) true to his promise and trustworthy. O Allāh! I beseech Thee not to tear off from me the (faith of) Islām as Thou hast guided me unto it, till Thou causest me to die a Muslim. O Allāh! cast in my heart a light, in my hearing a light and in my vision a light. O Allāh! enlarge my chest and make easy for me my affair. I betake myself for refuge to Thee against the mischief of the temptations of the heart, against the disorderliness of the affair, and against the trial of the grave. O Allāh! I

Allāh-u-Akbar, Allāh-u-Akbar, Allāh-u-Akbar wa lillāh-il-ḥamd. Allāhumma innī as-'aluka min khairi mā ta'lumu wa a'ūdhu bika min sharri mā tal'lamu wa astaghfiruka min kulli mā ta'lamu innaka anta 'allām-ul-ghuyūb, lā ilāha illallāh-ul-Malik-ul- Ḥaqq-ul-Mubīn, Muḥammad-ur-rasūl-ullāhi-ṣ – ṣādiq-ul-wa'd-il-amīn, Allāhumma innī as-'aluka kamā hadaitanī lil-Islāmi an-llā tanzi'ahū minnī ḥattā tatawaffanī wa ana Muslim, Allāhumm-aj-'al fī qalbī nūran wwa fī' sam'ī nūran wwa fī basarī nūran, Allāhummash-raḥ lī ṣadrī wa yassir lī amrī wa a-'ūdhu bika min sharri was-āwas-iṣ-ṣadri wa shatāt-il-amri wa fitnat-il-qabri, Allāhumma innī a'ūdhu bika min sharri mā yuliju fillaili wa sharri mā yuliju finnahāri, wa min sharri mā tahubbu bih-ir-riyāḥu, yā Ar-ḥam-ar-Rāḥimīn., subḥān-aka mā 'abadnāka ḥaqqa 'ibādatika yā Allāhu,subḥān-

also betake me for refuge to Thee against the mischief of that which penetrates at night time, against the mischief of that which penetrates at day—time, and against the mischief of all that blows along with the winds, O the Most Merciful of those who show mercy. Glory be unto Thee, we have not been able to worship Thee in the manner befitting Thy worship. Glory be unto Thee, O Allāh! We have not been able to remember Thee (to the extent) in the manner most befitting to Thine commemoration. (O my Lord! Forgive me and have mercy on me, pardon and do good unto me. Pass off my sins of which Thou art aware. Thou art Allah. Thou knowest what we know not. Thou art indeed the Most Powerful, the Most Noble) (Verily Ṣafā and Marwa are two signs of Allāh. Whosoever goeth on Pilgrimage to the House or visiteth it, shall not be to blame if he compass them both. And as for him who voluntarily performeth a good deed – Allāh is Grateful and Knowing.)

aka mā dhkarnaka ḥaqqa dhikrika yā Allāh. (Rabbighfir war-ḥam wa'fu wa takarram wa tajāwaz 'ammā ta'lamu innaka ta'lamu mā lā na'lamu innaka ant-Allāh-ul-a' Azz-ul-Akram.) (Inn-aṣ-Ṣafā wal-Marwata min Sha'ā'ir-illāh faman Ḥajj-al-baita awi'tamara falā iunāḥa 'alaihi an-yyaṭ-ṭawwafa bihimā wa man taṭaw-wa'a khairan fa-innallāha Shākirun 'Alīm.)

5. **Du'ā for Fifth Shawt of Sa'ī (from Safā to Marwa).**

اَللّٰهُ اَكْبَرُ اَللّٰهُ اَكْبَرُ اَللّٰهُ اَكْبَرُ وَلِلّٰهِ الْحَمْدُ ۔ سُبْحَانَكَ مَا

شَكَرْنَاكَ حَقَّ شُكْرِكَ يَا اَللّٰهُ ط اَللّٰهُمَّ حَبِّبْ اِلَيْنَا الْاِيْمَانَ وَ زَيِّنْهُ
فِيْ قُلُوْبِنَا وَكَرِّهْ اِلَيْنَا الْكُفْرَ وَالْفُسُوْقَ وَالْعِصْيَانَ وَاجْعَلْنَا
مِنَ الرَّاشِدِيْنَ (رَبِّ اغْفِرْ وَارْحَمْ وَاعْفُ وَتَكَرَّمْ وَتَجَاوَزْ عَمَّا
تَعْلَمُ اِنَّكَ تَعْلَمُ مَا لَا نَعْلَمُ اِنَّكَ اَنْتَ اللّٰهُ الْاَعَزُّ الْاَكْرَمُ)
اَللّٰهُمَّ قِنِيْ عَذَابَكَ يَوْمَ تَبْعَثُ عِبَادَكَ ط اَللّٰهُمَّ اهْدِنِيْ بِالْهُدٰى
وَنَقِّنِيْ بِالتَّقْوٰى ط وَاغْفِرْ لِيْ فِي الْاٰخِرَةِ وَالْاُوْلٰى ط اَللّٰهُمَّ
ابْسُطْ عَلَيْنَا مِنْ بَرَكَاتِكَ وَرَحْمَتِكَ وَفَضْلِكَ وَرِزْقِكَ ط اَللّٰهُمَّ
اِنِّيْ اَسْاَلُكَ النَّعِيْمَ الْمُقِيْمَ الَّذِيْ لَا يَحُوْلُ وَلَا يَزُوْلُ اَبَدًا ط
اَللّٰهُمَّ اجْعَلْ فِيْ قَلْبِيْ نُوْرًا ط وَّ فِيْ بَصَرِيْ نُوْرًا ط وَّ فِيْ
لِسَانِيْ نُوْرًا ط وَّعَنْ يَمِيْنِيْ نُوْرًا ط وَّ مِنْ فَوْقِيْ نُوْرًا ط
وَّاجْعَلْ فِيْ نَفْسِيْ نُوْرًا ط وَّعَظِّمْ لِيْ نُوْرًا ط رَبِّ اشْرَحْ لِيْ
صَدْرِيْ وَيَسِّرْ لِيْ اَمْرِيْ (اِنَّ الصَّفَا وَالْمَرْوَةَ مِنْ شَعَائِرِ اللّٰهِ
فَمَنْ حَجَّ الْبَيْتَ اَوِ اعْتَمَرَ فَلَا جُنَاحَ عَلَيْهِ اَنْ يَّطَّوَّفَ بِهِمَا
وَمَنْ تَطَوَّعَ خَيْرًا فَاِنَّ اللّٰهَ شَاكِرٌ عَلِيْمٌ)-

Allāh is Great, Allāh is Great, Allāh is Great and all praise is due to Allāh, Glory be unto Thee! We have not been able to thank Thee in a manner worthy of Thy thanks, O Allāh! Glory be unto Thee! We have not been able to

Allāh-u-Akbar, Allāh-u-Akbar, Allāh-u-Akbar wa lillāh-il ḥamd. Subḥānaka mā shakarn-aka ḥaqqa shukrika yā Allāhu, Allāhumma ḥabbib ilain-al-īmāna wa zayyin-hu fī qulū-binā wa · karrih ilain-al-kufra wal-fusūqa wal-'iṣyāna waj-

commemorate Thy name in a manner worthy of Thy commemoration, O Allāh! O Allāh! Make the faith amiable to us, and prepare the same in our hearts, and render infidelity, iniquity and disobedience hateful unto us, and (thereby) reckon us among Thy servants. (O my Lord! Forgive me and have mercy on me, pardon and do good unto me. Pass of my sins of which Thou art aware. Thou art Allāh. Thou knowest what we know not. Thou art indeed the Most Powerful, the Most Noble). O Allāh! Deliver us from Thy torment on the Day when Thou shall resurrect Thy servants.

O Allāh! Guide me on to the right path and cleanse me by virtue of the fear, and forgive me in the next world and here O Allāh! Of Thy blessings, Thy mercy, Thy grace and Thy provision spread a share for us. O Allāh! I beg of Thee the constant bliss which changeth not and waneth not.

O Allāh! Cast in my heart a light, in my hearing a light, in my vision a light, in my speech a light, and on to my right a light, from above me a light and cast for me in myself a light, and increase the light

'alnā min-ar-rāshid-īn.(Rabbighfir war-ḥam wa'fu wa takarram wa tajāwaz 'ammā ta'lamu innaka ta'lamu mā lā na'lamu innaka antallāh—ul-a'Azz-ul-Akram.)

Allāhumma qinī 'adhābaka yauma tab'athu 'ibād-aka, Allāhummahdinī bil-hudā wa naqqinī bittaqwā, waghfirlī fil-ākhirati wal-'ūla, Allā-humm-absuṭ 'alainā min barakātika wa raḥmatika wa faḍlika wa rizqika, Allāhumma innī as'aluk-an-na'īm-ul-muqim-al-ladhī lā yaḥūlu wa lā yazūlu abadan, Allāhumm-aj'al fī qalbī nūran wwa fī sam'ī nūran wwa fī baṣarī nūran, wwa fī lisānī nūran wwa 'an-yyamini nūran, wwa min fauqī nūran, wwaj'al fī nafsī nūran, wwa 'azzim lī nūran, Rabbi-shraḥ lī ṣadrī wa yassir lī amrī. (Inn-aṣ-Ṣafā wal-Marwata min sha'ā'ir-illāh faman Ḥajja-al-baita awi'tamara falā junāḥa 'alaihi an yyaṭṭawwafa bihimā wa man taṭawwa-'a khairan fa-innallāha Shākirun 'Alīm.)

for me, O my Lord! Increase my chest and make easy for me my affair. (Verily Ṣafā and Marwa are two of the eminent symbols of Allāh. Whoever therefore goeth on Pilgrimage to the House or visiteth it, shall not be to blame, if he compass them both. And as for him who voluntarily performeth a good deed, Allāh is Grateful and Knowing.[1]

6. Du'ā for Sixth Shawṭ of Sa'ī (from Marwa to Ṣafā):

اَللّٰهُ اَكْبَرُ اَللّٰهُ اَكْبَرُ اَللّٰهُ اَكْبَرُ وَلِلّٰهِ الْحَمْدُ ط لَآ اِلٰهَ
اِلَّا اللّٰهُ وَحْدَهٗ صَدَقَ وَعْدَهٗ وَنَصَرَ عَبْدَهٗ وَهَزَمَ الْاَحْزَابَ وَحْدَهٗ
لَآ اِلٰهَ اِلَّا اللّٰهُ وَلَا نَعْبُدُ اِلَّآ اِيَّاهُ مُخْلِصِيْنَ لَهُ الدِّيْنَ وَلَوْ
كَرِهَ الْكَافِرُوْنَ ط اَللّٰهُمَّ اِنِّيْ اَسْأَلُكَ الْهُدٰى وَالتُّقٰى وَالْعَافَ
وَالْغِنٰى ط اَللّٰهُمَّ لَكَ الْحَمْدُ كَالَّذِيْ نَقُوْلُ وَخَيْرًا مِّمَّا نَقُوْلُ
اَللّٰهُمَّ اِنِّيْ اَسْأَلُكَ رِضَاكَ وَالْجَنَّةَ وَأَعُوْذُبِكَ مِنْ سَخَطِكَ وَالنَّارِ
وَمَا يُقَرِّبُنِيْ اِلَيْهَا مِنْ قَوْلٍ اَوْ فِعْلٍ اَوْ عَمَلٍ ط اَللّٰهُمَّ بِنُوْرِكَ
اهْتَدَيْنَا وَبِفَضْلِكَ اسْتَغْنَيْنَا وَفِيْ كُنُفِكَ وَاِنْعَامِكَ وَعَطَائِكَ
وَاِحْسَانِكَ أَصْبَحْنَا وَأَمْسَيْنَا ط اَنْتَ الْاَوَّلُ فَلَا قَبْلَكَ شَيْءٌ
وَالْاٰخِرُ فَلَا بَعْدَكَ شَيْءٌ ط وَالظَّاهِرُ فَلَا شَيْءَ فَوْقَكَ ط وَالْبَاطِنُ
فَلَاشَيْءَ دُوْنَكَ ط نَعُوْذُبِكَ مِنَ الْاِفْلَاسِ وَالْكَسَلِ وَعَذَابِ الْقَبْرِ

وَفِتْنَةِ الْغِنٰى وَ نَسْأَلُكَ الْفَوْزَ بِالْجَنَّةِ (رَبِّ اغْفِرْ وَارْحَمْ
وَاعْفُ وَتَكَرَّمْ وَ تَجَاوَزْ عَمَّا تَعْلَمُ اِنَّكَ تَعْلَمُ مَا لَا نَعْلَمُ ط
اِنَّكَ اَنْتَ اللّٰهُ الْاَعَزُّ الْاَكْرَمُ) (اِنَّ الصَّفَا وَالْمَرْوَةَ مِنْ
شَعَائِرِ اللّٰهِ فَمَنْ حَجَّ الْبَيْتَ اَوِ اعْتَمَرَ فَلَا جُنَاحَ عَلَيْهِ اَنْ
يَطَّوَّفَ بِهِمَا وَ مَنْ تَطَوَّعَ خَيْرًا فَاِنَّ اللّٰهَ شَاكِرٌ عَلِيْمٌ)

Allāh is Great, Allāh is Great, Allāh us Great, and all praise is due to Allāh. There is none worthy of worship but Allāh, He is true to His promise. He helped His servant and routed the Confederates all by Himself. None has the right to be worshipped but Allāh and we offer sincere worship unto none but Him though infidels abhor it. O Allāh! I implore Thee for (the grant of) guidance, piety, continence and satisfaction. O Allāh! To Thee is all praise (due), like what Thou sayest, and better than what I can say. O Allāh! I beg of Thee Thy pleasure, and (thereby) the Paradise and I seek Thy refuge from Thy anger, from the Fire and from all those things — sayings, actions and acts — that should bring me near unto it. O Allāh! By virtue of Thy light are we rightly guided and by virtue of Thy grace do we feel satisfied.

Allāh-u-Akbar, Allāh-u-Akbar, Allāh-u-Akbar, wa lillāh-il-ḥamd. Lā ilāha illa-llāhu waḥdahū ṣadaqa wa'da-hū wa naṣara 'abdah , wa hazam-al-aḥzāba waḥdah, lā ilāha illallā-hu wa lā na'budu illā iyyāhu mukhliṣīna lah-ud-dīn wa lau karih-al-kā-firūn. Allā-humma innī as'aluk-al-hudā wat-taqā wal-āf-fa wal-ghinā Allāhuma lak-al ḥamda kalladhī naqūla wa khairam-mimmā naqūl, Allā-humma innī as'aluka riḍāka wal-jannata wa a'ūdhu bika min sakhaṭika wan-nār, wa mā yuqarribunī ilaihā min qaulin au fi'lin au 'amalin, Allāhumma bi-nūrik-ahta-dainā wa bi-faḍlik-as-taghnainā wa fī kunfika wa in'āmika wa 'aṭā'ika wa iḥsānika aṣ-baḥnā wa amsainā, antal-awwalu falā qablukashai-in, wal-ākhiru falā ba'daka shai'in, waz-zāhiru falā shai'in fauqaka, wal-bāṭinu falā shai'in dūnaka na'ūdhu bika min—al-aflāsi wal-kasali

In Thy protection, Thy grace Thy benevolence, and in Thy favour do we (live) morn and eve. Thou art the first and nothing existed before Thee, Thou art the Last, and nothing shall survive Thee. Thou art the Overpowering and nothing is above Thee. Thou art the Hidden and nothing is beside Thee (to grant protection). We fly for refuge unto Thee from destitution, laziness, torment of the grave and trials (associated with) wealth, and seek success (leading to) Paradise. (O my Lord! Forgive me and have mercy on me, pardon and do good unto me. Pass off my sins of which Thou art aware. Thou art Allāh. Thou knowest what we know not. Thou art indeed the most Powerful, the Most Noble.) (Verily Ṣafā and Marwa are two of the eminent symbols of Allāh. Whoever therefore goeth on Pilgrimage to the House or visiteth it, shall not be to blame if he compass them both. And as for him who voluntarily performeth a good deed, Allāh is Grateful and Knowing.)

wa 'adhāb-il-qabri wa fitnat-il-ghinā wa nas'aluk-al-fauza bil-jannati (Rabbighfir war-ḥam wa'fu wa takarram wa tajāwaz 'ammā ta'lamu innaka ta'lamu mā lā na'lamu innaka antallāh-ul-A'azẓ-ul-Akram.)

(Inn-aṣ-Ṣafā wal-Marwata min sha'ā'irillāh faman Ḥajj-al-baita awi'tamara falā junāḥa 'alaihi an yyaṭṭawwafa bihimā wa man taṭawwa'a khairan fa-innallāha Shākir-un-'Alīm.

7. Du'ā for seventh Shawṭ of Sa'ī (from Ṣafā to Marwa)

اَللّٰهُ اَكْبَرُ اَللّٰهُ اَكْبَرُ اَللّٰهُ اَكْبَرُ كَبِيْرًا وَالْحَمْدُ لِلّٰهِ كَثِيْرًا
اَللّٰهُمَّ حَبِّبْ اِلَيَّ الْاِيْمَانَ وَزَيِّنْهُ فِيْ قَلْبِيْ وَكَرِّهْ اِلَيَّ الْكُفْرَ

وَالْفُسُوْقَ وَالْعِصْيَانَ وَاجْعَلْنِيْ مِنَ الرَّاشِدِيْنَ (رَبِّ اغْفِرْ وَارْحَمْ
وَاعْفُ وَتَكَرَّمْ وَ تَجَاوَزْ عَمَّا تَعْلَمُ إِنَّكَ تَعْلَمُ مَا لَا نَعْلَمُ إِنَّكَ
أَنْتَ اللّٰهُ الْأَعَزُّ الْأَكْرَمُ) اَللّٰهُمَّ اخْتِمْ بِالْخَيْرَاتِ آجَالَنَا
وَحَقِّقْ بِفَضْلِكَ آمَالَنَا وَسَهِّلْ لِبُلُوْغِ رِضَاكَ سُبُلَنَا وَحَسِّنْ
فِيْ جَمِيْعِ الْأَحْوَالِ أَعْمَالَنَا ط يَا مُنْقِذَ الْغَرْقٰى ط يَا مُنْجِيَ
الْهَلْكٰى ط يَا شَاهِدَ كُلِّ نَجْوٰى ط يَا مُنْتَهٰى كُلِّ شَكْوٰى ط يَا
قَدِيْمَ الْإِحْسَانِ يَا دَائِمَ الْمَعْرُوْفِ ط يَا مَنْ لَا غِنٰى بِشَيْءٍ
عَنْهُ وَلَا بُدَّ لِكُلِّ شَيْءٍ مِّنْهُ ط يَا مَنْ رِزْقُ كُلِّ شَيْءٍ عَلَيْهِ وَمَصِيْرُ
كُلِّ شَيْءٍ إِلَيْهِ ط اَللّٰهُمَّ إِنِّيْ عَائِذٌ بِكَ مِنْ شَرِّ مَا أَعْطَيْتَنَا وَمِنْ
شَرِّ مَا مَنَعْتَنَا ط اَللّٰهُمَّ تَوَفَّنَا مُسْلِمِيْنَ وَأَلْحِقْنَا بِالصَّالِحِيْنَ
غَيْرَ خَزَايَا وَلَا مَفْتُوْنِيْنَ ط رَبِّ يَسِّرْ وَلَا تُعَسِّرْ ط رَبِّ أَتْمِمْ
بِالْخَيْرِ (إِنَّ الصَّفَا وَالْمَرْوَةَ مِنْ شَعَائِرِ اللّٰهِ فَمَنْ حَجَّ
الْبَيْتَ أَوِ اعْتَمَرَ فَلَا جُنَاحَ عَلَيْهِ أَنْ يَّطَّوَّفَ بِهِمَا وَ مَنْ
تَطَوَّعَ خَيْرًا فَإِنَّ اللّٰهَ شَاكِرٌ عَلِيْمٌ)

Allāh is Great, Allāh is Great, Allāh is Great, very great, and immense praise is due to Allāh. O Allāh! Make the faith amiable unto me and prepare the same in my heart, and render iniquity and disobed-

Allāh-u-Akbar, Allāh Akbar, Allāh-u-Akbar kabīra wal-ḥamdu lillāhi kathīra, Allā-humma ḥabbib ilayyal-īmāna wa zayyin-hu fī qalbī wa kar-rih ilayyal-kufra wal-fusūqa wal-'iṣyāna waj-'alnī min-ar-

ience hateful unto me, and (thereby) cause me to walk in the right way. (O my Lord! Forgive me and have mercy on me, pardon and do good unto me. Pass of my sins of which Thou art aware. Thou art Allāh. Thou knowest what we know not. Thou art indeed the Most Powerful, the Most Noble.) O Allāh! Close our ajals (i.e. fixed terms of life) with good (deeds on our part), establish our hopes with Thy grace. Make our paths easy for us to reach Thy pleaure. Grant beauty of nobility to our acts in all their aspects. O Thou the saviour of the drowning, O Thou the refuge of the perishing, O Thou the witness of all whispers, O Thou the final aim of all complaints, O Thou the eternal Benefactor, O Thou continuously Gracious, O Thou without whom nothing can be done, and who is inevitable for all things. O Thou on whom depends the subsistence of all things and to whom everything shall have to return. O Allāh! I take refuge with Thee from afflictions that Thou might give us and from afflictions that Thou shalt prevent from us. O Allāh! Cause us to die Muslims and to join the righteous - not disgraced and derāshidīn. (Rabbighfir war-ḥam wa'fu wa ta-karram wa tajāwaz 'ammā ta'lamu innaka ta'lamu mā lā na'lamu innaka antallāh-ul-A'azz-ul-Akram.)

Allāhumm-akhtim bil-khairāti ājālanā wa ḥaqqiq bi-faḍlika āmālanā wa sahhil-li-bulūghi riḍāka subulanā wa ḥassan fī jamī-'il-ahwāli a'mālanā yā munqidh-al-gharqā yā munjiyal-halkā, yā shāhida kulli najwā, yā muntahā kulli shakwā, yā qadīm-al-iḥsāni yā dā'im-ul-ma'rūfi, yā man lā ghanīyyan bi-shai-in 'anhu wa lā burra li-kulli shai-im-minhu, yā man rizqu kulli shaiin 'alaihi wa masiru kulli shai-in 'alaihi, Allāhumma innī ā'idhu bika min sharri mā a'ṭaitanā wa min sharri mā mana'tanā, Allāhumma tawaffanā Muslimīna wal-ḥiqna bis-ṣāliḥīn, ghaira khazāya wa lā maftūnīn Rabbi yassir wa lā tu'assir, Rabbi atmim bil-khair.

(Inn-aṣ-Ṣafā wal-Marwata min sha'ā'irillah, faman Ḥajjal-baita awi'tamara falā junāḥa 'alaihi an yyattawwafa bihima wa man taṭawwa'a khairan fa-innallāha Shākirun 'Alīm).

mented. O my Lord! Make (this) easy for me and make it not difficult. O my Lord! Help me accomplish it well.

(Verily Ṣafā and Marwa are two of the chief symbols of Allāh. Whosoever therefore goeth on Pilgrimage to the House or visiteth it, shall not be to blame if he compass them both. And as for him who voluntarily performeth a good deed, Allāh is Grateful and Knowing.)

RULES OF ACTION FOR SA'Ī

(1) If this Sa'ī is performed after Ṭawāf–e–Qadūm, the Pilgrim must recite Talbiya besides the prescribed invocations.

(2) If this Sa'ī is performed after Ṭawāf–e–Ziyāra (when Waqūf–e–'Arafāt is over) or for 'Umra, then Talbiya is not recited

(3) If the Iqāma for obligatory prayer is called, the Sa'ī should be discontinued; similarly it has to be discontinued for Ṣalāt–e–Janāza. Sa'ī is resumed after offering the prayers, and whatever Shawāṭ are remaining should now be completed.

(4) It is Sunna of the Messenger of Allāh (peace be upon him) to offer two rak'at of prayers by the side of Maṭāf, in the Ḥaram. It is, however, permissible to offer two rak'at somewhere at Bāb–ul–'Umra.

(5) Cleanliness, ablution, and clean clothes are Mustaḥab although Sa'ī can be accomplished otherwise.

AT THE END OF SA'Ī

(1) If you are only performing 'UMRA or ḤAJJ TAMATTU', the ceremony is over after performing Sa'ī. You can now, after the completion of Sa'ī, abandon Iḥrām and all the practices and conditions pertaining to Iḥrām have come to an end. You may now have your head shaven, (Ḥalaq) or at least have a little hair cut, equal to about an inch (Qaṣr). With the Ḥalaq or Qaṣr, Iḥrām formalities have ended. For Ḥājīs it is better to have Qaṣr now, and shaving (Ḥalaq) after the Ḥajj.

(2) If you are a Mufrid: You are still in Iḥrām from Mīqāt for Ḥajj. Therefore, the conditions and state of Iḥrām are still binding on you. So do not abandon Iḥrām, but continue to live in Mecca or Minā till 8th of Dhul-Ḥijja in the state of Iḥrām (on the 8th of Dhul-Ḥijja the ceremonies of Ḥajj start). So as a MUFRID you have completed only two Manāsik of Ḥajj so far, the Ṭawāf-e-Qadūm and the Sa'ī. You may have performed these two Manāsik on the 8th (or the 7th of Dhul-Ḥijja).

(3) If you are a QARIN: Again the Iḥrām is binding on you. After completing Sa'ī, it is better that you do only Qaṣr, and do not shave the head. The conditions and restrictions of Iḥrām are binding on you, as a Qārin and Mufrid. It is better to shave the head after the sacrifice on the 10th of Dhul–Ḥijja.

All Qārin, Mufrid and Mutamattī' should try to remain in Masjid–al–Ḥarām and spend most of their time in performing Nafl prayers and Ṭawāf of Bait–Allāh, recitation of the Holy Qur'ān and prayers. They should avoid useless activities, shopping etc. and wait for the start of Ḥajj which is to commence on the 8th of Dhul–Ḥijja.

(4) During the waiting period, the Ṭawāf which is Nafl, will not require the practice of Ramal and Iḍṭibā' and Sa'ī.

(5) If a Mutmattī' has brought Hadī i.e. an animal of sacrifice with him, then the state of restrictions of Iḥrām are binding on him as well, after the completing of Sa'ī. He acts in the manner of a Qārin or Mufrid, i.e. continues in the state of Ihrām till the 8th of Dhul–Ḥijja and makes the intention of Ḥajj in the same Iḥrām again on the 8th of Dhul-Ḥijja. A Mutamattī' must renew Iḥrām on the 8th of Dhul-Ḥijja if after Qaṣr or Ḥalaq he removed it.

ACTIVITIES OF THE PILGRIMS DURING THE INTERIM PERIOD OF WAITING

(1) During this period in Mecca, visit frequently Bait–Allāh and stay in Masjid–al–Ḥarām as much as possible, observing all the prayers. For it is one hundred thousand times more blessed to offer them in the Ḥaram than to offer them at home.

(2) Perform as many Ṭawāfs (nafli) as possible, without Ramal and Iḍṭibā'

(3) Worship in the state of I'tikāf and if possible visit Bait–Allāh from inside.

(4) Complete as many 'Umras as possible if you have arrived before the month of Dhul–Ḥijja.

(5) Recite completely at least once the whole of Holy Qur'ān.

(6) Do as many good deeds as possible for your fellow Ḥajjis. Every good deed carries a hundred thousand more Thawāb (reward) in Masjid–al–Ḥarām, Similarly avoid sins and misdeeds. Istilām of Ḥajr–al–Aswad is also part of worship.

(7) When you enter the Masjid–al–Ḥarām have the intention of I'tikāf and try to engage in worship all the time.

(8) The prayers should also be offered in Ḥaṭīm and supplication may be made here, as it is also a place of acceptance of invocations.

(9) Even to glance at the Ka'ba is an act of worship and can only be achieved here.

So do not stay away from Masjid-al-Ḥarām unless you have to.

CHAPTER TEN

THE HAJJ

There are five days of performing manasik of Ḥajj. These begin from the 8th of Dhul-Ḥijja and end on 12th or 13th of Dhul-Ḥijja. During these days you are moving from place to place, begging for Allah's mercy and forgiveness. Every step you take from now on will be only in His path, and only for His pleasure, to obey His commands.

The manasik of Ḥajj begin at Masjid-al-Ḥarām, with Ṭawāf of Bait-Allāh. Then you move to the Holy places, following Allah's commands, and in the steps of Prophet Ibrāhīm (peace be upon him), which were followed by the Holy Prophet Muḥammad (peace be upon him). From Masjid-al-Ḥarām you go to Minā, spend a day and a night there in worship and in tranquillity, preparing yourselves for harder days ahead, both spiritually and physically.

From Minā, you go for one day to the valley of 'Arafāt; the Mount of Mercy is here. Your stay there in 'Arafāt is the greatest Rukn of Ḥajj. Then you move to Muzdalifa from 'Arafāt, and try to spend the whole night in worship. This night is one thousand times more blessed than the night of Qadr.

From Muzdalifa, after the sunrise, you come back to Minā, (where your tent may have been pitched). Here you perform the ceremony of throwing pebbles at the Big Shaiṭān. This is called Ramī of Jamrat-al-'Aqaba.

Then you offer sacrifice and shave your head in Minā.

The second most important Rukn of Ḥajj is to go back to the Sacred House of Allah, and perform Ṭawāf. This Ṭawāf is called Ṭawāf-e-Ziyāra. Here in Masjid-al-Ḥarām you thus end the main manasik of Ḥajj.

You now go back to Minā, where you spend two or three more days. The main function now is to throw pebbles at the three Jamarāt, every day till you leave Minā for Mecca to perform the Farewell Tawāf.

The itinerary is given below for a reference.

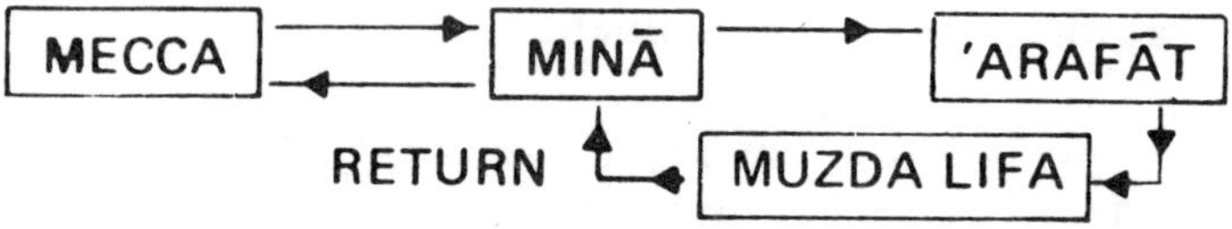

The itinerary during the five days of Hajj:

(1) On the 8th of Dhul-Ḥijja

a) In the Masjid-al-Ḥarām: After Fajr prayer, begin by performing Ṭawāf of Ḥajj. This Ṭawāf is called Ṭawāf-e-Qadūm, and is followed by Sa'ī depending on the kind of Ḥajj being performed. The ceremonies of Ṭawāf and Sa'ī are similar to those of 'Umra, the only difference is that these are performed with the intention of Ḥajj.

b) Proceed to Minā: There you offer five prayers of the day, including the Fajr prayer of the 9th day of Dhul-Ḥijja.

(2) On the **9th day** of Dhul-Hijja: (Waqūf-i-'Arafāt)

a) Proceed from Minā to the plains of 'Arafāt and spend the day in 'Arafāt till Maghrib prayers. Ẓuhr and 'Asr prayers are combined here at 'Aṣr time.

b) Proceed to Muzdalifa, after sunset from 'Arafāt. Maghrib and 'Ishā prayers are combined here at 'Ishā time. Spend the night in Muzdalifa and pray Fajr.

(3) On the 10th day of Dhul-Hijja:

The happiest dawn will be to-day for you here in Muzdalifa. This is now 'Īd-ul Aḍḥā.

i) Stay till sunrise

ii) Proceed to Minā for Ramī of Jamarāt-al-'Aqaba.

iii) Offer sacrifice, followed by

iv) Ḥalaq or Qaṣr

v) Proceed to Masjid-al-Ḥarām. Perform Tawāf-e-Ziyāra, the second most important Rukin of Ḥajj.

vi) Return to Minā, the same day.

(4) The 11th, 12th, 13th day of Dhul-Ḥijja

Main functions to be performed:-

a) Rami at all the three Jamrāt in Minā

b) Sacrifice if not offered on the 10th of Dhul-Ḥijja

c) Ḥalaq or Qaṣr if not performed on the 10th of Dhul-Ḥijja.

d) Ṭawāf-e-Ziyāra if not performed on the 10th of Dhul-Ḥijja.

Make sure you perform Ṭawāf-e-Sadr or the Farewell Ṭawāf before departure from Mecca. This is also called Tawāf-al-Wadā'

THE SCHEDULE FOR DAYS OF ḤAJJ

8th Dhul-Ḥijja, 1st Day

TAWĀF-E-QADŪM IN MASJID-AL-ḤARĀM

↓ PROCEED TO MINĀ

FIVE PRAYERS IN MINĀ

↓ PROCEED TO 'ARAFĀT

9th Dhul-Hijja 2nd Day

WAQŪF-E-'ARAFĀT — THE GREATEST RUKN OF ḤAJJ, COMBINE ẒUHR AND 'AṢR PRAYERS

↓ PROCEED TO MUZDALIFA AFTER SUNSET

The Night of the 10th of Dhul-Ḥijja

STAY IN MUZDALIFA TILL SUNRISE COMBINE MAGHRIB AND 'ISHĀ PRAYERS

↓ PROCEED TO MINĀ

10th Dhul-Ḥijja, 3rd Day

THE 'ĪD-UL-AḌḤA

↓

RAMĪ AT JAMARAT AL-'AQABA, SACRIFICE, ḤALAQ OR QASR IN MINĀ

↓ PROCEED TO MECCA

10th, 11th, 12th, Dhul-Hijja

ṬAWĀF-e-ZIYĀRA, THE 2ND MOST IMPORTANT RUKN OF ḤAJJ

↓ PROCEED TO MINĀ

RAMĪ AT THREE JAMARĀT IN MINĀ

↓ PROCEED TO MECCA

FAREWELL ṬAWĀF

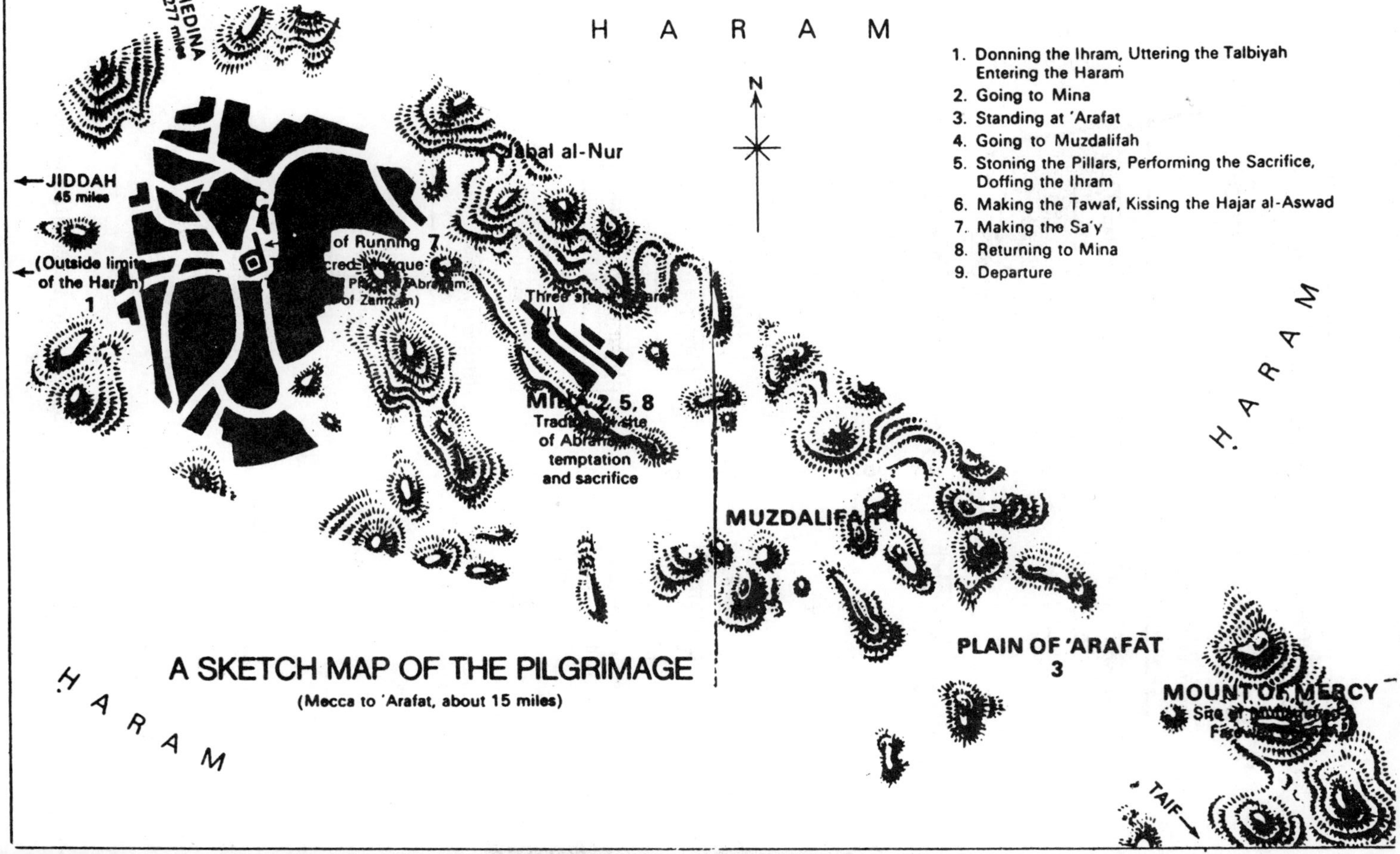

A SKETCH MAP OF THE PILGRIMAGE
(Mecca to 'Arafat, about 15 miles)

SUMMARY OF MANĀSIK OF ḤAJJ

	HAJJ–E–TAMATTU'	HAJJ–E–QIRĀN
1	Iḥrām of 'Umra condition	Iḥrām of Ḥajj and 'Umra together condition
2	Ṭawāf with Ramal Rukn	Ṭawāf with Ramal condition
3	Sa'i Wajib	Sa'i Wajib
4	Ḥalaq choice	*Ḥalaq*
5	Resumption of Ihram condition	*Reviving Ihram*
6	*Ṭawāf Qadūm*	Ṭawāf-e-Qadūm Sunna
7	*Sa'i*	Sa'i Wajib
8	Waqūf-e-'Arafāt Rukn-e-A'zam	Waqūf-e-'Arafāt Rukn-e-A'zam
9	Waqūf-e- Muzdalifa Wājib	Waqūf-e-Muzdalifa Wājib
10	Ramī Jamrāt al 'Aqaba Wājib	Ramī Jamrāt al 'Aqaba Wājib
11	Sacrifice Wājib	Sacrifice Wājib
12	Ḥalaq and Abandon Iḥrām Wājib	Halaq and Abandon Ihrām Wājib
13	Ṭawāf-e-Ziyāra Rukn	Ṭawāf-e-Ziyāra Rukn
14	Sa'i Wajib	*Sa'i*
15	Ramī Jamarāt Wājib	Rami Jamarát Wājib
16	Ṭawāf-e-Wadā' Wājib	Ṭawāf-e- Wadā' Wājib

Manāsik in shaded area are not Wājib, and can be excluded

SEQUENCE OF HAJJ CEREMONIES

Starting with Tawaf-a-Qudum and ending with Tawaf-e-Wadā' below.

The Ka bah, in Mecca's Sacred Mosque, with the Black Stone framed in silver, covered by the Kiswah, a black cloth with Koranic verse

Tent city at Mina (2)

The Mount of Mercy (3)

Muzdalifah (4)

The Stoning (5)

"The Circling" (6)

The Place of Abraham (6)

The Well of Zamzam (6)

"The Place of Running" (7)

ḤAJJ-E-IFRĀD

1. Iḥrām of Ḥajj condition
2. Ṭawāf-e-Qadūm Sunna
3. Sa'i
4. Halaq or Qasr
5. Second Iḥrām
6. Ṭawāf-e-Qadūm
7. Sa'i
8. Waqūf-e-'Arafāt Rukn-e-A'zam
9. Waqūf-e-Muzdalifa Wājib
10. Ramī Jamrāt-ul-'Aqaba Wājib
11. Sacrifice Mustahab
12. Ḥalaq and Abandon Iḥrām Wājib
13. Ṭawāf-e-Ziyāra Rukn
14. Sa'i Wājib
15. Ramī Jamār Wājib
16. Ṭawāf-e-Wadā' Wājib

MANĀSIK OF 'UMRA

1. Iḥrām of 'Umra condition
2. Ṭawāf with Ramal Rukn
3. Sa'i Wājib
4. Halaq or Qaṣr Wājib
5. Farewell Ṭawāf Wājib

The Manāsik

in the shaded area

are not Wājib

and can be excluded

CHAPTER ELEVEN

DETAILS OF MANĀSIK OF ḤAJJ

7TH OF DHUL–ḤIJJA

On the 7th Dhul–Hijja, the Imām delivers a Khuṭba (sermon) after Ẓuhr prayer in Masjid-al-Ḥarām. In this Khuṭba he expounds the laws and ceremonies of Ḥajj. This sermon is the Sunna of the Holy Prophet (peace be upon him).

8TH OF DHUL–ḤIJJA

1. It is Sunna to take a bath, adopt the Iḥrām and then come to the Masjid-al-Harām. It is Mustahab to join the Fajr prayer here.

2. The Qārin and Mufrid are already in the state of Ihrām (of Ḥajj). But a Mutamattī' will have to re-adopt his Ihrām, now with the intention of Hajj.

3. A Mutamattī' should say two Rak'at for Ihrām, and proclaim the Niyya for Ḥajj, viz:

اَللّٰهُمَّ إِنِّيْ أُرِيْدُ الْحَجَّ فَيَسِّرْهُ لِيْ وَ تَقَبَّلْهُ مِنِّيْ
نَوَيْتُ الْحَجَّ وَ اَحْرَمْتُ بِهٖ مُخْلِصًا لِلّٰهِ تَعَالٰى

O Allah! I prepare myself for Hajj, make it easy for me and accept it on my behalf. I hereby do the Niyya for Ḥajj and enter into its state of Ihram for the sake of Allah alone.

Allāhumma innī urīd-ul-Ḥajja fa-yassirhu lī wa taqabbalhu minnī, nawait-ul-Hajja wa ahramtu bihī mukhlisan lillāhi ta'āla.

With this declaration of Intention, they should repeatedly pronounce Talbiya.

An Aerial View of Minā
with Masjid-e-Khaif in Centre

لَبَّيْكَ اللّٰهُمَّ لَبَّيْكَ ، لَبَّيْكَ لَا شَرِيْكَ لَكَ لَبَّيْكَ
إِنَّ الْحَمْدَ وَالنِّعْمَةَ لَكَ وَالْمُلْكَ ، لَا شَرِيْكَ لَكَ

Here am I, O Allah! At Thy service at Thy service, at Thy service! There is no partner unto Thee. Here am I at Thy service. All praise and grace and sovereignty is due unto Thee. Thou hast no partner.

Labbaik Allāhumma Labbaika, Labbaika lā sharīka laka labbaik, Inn-al-ḥamda wan-ni-mata laka wal-mulk, Lā shrika lak.

No sooner is Talbiya recited than the Iḥrām for Ḥajj starts. Now all the aforementioned restrictions of Iḥrām are binding on the intending Pilgrim. All Pilgrims now perform Ṭawāf-e-Qadūm which means Ṭawāf of arrival. This Ṭawāf is Sunna for only those coming from outside the Ḥaram. It is not Sunna, for those residing in Mecca and within the boundaries of Haram.

The period of performing Tawāf-e-Qadūm is from the time of entering Mecca to the time of Waqūf-e-'Arafāt. This will cease (immediately) when one commences Waqūf-e-'Arafāt.

4. For a Qārin, Ṭawāf-e-Qadūm is Sunna, which is followed by Sa'i which is Wājib. Therefore Ramal and Idtiba' is Wājib in Ṭawāf-e-Qadūm.

5. For a Mufrid, Tawāf-e-Qadūm is Sunna. But it is better to do Sa'ī after Tawāf-e-Ziyāra.

6. It is Mustaḥab for Mutamattī', and for those who live in Mecca, to perform the Ṭawāf of Bait-Allah. Prescribed prayers for Ṭawāf-e-Qadūm and Sa'ī are the same as given in previous chapters.

7. All Pilgrims then offer two Rak'at of Ṭawāf. Now all Pilgrims proceed to Minā which is about 3 miles from Mecca. It is Sunna to offer five prayers from Ẓuhr of the 8th of Dhul-Ḥijja upto the Fajr Prayer of the 9th in Minā,

To 'Arafat from Minā on foot and by Buses

and to stay in Minā at night. This is actually preparing oneself for the rigorous ceremonies ahead. Today you compose yourselves and spend as much time in remembering Allah as possible.

8. It is Makrūh to spend the night of the 8th Dhul-Hijja in Mecca or to reach 'Arafāt.

9TH DHUL–HIJJA

1. Today you are to perform the most important Rukn of the Ḥajj, without which Ḥajj does not stand performed. This Rukn-e-A'zam is called Waqūf-e-'Arafāt

   Today, when the sun rises, you are to set out for 'Arafāt from Minā. Reciting Talbiya, with Dhikr and with passion, one should proceed with the idea that Allah has granted the Audience.

2. On the way to 'Arafāt, repeat Talbiya, Astaghfār, and Darūd innumerable times.

   Recite the following Du'ā on the way to 'Arafāt:

اَللّٰهُمَّ اجْعَلْهَا خَيْرَ غُدْوَةٍ غَدَوْتُهَا قَطُّ وَاَقْرِبْهَا مِنْ
رِضْوَانِكَ وَابْعِدْهَا مِنْ سَخَطِكَ ط اَللّٰهُمَّ اِلَيْكَ تَوَجَّهْتُ
وَعَلَيْكَ تَوَكَّلْتُ وَوَجْهَكَ اَرَدْتُّ فَاجْعَلْ ذَنْبِيْ مَغْفُوْرًا وَّحَجِّيْ
مَبْرُوْرًا وَّارْحَمْنِيْ وَلَا تُخَيِّبْنِيْ وَبَارِكْ لِيْ فِيْ سَفَرِيْ وَاقْضِ
بِعَرَفَاتٍ حَاجَتِيْ ط اِنَّكَ عَلٰى كُلِّ شَيْءٍ قَدِيْرٌ ط

O Allah! Make this day the best of my days (mornings), and make me nearer to Thy

Allāhummaj-'alha khaira ghudwatin ghadautuhā qaṭṭu, waqrabhā min rid wānika, wab'ad-

favours and farther from Thy wrath, O Allah! Towards Thee I turn, and in Thee have I placed my trust, and I intend to approach Thy Countenance (in attention). So forgive my sins and accept my Hajj, and have mercy on me, and do not deprive me (of Thy favours), and bless me in my journey, and fulfill my needs (both physical and spiritual) in 'Arafāt, for Thou hast Power over all things.

hā min sakhaṭika, Allā humma ilaika tawajjahtu wa 'alaika tawakkaltu wa wajhaka aradt-tu faj'al dhanbī maghfūran wwa Ḥajjī mabrūran-wwar-ḥamnī wa lā tukhayyibni, wa bārik lī lī safrī waqḍi bi' Arafā-tin ḥājatī, innaka 'alā kulli shai-'in Qadīr.

Do not stop on the way, this will cause discomfort to others.

3. Recite also:

لَآ إِلٰهَ إِلَّا اللّٰهُ وَحْدَهٗ لَا شَرِيْكَ لَهٗ ط لَهُ الْمُلْكُ
وَلَهُ الْحَمْدُ ط يُحْيِيْ وَيُمِيْتُ وَهُوَ حَيٌّ لَّا يَمُوْتُ
بِيَدِهِ الْخَيْرُ ط وَهُوَ عَلٰى كُلِّ شَيْءٍ قَدِيْرٌ ط

None has the right to be worshipped but Allah and He has no partner. To Him alone is the authority and to Him is the praise. It is He who gives life and gives death and He is eternal, ever existing, the good is in His power. He is all Powerful.

lā ilāha illallāhu waḥdahū lā sharīka lahū, lah-ul-mulku wa lah-ul-ḥamdu, yuḥyī wa yumītu wa huwa ḥayyu lā yamūtu biyadihil-khair, wa huwa 'alā kulli shai'in Qadīr.

4. If possible, after reaching 'Arafāt, take a bath, such that you do not rub the body, merely flush it with water. It is Sunna of The Prophet (Peace be upon him). If the bath is not possible Wuḍū is sufficient.

5. When you reach 'Arafāt, you or your Guide will be occupied in pitching a tent for the stay (Waqūf) here in 'Arafāt. Do not waste too much time in these worldly matters. Each step you take here is in the presence of Allah, be serene and self composed and recite Talbiya as much as possible, as well as other forms of Adhkār.

6. Just after the post-meridian or Zawāl (the earliest time of Ẓuhr) indulge in extensive Dhikr, ISTAGHFĀR and DU'Ā with the utmost humility and lowliness. Today is the day for the efficacy of prayers and forgiveness. Today the doors of Allah's mercy are open – so plead with Him as much as possible

7. It is Mustaḥab to proceed, after the bath, to Masjid–e–NAMRA. This is the mosque said to be built by Prophet Ibrāhīm and stands inside the entrance of 'Arafat. The portion below its western wall does not fall within the precincts of 'Arafāt itself. This portion is known as BAṬN URNA. Here the waqūf is not trustworthy. Many tents may be pitched in Baṭn Urna, but for the fulfillment of the Rukn-e-A'ẓam, the Waqūf, you will have to leave Baṭn Urna, if you happen to be there, and come to 'Arafāt proper, (Your Guide will know this).

8. Here, in the Masjid–e–Namra, the Imām or his nominee will deliver the second Khuṭba (sermon) of Ḥajj, which is Sunna but not Wājib.

9. Both the prayers of Ẓuhr and 'Aṣr are combined if they are offered behind the Imām. First the Ẓuhr prayer will be led immediately followed by the 'Aṣr prayer. These two prayers are offered with one Ādhān and two Iqāmas. The two rak'at of Sunna or any Nafl will not be offered between these two prayers. This is called Jama' Bain Ṣalātain. If for any reason, you could not attend the congregational combined prayers with the Imām, then you can offer (ladies, for example) Ẓuhr and 'Aṣr prayers separately as usual, with Sunna and Nafl Rak'at.

WAQŪF—E—'ARAFĀT ON 9TH DHUL—ḤIJJA

1. You can stay any where in 'Arafāt, but it is Sunna to stay near Jabal—ar—Rahma (the Mount of Mercy).
2. When you first see JABAL—AR—RAḤMA, recite:

اَللّٰهُ اَكْبَرُ اَللّٰهُ اَكْبَرُ اَللّٰهُ اَكْبَرُ وَلِلّٰهِ الْحَمْدُ ط سُبْحَانَ اللّٰهِ وَالْحَمْدُ لِلّٰهِ وَلَا اِلٰهَ اِلَّا اللّٰهُ وَاللّٰهُ اَكْبَرُ ط

Allah is Great, Allah is Great, Allah is Great and all praise is due to Allah, Glory be to Allah, and all praise is due to Allah and none has the right to be worshipped but Allah and Allah is Great.

Allāh-u-Akbar, Allāh-u-Akbar, Allāh-u-Akbar wa lillāh-il-ḥamd, Subḥān-allāhi wal-ḥamdu lillāhi wa lā ilāha illallāhu wallāhu Akbar.

The above is known as Takbīr, Tahlīl, Talbeeḥ
And also: recite the following Du'ā:

اَللّٰهُمَّ اغْفِرْلِیْ وَتُبْ عَلَیَّ وَاَعْطِنِیْ سُؤَالِیْ وَوَجِّهْ لِیَ الْخَيْرَ اَيْنَمَا تَوَجَّهْتُ سُبْحَانَ اللّٰهِ وَالْحَمْدُ لِلّٰهِ وَلَا اِلٰهَ اِلَّا اللّٰهُ وَاللّٰهُ اَكْبَرُ ط

O Allah! Forgive me, accept my penitence and reward me with what I have sought and in whichever direction I proceed, turn it into goodness. Glory be to Allah and all praise is due to Allah alone and none has the right to be worshipped but Allah and Allah is Great.

Allāhummaghfir lī wa tub 'alayya wa a'ṭinī sū'ulī wa wajjih lī al-khaira ainamā tawajjahtu subḥān-Allāhi wal-ḥamdu lillāhi wa lā ilāha illallāhu wallāhu Akbar.

3. The interval of the Waqūf in 'Arafāt begins after the Zawāl of the Sun (post–meridian) and ends on the morning of the Eidday, the 10th of Dhul–Ḥijja, just before Fajr. According to the Ḥadīth of the Holy Prophet, " 'Arafāt's Waqūf is Ḥajj, though it may only be for a short while"

4. It is also permissible to sit or lie down during the Waqūf. Talbiya at every step must be recited, and recited a lot. It is better that you continue Waqūf till sunset, facing Qibla. After the Ṣalāt, throughout the stay, continue Talbiya, Dhikr. Istaghfār, and Darūd, and recitation of the Holy Qur'ān or recitation of any Kalima of prayers, with humility and lowliness. You are one of the Wāqefīn in His presence, so entreat Him, plead, beg and pray for the welfare of your family, relatives, friends, neighbours, country and for the whole of the Muslim world. Ask for His Forgiveness and Mercy. This is the special occasion for acceptance of your prayers. Not a single moment is to be lost. Even legitimate things cannot be talked out, if not required.

5. If you have not offered the Jama' Bain–Ṣalātain behind the Imām, come back to your tent, and offer the 'Aṣr prayer. Try to go near to Jabal–ar–Raḥma prior to sunset and again indulge in prayers wholeheartedly. This is the Mount of Mercy, and Mercy will be granted to mankind, as it was to its Father (Adam).

6. In Waqūf, the raising of hands is Sunna of the Messenger of Allāh. If the hands are tired, then you can pray with joined hands. It is reported that the Prophet (peace be upon him) after raising his hands three times uttered Allāh-u-Akbar Wa Lillā hil Ḥamd and then recited the following Du'ā:

لَآ إِلٰهَ إِلَّا اللّٰهُ وَحْدَهٗ لَا شَرِيْكَ لَهٗ ط لَهُ الْمُلْكُ
وَلَهُ الْحَمْدُ ط اَللّٰهُمَّ اهْدِنِيْ بِالْهُدٰى وَ نَقِّنِيْ
بِالتَّقْوٰى وَاغْفِرْلِيْ فِي الْاٰخِرَةِ وَالْاُوْلٰى ط

None has the right to be worshipped but Allah. He is the One and He has no partner, to Him is the dominion and all praise is due to Him. O Allah! Keep me steadfast on Thy guidance and purify me thru piety and forgive me in this world and in the next.

Lā ilāha illallāhu waḥdahū lā sharīka lahū, lah-ul-mulku wa lah-ul-ḥamd, Allāhumma ahdinī bil-hudā wa naqqinī bit-taqwā waghfir lī fil-ākhirati wal-'ūlā.

After reciting this, the Holy Prophet dropped his hands for such a span of time as required in reciting Sūra Fātiḥa. He again raised his hands, uttered those words and repeated the Du'ā. He repeated this process three times.

PLAINS OF ARAFĀT

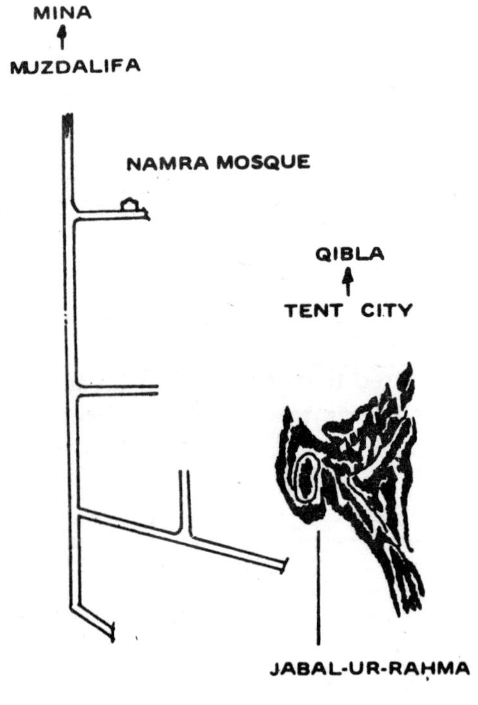

It is Sunna of the Prophet to recite the following Du a:

اَللّٰهُ اَكْبَرُ اَللّٰهُ اَكْبَرُ وَ لِلّٰهِ الْحَمْدُ وَلِلّٰهِ الْحَمْدُ
وَلِلّٰهِ الْحَمْدُ ط لَآ اِلٰهَ اِلَّا اللّٰهُ وَحْدَهٗ لَا شَرِيْكَ لَهٗ لَهُ الْمُلْكُ
وَلَهُ الْحَمْدُ ط اَللّٰهُمَّ اهْدِنِيْ بِالْهُدٰى وَنَقِّنِيْ وَاعْتَصِمْنِيْ بِا
التَّقْوٰى وَاغْفِرْلِيْ فِي الْاٰخِرَةِ وَالْاُوْلٰى ط اَللّٰهُمَّ اجْعَلْهُ حَجًّا
مَّبْرُوْرًا وَّ ذَنْبًا مَّغْفُوْرًا ط اَللّٰهُمَّ لَكَ صَلٰوتِيْ وَ نُسُكِيْ
وَمَحْيَايَ وَ مَمَاتِيْ وَاِلَيْكَ مَاٰلِيْ ط اَللّٰهُمَّ اِنِّيْ اَعُوْذُبِكَ مِنْ
عَذَابِ الْقَبْرِ وَ وَسْوَسَةِ الصَّدْرِ وَشَتَاتِ الْاَمْرِ ط اَللّٰهُمَّ اهْدِنَا
بِالْهُدٰى وَزَيِّنَّا بِالتَّقْوٰى وَاغْفِرْلَنَا فِي الْاٰخِرَةِ وَالْاُوْلٰى
اَللّٰهُمَّ اِنِّيْ اَسْاَلُكَ رِزْقًا حَلَالًا طَيِّبًا مُّبَارَكًا ط اَللّٰهُمَّ اَمَرْتَنِيْ
بِالدُّعَاءِ وَ لَكَ الْاِجَابَةُ وَاِنَّكَ لَا تُخْلِفُ وَعْدَكَ ط اَللّٰهُمَّ
مَا اَحْبَبْتَ مِنْ خَيْرٍ فَحَبِّبْهُ اِلَيْنَا وَيَسِّرْهُ لَنَا وَمَا كَرِهْتَ مِنْ
شَرٍّ فَكَرِّهْهُ اِلَيْنَا وَجَنِّبْنَا عَنْهُ وَلَا تَنْزِعْ مِنَّا الْاِسْلَامَ بَعْدَ
اِذْ هَدَيْتَنَا ط لَآ اِلٰهَ اِلَّا اللّٰهُ وَحْدَهٗ لَا شَرِيْكَ لَهٗ لَهُ الْمُلْكُ
وَلَهُ الْحَمْدُ يُحْيِيْ وَيُمِيْتُ وَهُوَ عَلٰى كُلِّ شَيْءٍ قَدِيْرٌ ط اَللّٰهُمَّ
اجْعَلْ فِيْ صَدْرِيْ نُوْرًا وَّفِيْ سَمْعِيْ نُوْرًا وَّ فِيْ قَلْبِيْ نُوْرًا ط
اَللّٰهُمَّ اشْرَحْ لِيْ صَدْرِيْ وَيَسِّرْلِيْ اَمْرِيْ وَاَعُوْذُبِكَ مِنْ وَسَاوِسِ
الصَّدْرِ وَتَشَتُّتِ الْاَمْرِ وَعَذَابِ الْقَبْرِ ط اَللّٰهُمَّ اِنِّيْ اَعُوْذُبِكَ

مِنْ شَرِّ مَا يَلِجُ فِى اللَّيْلِ وَشَرِّ مَا يَلِجُ فِى النَّهَارِ وَشَرِّ مَا
تُهِبُّ الرِّيَاحُ وَشَرِّ بَوَائِقِ الدَّهْرِ ۝ رَبَّنَا اٰتِنَا فِى الدُّنْيَا
حَسَنَةً وَّفِى الْاٰخِرَةِ حَسَنَةً وَّقِنَا عَذَابَ النَّارِ ۝ اَللّٰهُمَّ اِنِّىْ
اَسْأَلُكَ مِنْ خَيْرِ مَا سَأَلَكَ بِهٖ نَبِيُّكَ وَاَعُوْذُبِكَ مِنْ شَرِّ
مَا اسْتَعَاذَ مِنْهُ نَبِيُّكَ صَلَّى اللّٰهُ عَلَيْهِ وَسَلَّمَ ۝ رَبَّنَا ظَلَمْنَا اَنْفُسَنَا
وَاِنْ لَّمْ تَغْفِرْلَنَا وَتَرْحَمْنَا لَنَكُوْنَنَّ مِنَ الْخَاسِرِيْنَ ۝ رَبِّ اجْعَلْنِىْ
مُقِيْمَ الصَّلٰوةِ وَمِنْ ذُرِّيَّتِىْ رَبَّنَا وَتَقَبَّلْ دُعَاءِ ۝ رَبَّنَا اغْفِرْلِىْ
وَلِوَالِدَىَّ وَلِلْمُؤْمِنِيْنَ يَوْمَ يَقُوْمُ الْحِسَابُ ۝ رَبِّ ارْحَمْهُمَا كَمَا
رَبَّيَانِىْ صَغِيْرًا ۝ رَبَّنَا اغْفِرْلَنَا وَلِاِخْوَانِنَا الَّذِيْنَ سَبَقُوْنَا
بِالْاِيْمَانِ وَلَا تَجْعَلْ فِىْ قُلُوْبِنَا غِلًّا لِّلَّذِيْنَ اٰمَنُوْا رَبَّنَا اِنَّكَ
رَءُوْفٌ الرَّحِيْمُ ۝ رَبَّنَا اِنَّكَ اَنْتَ السَّمِيْعُ الْعَلِيْمُ وَتُبْ عَلَيْنَا
اِنَّكَ اَنْتَ التَّوَّابُ الرَّحِيْمُ ۝ لَاحَوْلَ وَلَا قُوَّةَ اِلَّا بِاللّٰهِ الْعَلِىِّ
الْعَظِيْمِ ۝ اَللّٰهُمَّ اِنَّكَ تَعْلَمُ وَتَرٰى مَكَانِىْ وَتَسْمَعُ كَلَامِىْ
وَتَعْلَمُ سِرِّىْ وَعَلَانِيَّتِىْ وَلَا يَخْفٰى عَلَيْكَ شَىْءٌ مِّنْ اَمْرِىْ
وَاَنَا الْبَائِسُ الْفَقِيْرُ الْمُسْتَغِيْثُ الْمُسْتَجِيْرُ الْوَجِلُ الْمُشْفِقُ الْمُقِرُّ
الْمُعْتَرِفُ بِذَنْبِهٖ اَسْأَلُكَ مَسْأَلَةَ الْمِسْكِيْنِ وَاَبْتَهِلُ اِلَيْكَ
اِبْتِهَالَ الْمُذْنِبِ الذَّلِيْلِ وَاَدْعُوْكَ دُعَاءَ الْخَائِفِ الضَّرِيْرِ مَنْ
خَضَعَتْ لَكَ رَقَبَتُهٗ وَفَاضَتْ عَيْنَاهُ وَنَحَلَ لَكَ جَسَدُهٗ وَرَغِمَ لَكَ
اَنْفُهٗ اَللّٰهُمَّ لَا تَجْعَلْنِىْ بِدُعَائِكَ شَقِيًّا وَّكُنْ لِىْ رَءُوْفًا رَّحِيْمًا

يَا خَيْرَ الْمَسْئُوْلِيْنَ وَيَا خَيْرَ الْمُعْطِيْنَ يَا اَرْحَمَ الرّٰحِمِيْنَ وَالْحَمْدُ
لِلّٰهِ رَبِّ الْعٰلَمِيْنَ آمِيْنَ ۔ يَا مَنْ لَّا يُبْرِمُهُ الْحَاحُ الْمُلِحِّيْنَ
فِي الدُّعَاءِ وَلَا تَضْجِرُهُ مَسْأَلَةُ السَّائِلِيْنَ اَذِقْنَا بَرْدَ عَفْوِكَ
وَحَلَاوَةَ مَغْفِرَتِكَ وَلَذَّةَ مُنَاجَاتِكَ وَرَحْمَتِكَ ۔ اِلٰهِيْ مَنْ
مَدَحَ اِلَيْكَ نَفْسَهٗ فَاِنِّيْ لَائِمٌ نَفْسِيْ اَخْرَسَتِ الْمَعَاصِيْ
لِسَانِيْ فَمَا لِيْ وَسِيْلَةٌ مِّنْ عَمَلٍ وَّلَا شَفِيْعٌ سِوَى الْاَمَلِ ط

Allah is Great, Allah is Great, Allah is Great, All praise is due to Allah, All praise is due to Allah and All praise is due to Allah, None has the right to be worshipped but Allah, He is One without partner. For Him alone is the the kingdom and all praise. O Allah! Guide me to the right path, and purify me and perfect me in piety, and forgive me in this world and the next. O Allah! Render this Hajj of mine acceptable and a means of forgiveness of my sins. O Allah! For Thy pleasure is my prayer, my sacrifice my life and my death, and for You is all I have. O Allah! I seek Thy refuge from the torment of the grave, and the evil suggestion of the heart and from harm of my affairs. O Allah! Guide us to the right path, and

Allāh-u-Akbar, Allāh-u-Akbar. Allāh-u-Akbar, wa lillāh-il-ḥamd, wa lillāh-il-ḥamd, wa lillāh-il-ḥamd, Lā ilāha illalāhu waḥdahū lā sharīka lahū, la-hul-mulku wa lahul-ḥamd. Allāhummahdinī bil-hudā, wa naqqinī wa'taṣimnī bit-taqwā waghfir lī fil-ākhirati wal-'ūla Allāhummaj'alhu Ḥajjam-mabrūran wwa dhanbam-maghfūra. Allāhumma laka ṣalātī wa nusukī maḥyāya wa mamātī, wa ilaika ma'āli. Allāhumma innī a'ūdhu bika min 'adhāb-il-qabri wa waswasat-is-ṣadri wa shatāt-il-amr. Allāhummahdina bil-hudā wa zayyinnā bit-taqwā waghfir lanā fil-ākhirati wal-'ūlā. Allāhumma innī as'aluka rizqan ḥalālan ṭayyibam mubārakan. Allāhumma amartanī bid-du'āi wa lak-al-ijāba, wa innaka lā tukhlifu wa'dak.

forgive us in this world and the next. O Allah! I ask you for lawful subsistence, pure and blessed. O Allah! Thou hast instructed me to pray to Thee and it is upto Thou to accept my prayer. Of course Thou does not break Thy promise.

O Allah! Whatever of goodness Thou preferest, make that likeable to us, and easy for us, and whatever evil Thou abhorst make that hateful to us, and remove it from us. And do not take away Islam from us after having guided us to it. None is worthy of worship except Allah, who is One and has no partner, for Him is the kingdom and all praise, He gives the life and takes it away and He is all Powerful. O Allah! Make light in my chest, and light is my hearing, and light in my vision and light in my heart. O Allah! Expand my chest and make my affairs easy for me. And I seek your refuge from evil suggestions in my heart and harm of my affairs, and from the torment of the grave. O Allah! I seek Thy refuge against the evil of that which penetrates at night and against the evil of that which penetrates at day-time, and against the evil of that which blows along with the

Allāhumma ma aḥbabta min khairin, fa-aḥibbahū ilaina wa yassirhu lanā, wa mā karrihta min sharrin fa-karrih-hu ilainā wa jannibnā 'anhu wa lā tanzi' minn-al-islāma ba'da idh hada-ita-nā, Lā ilāha illallāhu waḥ-dahū lā sharīka lahū, lah-ulm-ulku wa lah-ul-ḥumdu, yuḥyi wa yumīt, wa huwa 'alā kulli shai'in Qadīr. Allāhummaj-'al fī ṣadrī nūran wwa fī sam'ī nūran wwa fī qalbī nūran, Allāhummashraḥ lī sadrī wa yassir lī amrī, wa a'ūdhu bika min wasāwis-iṣ-ṣadri wa tas-hattut-il-amri wa 'adhāb-il-qabr. Allā humma innī a'ūdhu bika min sharri mā yaliju fill-aili wa sharri mā yaliju finna-hāri wa sharri mā tuḥibb-ur-riyāḥu wa sharri bawā 'iq-id-dahri, Rabbanā ātinā fidduni-ya hasa-natan wwa fil-ākhirati ḥasanatan wwa qinā 'adhāb-an-nār. Allāhumma innī as' aluka min Khairi mā sa'alaka bihī nabiyyuka wa a'ūdhu bika min sharri masta'ādha minhu nabiyyuka ṣallallāhu 'alaihi wa sallam. Rabbanā ẓalamnā anfusanā wa in-llam taghfir lanā wa tarḥamnā lanakūnannā min-al-khāsirīn. Rabbij'alnī muqīm-aṣ-ṣalāti wa min dhurri-yyati Rabbanā wa taqabbal du'ai, Rabbana ghfir lī wa li-wālidayya wa lil-mu'minīna

wind, and from the calamities of time. O Allah! Grant us goodness in this world and goodness in the hereafter, O Allah! I ask Thee for the goodness for which Thy Prophet asked and I seek Thy refuge from evil for which Thy Prophet (may peace and blessings of Allah be upon him) sought, O our Lord! We have been cruel to ourselves and if Thou wilt not forgive us and have mercy on us, we will become like those among the losers. O my Lord! Make me one who establishes regular prayers and also my offspring, O our Lord! Accept Thou my prayer. O our Lord! Forgive me and my parents and all Believers on the Day of Reckoning. O Lord! Have mercy on them (my parents) as they brought me up from childhood. O Our Lord! Forgive us and our brothers who preceded us in faith and do not let us bear any malice against those who have faith, Thou art the Most Kind, the Most Merciful. O our Lord! Thou art all Hearing All Knowing and turn unto us (in mercy), Thou art Oft returning Most Merciful. And there is none who has the power of goodness nor of security from evil except with

yauma yaqūm-al-ḥisāb. Rabb-ir-ḥamhumā kamā rabb-iyānī ṣaghīran, Rabbanaghfir lanā wa li-ikhwānina-lladhīna sabaqūnā bil-īmāni wa lā taj'al fī qulūbinā ghill-al-ladhīna āmanū, Rabbanā innaka Ra'ūf-ur-Raḥīm. Rabbanā innaka ant-as-Samī'-ul-'Alīm, wa tub 'alainā innaka ant-at-Tawwāb-ur-Raḥīm. Lā ḥawla wa lā quwwata illā billāh-il-'Aliyy-il-'Aẓīm. Allāhumma innaka ta' lamu wa tarā makānī wa tasma'u kalāmī wa ta'lamu sirrī wa 'alāniyyatī wa lā yakhfa 'alaika shai-un-mmin amrī wa an-al-bā'is-ul-faqīr-ul-mustaghīth-ul-mustajīr-ul-wajil -ul-mush-fiq-ul-muqirr-ul mu'-tarifu bi-dhanbihī as-'aluka mas'alatal-miskīna wabtahilu ilaika ibtihāl-al-mudhnib-idh-dhalīli wa ad'ūka du'ā-al-khā'if -iḍ ḍarīri man khaḍa'at laka raqabatuhū wa fāḍat 'aināhu wa nubila laka jasaduhū wa raghima laka anfuhū, Allāhumma lā taj'alnī bi-du'ā'ika shaqiyyan wwa kun-lli Ra'-ūfan-r-Raḥīm. Yā khair-al-mas'-ūlīna wa yā khair-al-mu'ṭīna yā Arḥam-ar-Rāhimīn, wal-ḥamdu lillāhi Rabb-il-'ālamīn, Āmīn. Yā man-llā yubrimuh-ul-ḥāḥ-ul-mulḥīna fid-du'āi wa lā taḍjiruhū mas'alat-us-sā'ilīna adhiqnā barda 'afwika wa halāwata maghfirati ka wa

the assistance of Allah, the High, the Great, O Allah! Thou knowest and seest my place and listenest to me and Thou knowest my secrets and the obvious, and none is hidden from Thee of my affairs. I am non-entity, afflicted, destitute and humble beggar, and am a petitioner who begs Thou for reward, I am one who confesses his sins humbly and I beseech Thee and beg Thee like a blind man whose neck is bowed before Thee and whose eyes are tearful, and whose body has weakened (in Thy rememberance) and whose nose is full of dust (remaining in prostration) and begging Thy mercy. O Allah! Do not disappoint me concerning my prayers to Thee and be Kind and Merciful to me, O the best of those who are asked, O the best of the Givers, and O the most Merciful of the Mercifuls. All praise is due to Allah, the Lord of the worlds, Amen. O the one who never gets tired of the insistence of asking, begging in prayers and who is not weary of the requests. Make us taste the coolness of Thy pardon and sweetness of Thy forgiveness and to the pleasure of pleading to Thee and Thy mercy, O my Allah! Let who-

ladhdhata munājatika wa raḥmatika, Ilāhī man madaḥa ilaika nafsahū fa-innī lā-imu nafsī akhrasat-il-ma'āṣī lisānī fa-mā lī wasīlatum-min 'amalin wa lā shafi'un siw-al-amal.

soever wishes to praise himself to you do so, I Only praise Thee and blame myself in front of Thee, although my sins have made me speechless and there is none in my affairs to give me deliverance except my hope of Thy mercy.

7. If you leave the ground of 'Arafāt before sunset, then a sacrifice of an animal will become obligatory. If for some unavoidable circumstance you cannot comply with the Waqūf from noon until sunset of 9th Dhul-Ḥijja then you can do it even after sunset. You will then be absolved of the obligation of Waqūf. If one returns to 'Arafāt before sunset, then the Damm (the sacrifice) will be waived. But if one returns after sunset, Damm will not be waived, though the obligation of Waqūf is fulfilled.

8. It is Makrūh to delay the departure from 'Arafāt after sunset. It was here in 'Arafāt, that the Messenger of Allah (peace be upon him) humbled himself like a beggar, asking Allah to grant forgiveness to all his 'Umma. He prayed, cried, appealed and humbled himself like a helpless creature in front of his Creator. The aim is to pray to Allah, and people who are not conversant in Arabic, can pray to Him in their own language. These invocations should include all the human beings close to you and especially the Muslims of the rest of the world.

For all our mundane and heavenly designs no one can suggest more adequate or more comprehensive invocations than those taught by the Messenger of Allah (peace be upon him). These invocations have been compiled by learned people, the books recommended are Hizbul-A'ẓam and Munājāt-e-Maqbūl. According to the Ḥadīth of the Holy Prophet: The best invocation on the day of 'Arafāt and the best of all the invocations I have ever offered, is:

لَا إِلٰهَ إِلَّا اللّٰهُ وَحْدَهٗ لَا شَرِيْكَ لَهٗ ط لَهُ الْمُلْكُ
وَلَهُ الْحَمْدُ وَ هُوَ عَلٰى كُلِّ شَيْءٍ قَدِيْرٌ۔

None has the right to be worshipped but Allah, He is the One, there is no partner with Him, to Him belong the dominions and all praise is due to Him and He is Powerful over all things.

Lā ilāha illallāhu waḥdahū lā sharīka lahū, lah-ul-mulku wa lah-ul-ḥamdu wa huwa 'alā kulli shai'in Qadīr.

Whatever invocations are to be recited, their meaning should be fully understood and implied.

The Waqūf-e-'Arafāt is fulfilled even if you put your foot for a second before the sunset in the plain of 'Arafāt.

PROCEEDING FROM 'ARAFĀT TO MUZDALIFA, ON THE NIGHT OF 10TH DHUL-ḤIJJA

1. It is Mustaḥab to walk on foot when approaching Muzdalifa. One should not isolate oneself from the people either in 'Arafāt or Muzdalifa.

2. It is Mustaḥab to leave for Muzdalifa after sunset in 'Arafāt. In Muzdalifa it is Wājib to combine the prayers of Maghrib and 'Ishā at the time of 'Ishā after the Sunna of the Holy Prophet (peace be upon him). So do not offer Maghrib or 'Ishā on the way until you reach Muzdalifa. On the way to Muzdalifa, engage yourself in extensive Talbiya, Dhikr, Darūd and Istaghfār.

3. When you reach Muzdalifa, offer Maghrib and 'Ishā Farḍ prayers jointly at the time of 'Ishā. The Farḍ prayers of 'Ishā should be offered immediately after the Farḍ prayers of Maghrib. Sunna prayers of Maghrib, as well as Sunna and Witr of 'Ishā should be offered afterwards.

4. In Muzdalifa, both prayers combined for Maghrib and 'Ishā should be offered with one Solitary Ādhān and one Iqāma. A congregational prayer is not a precondition, but it is better to offer it in congregation.

It is Mustaḥab to stand in Waqūf near Mash'ar-al-Ḥarām in Muzdalifa.

THE RULES OF ACTION IN MUZDALIFA

1. Maghrib prayers, if offered in 'Arafāt or on the way to Muzdalifa, will have to be repeated on reaching Muzdalifa.

2. If the Pilgrims arrive in Muzdalifa before the time of 'Ishā prayers, they should wait until the time for 'Ishā and then combine Maghrib and 'Ishā prayers.

3. It is Sunnat-e-Mu'akkada to stay at Muzdalifa on the night of 10th Dhul-Ḥijja i.e. after the Waqūf of 'Arafāt (or on the night of 'Īd-ul-Aḍḥā). (Remember in the Islāmic calendar night comes first and the day of 10th Dhul-Ḥijja follows). This night spent in Muzdalifa, in worship and Waqūf, is one hundred thousand times better in Thawāb than the Night of Qadr, (Lailatul Qadr). So do not waste a single moment. Spend the night, if you can, in Dhikr, prayers, Istaghfār, Darūd and Salām.

4. Just before sunrise, collect small pebbles of the size of a chickpea (about 72 in case you lose some) from Muzdalifa. These will be used to cast at the three Jumarāt in Minā, at the time of Ramī.

5. On the way to Muzdalifa repeat Talibiya, Takbīr, Tahlīl and Ḥamd and Istaghfār and also recite:

اَللّٰهُمَّ اِلَيْكَ اَفَضْتُ وَمِنْ عَذَابِكَ اَشْفَقْتُ وَاِلَيْكَ رَغِبْتُ
وَمِنْ سَخَطِكَ رَهِبْتُ فَاقْبَلْ نُسُكِيْ وَاَعْظِمْ اَجْرِيْ وَتَقَبَّلْ تَوْبَتِيْ

وَارْحَمْ تَضَرُّعِيْ وَاسْتَجِبْ دُعَائِيْ وَاَعْطِنِيْ سُؤَالِيْ يَا اَرْحَمَ الرَّاحِمِيْنَ

O Allah! I have come unto Thee, and am apprehensive of Thy wrath, and I approach Thee, and am afraid of Thy anger, so accept my Hajj, and reward me greatly, and accept my repentance and have mercy on my supplication, and accept my prayers and answer my requests, O, the Most Merciful of the Mercifuls!

Allāhumma ilaika afaḍtu wa min 'adhābi-ka ashfaqtu wa ilaika raghibtu, wa min sakha-ṭika rahibtu faq-bal nusu-kī wa a'ẓim ajrī wa taqabbal tauba-tī war ḥam taḍarru'ī was-tajib du'ā'ī wa a'ṭinī su'ālī yā Ar-ḥam-ar-Rāḥimīn.

6. When passing through Wādī-e-Muḥaṣṣir, now known as Wādī-un-Nār, recite:

اَللّٰهُمَّ لَا تَقْتُلْنَا بِغَضَبِكَ وَلَا تُهْلِكْنَا بِعَذَابِكَ

وَعَافِنَا قَبْلَ ذٰلِكَ

O Allah! Do not curse us with Thy wrath, not with Thy torture, and forgive me before this (happens).

Allāhumma lā taqtulnā bigha-ḍabika wa lā tuhliknā bi-'adhā-bika wa 'āfinā qabla dhālik.

7. When entering **Muzdalifa**, recite:

اَللّٰهُمَّ هٰذِهٖ جَمْعٌ اَسْاَلُكَ اَنْ تَرْزُقَنِيْ جَوَامِعَ الْخَيْرِ كُلِّهٖ فَاِنَّهٗ

لَا يُعْطِيْهَا غَيْرُكَ ۔ اَللّٰهُمَّ رَبَّ الْمَشْعَرِ الْحَرَامِ وَرَبَّ زَمْزَمَ

وَالْمَقَامِ وَرَبَّ الْبَيْتِ الْحَرَامِ وَالْمُعْجِزَاتِ الْعِظَامِ اَسْاَلُكَ اَنْ

تُبَلِّغَ رُوْحَ سَيِّدِنَا مُحَمَّدٍ اَفْضَلَ الصَّلٰوةِ وَالسَّلَامِ وَاَنْ تُصْلِحَ لِيْ

ذُرِّيَّتِيْ وَدِيْنِيْ وَتَشْرَحَ لِيْ صَدْرِيْ وَتُطَهِّرَ قَلْبِيْ وَتَرْزُقَنِيْ

الْخَيْرَ الَّذِيْ اَسْاَلُكَ اَنْ تَجْمَعَهٗ فِيْ قَلْبِيْ وَاَنْ تَقِيَنِيْ جَوَامِعَ

الشَّرِّ فَإِنَّكَ وَلِيُّ ذَالِكَ وَالْقَادِرُ عَلَيْهِ ط

O Allah! This is a gathering in Thy presence and I ask Thee to give me all goodness for none except Thee can. O Allah! Lord of Mash'ar-al-Haram, Lord of Zamzam and Maqām (of Ibrahim), Lord of Bait-ul-Ḥarām and Lord of Great Miracles! I ask Thee to please convey to the soul of our Chief, Muhammad, the best of salutation and peace, and correct for me my offspring, and in my religion, and expand my chest, and cleanse my heart, and bestow on me that good which I beseech Thee to collect in my heart and save me from all evil, for Thou art the Guardian and Thou hast the Power over these (things).

Allāhumma hādhihi jam'un as-'aluka an tarzuqanī jawami-'alkhairi kullihī fa-innahū lā yu'-tiha ghairuka, Allāhumma Rabb-al-Mash'ar-il Harāmi wa Rabba Zamzamin wal-Maqāmi wa Rabb-al-Bait-il-Ḥarāmi wal-mu'jizāt-il-'izāmi as'aluka an tuballigha rūḥa sayyidina Muḥammad afdal-as-salāti was-salāmi wa an tus-liha li dhurriyya-tī wa dīni wa tashrah lī sadrī wa tuṭahhira qalbī wa tarzuqaniyalkhair-al-ladhī as'aluka an tajma'ahū fī qalbī wa an taqiyanī jawāmi'-ash-sharri fa-innaka walīyyu dhālika wal-qādiru 'alaihi.

8. It is Mustahab to stay near Mash'-ar-al-Harām in Muzdalifa, if possible.

9. During the night recite:

اَللّٰهُمَّ إِنِّيْ أَسْأَلُكَ أَنْ تَرْزُقَنِيْ فِيْ هٰذَا الْمَكَانِ
جَوَامِعَ الْخَيْرِ كُلِّهِ وَأَنْ تَصْرِفَ عَنِّي السُّوْءَ كُلَّهُ
فَإِنَّهُ لَا يَفْعَلُ ذَالِكَ غَيْرُكَ وَلَا يَجُوْدُ بِهِ إِلَّا أَنْتَ

O Allah! I implore Thee to give me in this (sacred) place a collection of all goodness, and take away from me all evil, for none can do this except

Allāhumma innī as'aluka an tarzuqanī fī hādh-al-makāni jawāmi'al-khairi kullihī wa an tasrifa ann-is-sū'a kullahū fa-innahū lā yaf'alu dhālika

Thee, and none can forgive except Thee.	ghairuka wa lā yaj-udu bihī illā anta.

MORNING OF 10TH OF DHUL-ḤIJJA, THE THIRD DAY OF ḤAJJ

WAQŪF-E-MUZDALIFA – THE FIRST WĀJIB

Today, the Ḥajis have to perform a number of Wājibāt of ceremonies, and therefore they have been exempted from saying 'Īd prayers. To-day is the 'Īd day.

1. The first Wājib is that of Waqūf in Muzdalifa. The duration of this Waqūf is from the appearance of Fajr to the actual sunrise. This Wājib is accomplished if someone goes to Minā after Fajr prayer without waiting for sunrise. But it is Sunna that the sunrise should be awaited.

2. Waqūf in Muzdalifa is Wājib, but for women and the elderly, weak and ailing, it is permissible to abandon the Waqūf and head for Minā after Fajr prayer. But if a male Pilgrim abandons Waqūf of Muzdalifa without any valid excuse, a Damm, (the sacrifice of a sheep or a goat) becomes obligatory.

3. This exemption from Damm for elderly, weak and ailing people is exclusively related to Waqūf at Muzdalifa. Violation of any of the other abstinances of Ihram of Waqūf-e-'Arafāt, on account of illness etc., will impose the obligation of Damm (Zubda).

4. Waquf in Muzdalifa can be observed anywhere within the surroundings of Muzdalifa's open field with the exception of Wādi-e-Muḥaṣṣir. This is the place where the divine punishment had descended upon the people of the Elephant (Aṣḥāb-e-fīl). This is pointed out by a placard.

MAP OF MINĀ

SCALE 1" = 1.5 Mile.

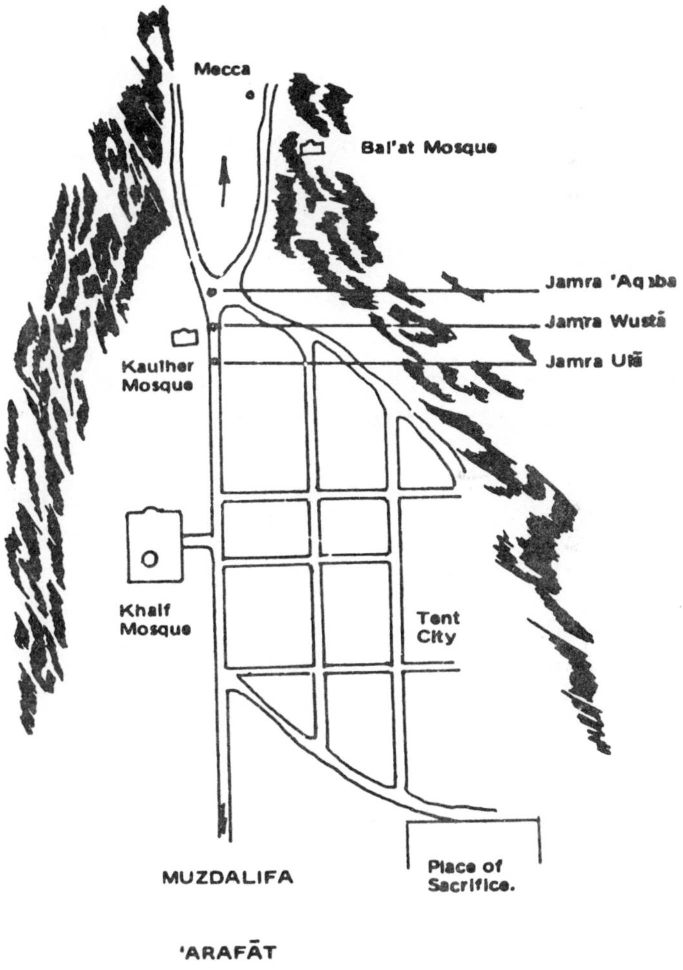

5. In the morning, after Fajr, during the Waquf of Muzdalifa, recite:

اَللّٰهُمَّ بَلِّغْ رُوْحَ مُحَمَّدٍ مِّنَّا التَّحِيَّةَ وَالسَّلَامَ وَاَدْخِلْنَا
دَارَ السَّلَامِ يَا ذَا الْجَلَالِ وَالْاِكْرَامِ۔

O Allah! convey to the soul of Prophet Muḥammad our salutation and greetings, and enter us in Paradise, O Lord of Majesty and Honour!

Allāhumma, balligh rūḥa Muḥammad minn-at-taḥi-yyata was-salām, wa adkhilnā dār-as-salāmi ya dhal-Jalāli wal Ikrām.

II SECOND WĀJIB ON 10TH OF DHUL–ḤIJJA THE RAMĪ AT JAMRAT–UL–'AQABA

1. Departure from Muzdalifa: A short while before the sunrise, proceed to Minā. Delaying the departure after sunrise, is contrary to Sunna.

2. It is Sunna to collect very small pebbles from Muzdalifa before Fajr. These should be equal to a big chick-pea or date-stone in size for the purpose of Ramī at Jamarat.

3. Today on reaching Minā, the first thing to do is the Ramī at Jamrat-ul-'Aqaba, which is Wājib on this very day.

4. What is a Jamra? These are three spots in Minā which indicate the three historical places where Prophet Ibrāhīm (may peace be on him) had cast

From Mazdalifa to Minā

pebbles at Shaiṭān, to repel him from tempting him to disobey Allāh's will. These three places are called Jamrāt (جمرات). Pelting these spots with pebbles (picked from Muzdalifa) is to commemorate the great event of Prophet Ibrāhīm's obedience to Allāh's will. This is one of the Wājibāt of Ḥajj and is called Ramī-al-Jamrāt.

The last Jamra, as you approach Minā from Muzfalifa is called Jamrat-ul-'Aqaba. The second Jamra is called Jamrat-al-Wusṭā (the middle one) and the first one, is called Jamrat-ul-'ūlā which is near Masjid-e-Khaif in Minā. The location of these Jamrāt is clearly posted by means of pillars and sign boards. (Fig. 5).

5. The second Wājib of this day is therefore to cast seven pebbles at Jamrat-al-'Aqaba as you approach Minā from Muzdalifa. Today you are to perform Ramī on Jamrat-ul-'Aqaba only.

Following are the Rules of action for Ramī:

RULES OF ACTION FOR RAMĪ ON 10TH OF DHUL-ḤIJJA

i) It is Mustaḥab to bring seven pebbles for Ramī of Jamrat-ul-'Aqaba from Muzdalifa, although collecting them from anywhere else is allowed. But they should NEVER be collected from the vicinity of the Jamrāt themselves, as the pebbles lying near Jamrāt are reprobated in the eyes of Allāh as clearly stated in Ḥadīth.

ii) For Ramī of the Jamrāt on the 11th, 12th and 13th of Dhul-Hijja it is not Sunna to bring pebbles from Muzdalifa, they may be picked from somewhere else but not from the vicinity of Jamrāt (Zubda).

iii) The pebbles should be of the size of a big chick-pea or date-stone. It is Makrūh to use big stones for Ramī.

iv) Masnūn time for Ramī on Jamrat-ul-'Aqaba on the 10th of Dhul-Hijja is from sunrise to sunset. It is Makrūh after sunset, though it may also be performed between noon and sunset.

v) For Women: If it is not convenient for ladies to perform Ramī due to the crowd, they should perform Ramī after sunset, like-wise elderly, sick and weak people may also perform Ramī after Maghrib.

vi) It is Makrūh to use impure pebbles for Ramī, it is better to wash them before use.

vii) When you reach Minā, on the 10th of Dhul-Hijja, you may recite:

اَللّٰهُمَّ هٰذِهٖ مِنًى قَدْ اَتَيْتُهَا وَ اَنَا عَبْدُكَ وَ ابْنُ عَبْدِكَ
اَسْأَلُكَ اَنْ تَمُنَّ عَلَيَّ بِمَا مَنَنْتَ بِهٖ عَلٰى اَوْلِيَائِكَ ط اَللّٰهُمَّ
اِنِّيْ اَعُوْذُبِكَ مِنَ الْحِرْمَانِ وَالْمُصِيْبَةِ فِيْ دِيْنِيْ يَا اَرْحَمَ
الرّٰحِمِيْنَ ط اَلْحَمْدُ لِلّٰهِ الَّذِيْ اَبْلَغَنِيْ سَالِمًا مُعَافِيًا ط

O Allāh! This is Minā. I have reached it as Thy servant, and the son of Thy servant. I pray that thou bestoweth upon me, that which Thou hast bestoweth on Thy favourites. O Allāh! I seek Thy refuge from deprivation and calamity in my faith, O Most Merciful of the Mercifuls! All praise is due to Allah who made me reach this place safe and sound.

Allāhumma hādhihī Minā qad ataitu-hā wa ana 'abduka wab nu 'abdika as- aluka an tamun na 'alayya bimā mananta bihī 'alā auliyā'ika, Allāhumma innī a'ūdhu bika min-al-hirmāni wal-muṣībati fī dīni yā Arḥam-ar-Rāḥimīn, Al-ḥamdu lillāh-il-ladhī ablaghanī sāliman mu'āfi-ya.

viii) To cast the pebbles: You should be at least 8 feet away from the Jamrat-ul-'Aqaba or further than this. You should then throw pebbles one by one with your right hand, holding the pebble between the first finger (of Shahāda) and the thumb. At the same time you should recite with the throw of every pebble:

بِسْمِ اللّٰهِ اَللّٰهُ اَكْبَرُ رَغْمًا لِّلشَّيْطَانِ

In the name of Allah, Allah is Great, The casting of pebbles is against the Devil.	Bismillāhi Allāh-u-Akbar, Raghmal-li-sh-shaitān.

If you can remember, recite:

اَللّٰهُمَّ اجْعَلْهُ حَجًّا مَّبْرُوْرًا وَّ سَعْيًا مَّشْكُوْرًا وَّ ذَنْبًا مَّغْفُوْرًا

"O Allah render my Hajj approved (accepted) and accord thy appreciation to my struggle and forgive my sins"	Allāhummaj-'lhu Hajjam-Mabrūran wwa sa'iyam-mash-kūran wwadhambam-maghfūra

ix) The seven pebbles thrown at once will be counted only once, and you will have to complete the seven throws.

x) Talbiya is to be DISCONTINUED as soon as you start Ramī at Jamrat-ul-'Aqaba.

xi) If the pebble did not hit the Jamra itself but fell nearby, this is also acceptable provided it did not fall far from it.

xii) It is not advisable to stay near Jamra after Ramī is completed for invocations, as the Messenger of Allah did not stay there after the Ramī.

xiii) Today you are not supposed to perform Ramī at the Jamrāts other than Jamrat-al-'Aqaba.

xiv) The wajib of Rami is fulfilled within the time before appearance of Fajr.

xv) In case the night after 10th Dhul-Ḥijja is spent and Ramī is still not performed, its accomplishment after this due time will stand Wājib, and at the same time you would be bound to offer a Damm,(sacrifice of a sheep or goat as a penalty) for delaying the Ramī.

xvi) All Pilgrims are required to perform Ramī by themselves. The substitute for oneself is only allowed in case of illness or weakness on account of which one may be allowed to offer one's prayers while sitting. These people can also ask a substitute to perform Ramī if going to the Jamrat will aggravate the illness for the one who is unable to walk on foot and there is no conveyance available.

xvii) For the Substitute: Who is to perform Ramī on behalf of someone else, it should be that he observes his own Ramī first and then fulfills the act of Ramī as a substitute.

It is permissible that on the first Jamra, he throws his own seven pebbles immediately followed by another seven pebbles on another's behalf and completes the Ramī on the 2nd and 3rd Jamra in the same way.

xviii) It is Makrūh to throw his own pebble followed by another for another person.

xix) A Ramī performed by a substitute without deputation by the excused person does not stand valid. Any how, on behalf of the children, or invalid people, their guardians are lawfully allowed to perform Ramī of their own accord.

III. THE THIRD WĀJIB ON THE 10TH OF DHUL-ḤIJJA

THE SACRIFICE

WĀJIBAT:

1. It is Wājib for a Qārin and a Mutammattī' that, being free from Ramī, they do not have their heads shaven or their hair cut (Qasr or Halaq), until they discharge their Wājib of offering sacrifice.

2. For a Qārin and a Mutammatī', if they shave their head, or cut the hair before offering sacrifice, they will fall under the obligation of a Damm.

3. For a Mufrid, it is not Wājib to offer sacrifice, but it is Mustaḥab. It is lawful for him not to offer a sacrifice and to have his head shaven, or cut his hair short.

4. After the sacrifice, it is Sunna to shave the head, (Halaq) of Ḥajj in Minā. You are allowed to do Halaq anywhere within the precincts of the Ḥaram. But if you do it outside the precincts of the Haram you will be liable to offer a Damm.

IV. THE FOURTH WĀJIB ON THE 10TH OF DHUL-ḤIJJA

ḤALAQ and/or QAṢR

1. After offering sacrifice, it is Wājib to have your head shaven or your hair cut equal in length to a joint of a finger (about one inch). But it is not necessary for it to be done on the 10th of Dhul-Hijja. It may be done up to the 12th of Dhul-Hijja. You will remain under the restrictions of Ihrām whatever length of time you may pass until you have your head shaved or your hair cut.

2. If Halaq or Qaṣr is done on the 10th of Dhul-Hijja, you will be relieved from the Ihrām restrictions from that time. Now wearing sewn garments, perfumes, clipping nails etc., becomes lawful. But still, sexual intercourse will not be lawful

until you have performed the last important Rukn of Hajj i.e. Tawāf-e-Ziyāra (or Tawāf-e-Fard)

3. It is prohibited for a Woman to have her head shaved. She should only have her hair cut. She should cut off about one inch (length of a finger joint). However, the hair cut of one fourth of her head will also suffice for her being relieved from Ihram restrictions (Zubda).

4. It is not lawful to clip your nails or trim your mustaches before Halaq or Qasr. In case of this, you will be liable for its atonement.

RULES OF ACTION

1. After being free from Ramī, it is not essential to offer sacrifice and do Halaq or Qasr on the same day as the 10th of Dhul-Hijja. If for any unavoidable reasons, you are unable to offer sacrifice on the 10th, then you can offer it in the next two days up to the 12th of Dhil-Hajja, but until such time and till after the Halaq or Qasr, you will remain under the obligation of Iḥrām.

2. If a Qārin and Mutammattī' can not afford to spend money on offering a sacrifice, they have to keep ten fasts in compensation thereof. This is subject to the condition that three of the ten fasts must be observed by the day of Waqūf-e-'Arafāt i.e. by the 9th of Dhul-Ḥijja. The remaining seven fasts can be observed after returning from the Hajj, anywhere and whenever convenient.

3. If the three fasts are not kept up to the day of 'Arafāt the sacrifice will be binding.

4. In case the Pilgrim can not afford sacrifice, he will be relieved from the restrictions of Iḥrām after Ḥalaq or Qaṣr, but he will be obliged to offer two Damms. One for Qirān Hajj or Tamattu', and the other for Jināyat or violation of the restrictions of Ihrām, which becomes WĀJIB on account of having his head shaved (or hair cut) before offering sacrifice (Zubda).

V-TAWĀF-E-ZIYARA – (ṬAWĀF-E-FARḌ) THE FIFTH WĀJIB AND THE SECOND IMPORTANT RUKN OF HAJJ ON THE 10TH OF DHUL-HIJJA

Ṭawāf-e-Ziyāra is the second fundamental Rukn of Ḥajj. The first fundamental was Waqūf-e-'Arafāt, (The Rukn-e-A'zam).

According to the Sunna of the Messenger of Allah (peace be upon him), this Ṭawāf is to be performed, after being free from Wājibāt of Ramī, sacrifice, and Halaq (or Qaṣr), but the Farḍ (obligatory Rukn) stands discharged even if Ṭawāf-e-Ziyāra is performed prior to all these practices.

This Ṭawāf is performed in the manner which has been described in the chapter of the Ṭawāf (Ṭawāf-e-Qadūm etc.) The only difference is that of the declaration of Intention. For this you say the Niyya, for Ṭawāf-e-Ziyāra. It is a great feeling to perform Ṭawāf-e-Ziyāra. Here the tears will flow in streams as you are now in the presence of Allāh, at the end of your Ḥajj. Here you will cry for gratitude, for Mercy and for fulfillment. It gives a great feeling of fulfillment. You thank Allah, the Almighty for enabling you to perform this Holy duty and making it easy for you. Today is a feeling of great intensity, only to be experienced and not described.

This Ṭawāf is also known as Ṭawāf-e-Ifāḍa, Ṭawāf-e-Ayyam-e-Naḥr or Tawāf-e-Wajib or Farḍ. This is the last Rukn of Ḥajj, after this you would have completed all the Manāsik of Ḥajj and now you are Ḥaji, may Allāh accept your Ḥajj and appreciate your efforts for it.

IMPORTANT RULES OF ACTION FOR TAWĀF-E-ZIYĀRA

1 The time for this Ṭawāf is from the morning of the 'Īd, the 10th of Dhul-Ḥijja upto the end of the days of Naḥr i.e. upto the 12th of Dhul-Ḥijja before sunset.

2. In case of any delay beyond the 12th Dhul-Ḥijja, a Damm will be obligatory and even then the Ṭawāf as an obligation will

remain UNDISCHARGED. This Ṭawāf can neither be nullified in any case, nor can it be discharged by any substitute.

3. It remains obligatory throughout your life until it is rendered discharged, and until then your intimacy and sexual intercourse with your spouse will remain unlawful and forbidden (Ghunya).

4. After completing Ṭawāf-e-Ziyāra, all the abstinences of Iḥrām are rendered lawful. So your spouse now becomes Ḥalāl to you and the normal sexual relationship can be resumed.

5. For a Woman: who is having mensus or a blood discharge of a child-birth, the completing of Ṭawāf-e-Ziyāra is not allowed. If the mensus or the blood discharge of child-birth commences on the 10th of Dhul-Ḥijja and she does not attain cleanliness till the 12th of Dhul-Ḥijja, she will have to postpone Ṭawāf-e-Ziyāra till she is clean, and no Damm will be obligatory on her for this postponement. It is better for her to wait till she becomes clean. Without Ṭawāf-e-Ziyāra she can not return home and if she does, Ṭawāf will remain obligatory till she returns to Mecca and performs it. Otherwise she will remain Ḥárām or unlawful to her husband till such time.

THE SA'Ī OF ḤAJJ

1. A Qārin and Mutamattī', who has already performed the Sa'ī after their Ṭawāf-e-Qadūm is not supposed to perform Sa'ī again.

2. A Mufrid who did not perform Sa'ī with Ṭawāf-e-Qadūm as well as a Qārin and Mutamattī' who have performed only a Sa'ī for 'Umra, before Waqūf-e-'Arafāt, and have not performed Sa'ī of Ḥajj, it is Wājib for them to perform Sa'ī after their Ṭawāf-e-Ziyāra.

3. They are also to practice Ramal and Iḍṭiba' in the first three rounds of their Tawāf-e-Ziyāra.

4. After completing Ṭawāf-e-Ziyāra and Sa'ī of Ḥajj, all the practices of 10th Dhul-Ḥijja have come to an end. You are now to go back to Minā. It is your real 'Īd today.

THE 11TH OF DHUL–ḤIJJA
THE FOURTH DAY OF ḤAJJ

1. Only a few of the Wājibāt of Ḥajj are remaining to be practised now. You are to stay at Minā for two or three more days and to perform Ramī on all three Jamarāt. These days are called the days of Naḥr.

2. To spend the nights of these days as well in Minā is Sunnat-e-Mu'akkida, while according to some other authors it is Wājib. It is forbidden to spend the nights anywhere outside Minā. (Not even in Mecca)

3. You are to accomplish the offering of sacrifice and Ṭawāf-e-Ziyāra on 11th Dhul-Ḥijja if you have not already performed hese on the 10th of Dhul-Ḥijja.

4. It is better to be free from sacrifice and Ṭawāf-e-Ziyāra before Ẓuhr prayer.

5. After Ẓuhr prayer, in the afternoon you should proceed for Ramī on all the three Jamarāt.

6. The Mustaḥab time for Ramī on the 11th of Dhul-Ḥijja is after the noon to sunset. After sunset it is Mukrūh, but if it is performed before the sunrise of the 12th of Dhul-Ḥijja, it stands accomplished without falling under the obligation of Damm.

7. After the Fajr of the 12th of Dhul-Ḥijja, the Ramī of the 11th of Dhul-Ḥijja becomes Qaḍā (amiss) and it is obligatory to perform its Qaḍā and expiation of Damm has also become Wājib for missing it on the 11th of Dhul-Ḥijja.

8. On the 12th of Dhul-Ḥijja, you are to perform Ramī at three Jamrāt for this day

9. The way to perform Ramī, on the 11th and 12th and 13th of Dhul-Hijja is as follows:

(i) First perform Ramī at the first Jumra, near Masjid-e-Khaif with seven pebbles in the same manner as you did on the 10th of Dhul-Hijja.

(ii) Then move aside from the crowd and pray to Allāh with raised hands facing the Ka'ba. This invocation should last as long as the duration of recitation of 20 verses (Āyas) of the Holy Qur'ān. During this period remain busy in Takbīr, Taḥlīl, Istaghfār and Darūd. Pray to Allāh for yourselves, friends and Muslims in general. This is a place of acceptance of prayers.

(iii) Then reach Jamrat-ul-Wusṭā, the middle Jamra, where you are to throw seven pebbles at it in the same manner as before.

(iv) Here too, you are to move aside from the crowd and remain busy in Istaghfār and invocation facing the Ka'ba.

(v) You are then to reach Jamraṭ-ul-'Aqaba. There perform Ramī in the same manner as you did on the two previous occasions with seven pebbles. Here you should not stay for invocation as the Messenger of Allāh (peace be upon him) did not stay here.

For to-day (the 11th or 12th or 13th of Dhul-Ḥijja) this is all you have to accomplish if you are free from any obligation of sacrifice etc. The rest of the time should be spent in Minā at your own place, remaining busy with invocations, recital of the Holy Qur'ān and Dhikr of Allāh. These days should not be wasted in useless pursuits.

THE 12TH AND 13TH OF DHUL-ḤIJJA

1. In case of failure in offering sacrifice on the 10th or 11th of Dhul Ḥijja, or performing Ṭawāf-e-Ziyāra, you are now to perform these on 12th Dhul-Ḥijja.

2. If the sacrifice etc. has been performed on the 10th or 11th of Dhul-Ḥijja, the only practice you are to follow to-day is Ramī of the three Jamrāt. The manner of performing Ramī is the same as described above for the 11th of Dhul-Ḥijja.

3. After Ramī on the 12th of Dhul-Ḥijja, if you choose to stay in Minā then Ramī of the 13th of Dhul-Ḥijja becomes Wājib after sunset of 12th of Dhul-Ḥijja. If you desire, you may proceed to Mecca after the Ramī of the 12th of Dhul-Ḥijja, provided you leave Minā before sunset. After sunset it is Makrūh to leave Minā.

4. It is better to stay the night of the 12th of Dhul-Ḥijja in Minā if you have not left for Mecca before sunset. Proceed to Mecca after performing Ramī on the 13th of Dhul-Ḥijja.
The dawning of the 13th of Dhul-Ḥijja while still in Minā, renders you liable to observe another Wājib Ramī for this day. if you leave Mina on the 13th of Dhul-Ḥijja without performing Ramī a Damm will be obligatory. However, the Ramī on the 13th of Dhul-Ḥijja can be performed before noon. If someone missed Ramī on all three days then he should perform it before the sunset of the 13th of Dhul-Ḥijja.

RETURN TO MECCA

1. Return to Mecca from Minā, after the completion of Ramī at three Jamrāt.

2. It is Sunna to stay for a while at the valley of Muḥaṣṣab while returning to Mecca from Minā. It may be impossible to stop at Muḥaṣṣab due to the difficulties of conveyance.

3. The only responsibility of Ḥajj that now remains to be discharged is Ṭawāf-e-Wadā'. This is the farewell Ṭawāf and is also called Ṭawāf-e-Ṣadr. It is Wājib to perform this Ṭawāf on your departure from Mecca.

4. As long as you now stay in Mecca, perform innumerable Nafl Ṭawāfs, as many as you can. Presence in Ḥaram, Ṭawāf of

Bait-Allāh, looking at the Ka'ba itself, recital of the Holy Qur'ān, Dhikr and invocations are to be considered a great opportunity given to you by Almighty and Most Merciful Allāh. Now you are to leave this place full of Barakāt for your home, so avail of it as much as you can. Alms and charity should be extended as much as possible. Love and respect to people of Mecca is one of the ceremonies of respects of this Holy place. Any discomfort should be ignored and criticising of this place and people of the Ḥaram should be avoided. All kinds of sins, big or small should be carefully avoided. As in Mecca one act of kindness has one hundred thousand times the Thawāb (rewards). You are in Bait-Allāh and its vicinity, remain respectful and humble in His Presence.

TAWĀF-E-WADĀ

1. For those living outside the boundaries of Mīqāt, it is Wājib to perform Ṭawāf-Wadā' at the time of departure from Mecca.

2. This is the last Wājib of Ḥajj and has to be performed by all, Qārin, Muttmattī' of Mufrid alike.

3. This Ṭawāf is not Wājib for the people of the Ḥaram and the inhabitants within the boundaries of Miqat.

4. A woman, who enters the period of menses or birth blood discharge at the time of Ṭawāf-e-Wadā' if her Muḥram can no longer stay in Mecca, is exempted from Ṭawaf-e-Wadā' in such circumstances. It is no more Wājib for her. She should stand near the gaṭe of the Haram and depart after invocations. It is not binding on the Muhram to wait for her to be clean.

5. A particular Niyya (intention) is not necessary for Tawāf-e-Wadā'.A Nafl Tawaf already performed before the departure can be sufficient as a substitute for it. But it is preferable to perform Ṭawāf-e-Wadā' before your departure.

6. **If you stay** in Mecca after performing Ṭawāf-e-Wadā', the

repetition of Ṭawāf at the time of departure is Mustaḥab (Zubda).

7. AFTER TAWĀF-E-WADĀ', offer two Rak'at of Ṭawāf. Pray at Maqām-e-Ibrāhīm. Drink Zamzam facing the Ka'ba and then depart from Bait-Allāh.

8. Before Ṭawāf-e-Wadā' and during the stay in Mecca, you can perform a number of 'Umras. For this, you are to go outside the precincts of Ḥaram (a taxi takes you about 3 miles outside Mecca), for adopting Iḥrām. The nearest of these places is Tan'īm.

Different viewpoints prevail, For sure it is better to accomplish many Ṭawāfs which used to be the practice of the Companions of the Holy Prophet (peace be upon him). After Ṭawāf-e-Wadā', recite the following Du'ā (near the Multazim, if you can):

اَلسَّائِلُ بِبَابِكَ يَسْأَلُكَ مِنْ فَضْلِكَ وَمَعْرُوْفِكَ وَيَرْجُوْ رَحْمَتَكَ

The beggar at Thy door asking Thy favour and Thy recognition, and I seek Thy mercy.

As sā'ilu bi-bābika yas'aluka min faḍlika wa ma'rūfika wa yarjū Raḥmataka.

and also recite:

اَللّٰهُمَّ اِنَّ هٰذَا بَيْتُكَ الَّذِيْ جَعَلْتَهٗ مُبَارَكًا وَّهُدًى لِّلْعٰلَمِيْنَ

فِيْهِ اٰيَاتٌ بَيِّنَاتٌ مَّقَامُ اِبْرَاهِيْمَ ۚ وَمَنْ دَخَلَهٗ كَانَ اٰمِنًا ۚ

اَلْحَمْدُ لِلّٰهِ الَّذِيْ هَدٰنَا لِهٰذَا وَمَا كُنَّا لِنَهْتَدِيَ لَوْلَآ اَنْ

هَدٰنَا اللّٰهُ فَكَمَا هَدَيْتَنَا فَتَقَبَّلْ مِنَّا وَلَا تَجْعَلْ هٰذَا اٰخِرَ

الْعَهْدِ مِنْ بَيْتِكَ الْحَرَامِ وَارْزُقْنَا الْعَوْدَ اِلَيْهِ حَتّٰى تَرْضٰى

عَنَّا بِرَحْمَتِكَ يَا اَرْحَمَ الرَّاحِمِيْنَ ۚ

O Allah! Verily Thy House, that Thou Blessed and made a guidance for the (people of the) worlds, in it are the signs manifest, Maqam-e-Ibrahim, whosoever enters it attains security. All praise is due to Allah who guided us to this, and we were not the guided ones if Allāh had not guided us. So as Thou guideth us, so accept this from us and do not make this visit to Thy Sacred House our last one, and grant us return to it until Thou hath become pleased with us with Thy mercy, O the Most Merciful of the Mercifuls!

Allāhumma inna hādhā baituk-al-ladhi ja'altahū mubārakan wwa hudan-llil-'ālamīn, fīhi āyātum-bayyinātum-Maqāmu-Ibrāhīm, wa man dak-halahū kāna amınan, Alḥam-du lillāh-il-ladhī hadānā lihadhā wa mā kunna li-nahta-diya lau lā an hadanallahu fak-amā hadaitanā fataqabbal minnā wa lā taj'al hādhā ākhir-al-'ahdi mim-Baitik-al-Ḥarāmi warzuqn-al-'auda ilaihi ḥattā tarḍā 'annā bi-raḥmatika yā Arḥam-ar-Rāḥimīn.

Give alms to the poor and the needy as you come out of the Sacred House of Allāh as a token of thanks.

While saying good-bye to the Ka'ba (you will be too and for it to depart), recite the following Du'ā:

اَللّٰهُمَّ لَا تَجْعَلْهُ آخِرَ الْعَهْدِ مِنْ بَيْتِكَ الْحَرَامِ وَإِنْ جَعَلْتَ
فَعَوِّضْ مِنْهُ الْجَنَّةَ ۔ آئِبُوْنَ تَائِبُوْنَ عَابِدُوْنَ لِرَبِّنَا حَامِدُوْنَ
لِلرَّحْمَةِ قَاصِدُوْنَ صَدَقَ اللّٰهُ وَعْدَهٗ وَنَصَرَ عَبْدَهٗ وَهَزَمَ
الْاَحْزَابَ وَحْدَهٗ لَا حَوْلَ وَلَا قُوَّةَ اِلَّا بِاللّٰهِ الْعَلِيِّ الْعَظِيْمِ ۔

O Allāh! Do not make this visit to Thy Sacred House our last one, And if Thou did, then reward us with Paradise in return, (We are) yearning (for

Allāhumma lā taj'alhu ākhir-al-ahdi mim-Baitik-al-Ḥaramı wa in ja'alta fa- awwid minh-ul-jannata, a'ibuna tā'ibūna' 'ābidūna li-Rabbina ḥāmiduna

return to Thy House) the repenters, the worshippers for our Lord, praising, heading for His mercy, True is His promise, He helped His servant (Prophet Muḥammad) and defeated the army of non-believers alone, all by Himself, There is none who has the Might and Power, except with the help of Allāh, the High, the Great.

lir-raḥmati qāṣidūna, ṣadaqallāhu wa'dahū, naṣara 'abdahū wa hazam-al-aḥzāba waḥdahū, lā haula wa lā quwwata illā billāh-il-'Aliyyil 'Aẓīm.

CHAPTER 12

A Summary of Important Rules of Action For Women During Ḥajj and 'Umra

Women perform all the Manāsik of Ḥajj and 'Umra just as men do except for a few exceptions under different circumstances.

1. IHRĀM:
   a) They can wear their usual, stitched garments.
   b) They should be adequately covered up to their wrists and ankles and hair. Only their faces should be uncovered.
   c) Avoid wearing bright colours, and inadequate dress.
   d) They should not use any perfumes.
   e) They can wear jewelry, socks, gloves, etc.

2. TALBIYA:
   a) They are not to recite the Talbiya loudly.
   b) They should recite in such a way that their voices may not be heard by men.

3. TAWĀF:
   a) They are exempted from Ramal and Iḍṭibā' in Ṭawāf.
   b) Their faces should be uncovered during Ṭawāf.
   c) They are not to perform Ṭawāf if they are menstruating or having a child-birth discharge of blood.
   d) In this case they have to take bath, adopt a new Iḥrām and perform all other Manāsiks of Ḥajj. They can perform Ṭawāf after they are clean.
   e) It is preferable for them to perform Ṭawāf at night.

4. SA'Ī:
   a) Since they cannot perform Ṭawāf during the menstruating period, they are not supposed to perform Sa'ī as it is only

Wājib after the Ṭawāf.

b) Women are not supposed to run between Meelain Akhḍarain during Sa'ī.

c) They may not climb atop Ṣafā and Marwa due to the crowd of men there.

d) They should recite invocations in a low voice.

5. ḤALAQ OR QAṢR: At the end of Sa'ī or 'Umra or Ḥajj or Sacrifice they are allowed only to cut their hair (about 1" in length). Shaving of their heads is prohibited.

6. WAQŪF-E-'ARAFĀT AND MUZDALIFA:

Women have to perform all the ceremonies of Ḥajj in exactly the same manner as men. They have to perform Ṭawāf-e-Qadūm, Sa'ī, stay in Minā, Waqūf-e-'Arafāt, Muzdalifa etc. The only problem arises when they start menstruating. In this situation, they can perform all the ceremonies like any other person, except "Ṭawāf". They can not go in the Holy Mosque and perform Ṭawāf. But they can observe Waqūf-e-'Arafāt etc., as usual. They cannot offer ceremonial prayers just as they cannot perform Ṭawāf. But their Ḥajj stands fulfilled even if they cannot perform Ṭawāf, except Ṭawāf-e-Ziyāra, for which they have to wait untill they are clean to perform it. They can be busy in Adhkar and recitation of Du'ā and supplication in the state of Iḥrām all the time.

7. RAMĪ: A substitute can perform the Ramī of Jamarāt for her if she is unable to reach Jamarāt due to the crowd or illness or fatigue.

8. SACRIFICE: A substitute can perform sacrifice on her behalf due to the crowd of men at the sacrificial place in Minā. It should be performed after Ramī.

9 TAWAF-E-ŻIYARA There is NO substitute for Ṭawāf-e-Ziyara. This is the second most important Rukn of Hajj. If she has to postpone this Ṭawaf, due to mensus or discharge of child-birth blood, she should wait till she becomes clean. Until such time she will not become Ḥalāl to her husband. No Damm will be obligatory for her for this postponement. If she is with mensus till the end of the 12th of Dhul-Ḥijja even then she is supposed to wait to perform this Ṭawāf, otherwise, her Ḥajj will remain incomplete.

10. ṬAWAF-E WADA She is exempted from Ṭawaf-e-Wadā' if she is having her mensus or discharge of child-birth blood A Nafl Tawaf can be substituted for the Farewell Ṭawaf

CHAPTER THIRTEEN

BOOK OF JINAYAT

Violations of the restrictions of Iḥram and other dictates of Ḥajj are called Jināyat. For these Jinayat the revealed law of Islām (Sharī'at) has imposed some penalties details of which may be seen in comprehensive books. We give here an account of only very necessary dictates for often occurring events.

Jinayat of Ḥajj are divided into two kinds. Firstly the violation of restrictions of Iḥrām that is to say the commission of those practices which have been prohibited during Iḥrām. Secondly to abandon any Wājib out of the Wājibāt of Ḥajj or to be lacking therein in any way.

JINAYAT OF IḤRAM

At first, we formally detail below some necessary instructions about Jinayat of Iḥram.

INSTRUCTION NO. 1

Jinayat of Iḥram are as follows:

(1) To use perfume.
(2) Males to wear sewn clotnes.
(3) Males to cover their heads and faces while females to cover their faces only.
(4) To remove hair from any part of one's body.
(5) To prune nails.
(6) To Kill a louse or to remove it from one's body.
(7) To have sexual intercourse or to enjoy kissing and embracing lustfully.
(8) To hunt any of the lana animals. (Ghunya).

INSTRUCTION NO. 2

Restrictions of Iḥram are quite different in nature from common practices of adoration. Whether the violation is committed by mistake, oblivion or by some excuse or without excuse, in any case, penalty is always obligatory for it. Every

Jinayat or violation of the restriction of Iḥrām is always followed by a penalty irrespective of the violation being on account of ignorance, mistake, oblivion, under some compulsion, whether it is done while waking or sleeping, in a state of senselessness or intoxication, out of destitution or under some compulsion and whether it is committed by oneself or committed by another person. Males and females are equal in this respect (Zubda). But of course, the violation by way of mistake, oblivion or excuse is not a sin. It necessitates only penalty while the violation without any excuse is a sinful act as well as it necessitates penalty. If a rich person violates any restriction of Iḥrām without any excuse just because of the fact that he can afford the penalty i.e. Damm, he is a grevious sinner and his Ḥajj is not Mabrūr (approved). The second difference lies in the fact that the penalty for a violation without excuse is obligatory to be paid exactly as defined. Keeping fasts cannot suffice in exchange. It is of course unlike the violation with excuse where such facilities have been provided as will be described further.

INSTRUCTION NO. 3

The penalty for Jināyat is not necessarily to be paid forthwith yet it is preferable to pay it soon. It is however Wājib to be paid before death, otherwise making a will for its payment is Wājib. In the absence of such a will if the heirs pay the penalty on behalf of the deceased person by way of benevolence towards him, it is hoped that Allah may admit it as a payment on behalf of the deceased person. The heir cannot however keep fasts on behalf of the deceased (Zubda).

INSTRUCTION NO. 4
EXPLANATION OF TERMINOLOGY

Damm: Wherever the word Damm is used it means sacrifice of a goat, a sheep or one seventh part of a cow or a camel. This word is subject to all the conditions defined necessary for an animal of sacrifice.

Badana. Wherever this word is used it means the whole cow or camel. The sacrifice of a whole cow or a whole camel is obligatory only in two Jināyat. Firstly, in case of performing Ṭawaf-e-Ziyāra while one is with menses, birth-blood discharge or with pollution. Secondly, in case of having sexual intercourse after one's Waqūf of 'Arafāt but before Ḥalaq.

Ṣadaqa. This word, when used restricted, means the fixed quantity of Ṣadaqat-ul-Fiṭr that is one and three fourths of a Kilo of wheat or its price. Sometimes it also happens that instead of using the unrestricted word 'Ṣadaqa', you are asked to give "some Ṣadaqa". At that time it is enough to give a handful grain or its price or a loaf of bread or a Qursh in cash. But indeed, when this word "Ṣadaqa" has been mentioned while defining penalty for wearing sewn clothes, using perfume, pruning nails and shaving hair, it means three Sā[2] of wheat to be distributed among six Masākin (indigent persons). This penalty has been defined in case of a complete Jināyat with excuse, details of which are to follow.

THE DIFFERENCE BETWEEN THE JINĀYAT WITH AND WITHOUT EXCUSE

The word 'Excuse' used here stands for fever, suffering from cold, wound, pain, lice and all that which carries intense labour and hardship. Everlasting of ailment or the risk of life is not a condition in this connection (Zubda). Mistake, oblivion, senselessness, sleep and poverty are not excuses (Zubda).

With an excuse of ailment etc., if a person wears sewn clothes, uses perfume, has a hair cut or covers his head or face with a piece of cloth; or a woman covers her face with a piece of cloth in such a way that it keeps touching her face; in all such cases if the Jināyat is perfect, you have the option either to offer a Damm or to keep three fasts or otherwise a Ṣadaqa equivalent to Ṣadaqat-ul-Fiṭr should be distributed to each of the six Masākin. Every Miskīn will be given one and three fourths of a Kilo of wheat or its equivalent price. In case the Jināyat is not perfect the choice lies only in two things. Either three fasts are kept or Ṣadaqa is distributed to six Masākin. To exercise an

1. Weighing about 2.2 Lbs.
2. Sā' is a measure, half of its quantity is given in Ṣadaqat-ul-Fiṭr, which is already mentioned above.

option among three or two penalties is admissable only in the case of Jināyat being with excuse. In case the Jināyat is without excuse a penalty of Damm has been defined for a perfect Jināyat and that of Ṣadaqa for its being imperfect. This penalty will not stand as paid by keeping fasts. The details of perfect and imperfect Jināyat are as explained below:—

EXPLANATION OF PERFECT AND IMPERFECT JINĀYAT

Perfection and imperfection of a Jināyat is different in respect of different kinds of Jināyat. The explanation thereto is as under:--

THE JINĀYAT PERTAINING TO USE OF PERFUMERY ON THE BODY

If someone perfumed any complete part of the major parts of his body like head, beard, palm thigh or a calf of his leg, the Jināyat became perfect though the perfume was used for a little time. In this case, if the Jināyat was without excuse, a Damm would be obligatory. Even if he might have washed off the perfume forthwith, yet it would not eliminate Damm obligation. In case the Jināyat was committed under some excuse there would stand the above mentioned three choices under his discretion. He might offer a Damm or keep three fasts or give charity equivalent to Ṣadaqat-ul-Fiṭr to each of the six Masākīn. On the other hand if someone perfumed any of the minor parts of his body like nose, ear, eye, mustaches and finger or he used perfume on a portion of any major part of his body, the Jināyat remained imperfect wherefor Ṣadaqa equivalent to Ṣadaqat-ul-Fiṭr became Wājib and in case of any excuse three fasts might also suffice in place of Ṣadaqa (Zubda).

IMPORTANT NOTE

All that which is stated above is subject to the perfume being a little in quantity. In case the perfume is in a large quantity there remains no difference whether the perfumed part is major or minor and whether it is a full part of the body or a portion thereof. In every case a Damm will be obligatory. The criterion for determining a little or a large quantity of a perfume differs in respect of different perfumery. A large quantity of a perfume is that quantity which is treated to be as such in common usage. For instance, a little quantity of musk which stands as large in its usage, will of course be considered as large. (Ghunya)

THE JINAYAT PERTAINING TO USE OF PERFUME IN CLOTHES

RULE OF AÇTION

Suppose a person wears the clothes which have been smeared with some fragrant commodity. If the fragrance is in a large quantity but it has been spread on a portion less than a span or two, or the fragrance is in a little quantity but it has been spread on a portion more than a span or two, in each case a Damm is obligatory if the clothes are worn for a full day or a full night.

If a little perfume has been used on a portion less than a span or two, a Ṣadaqa is to be given (though the clothes might have been worn for a full day). On wearing such clothes for a time less than a day also, there is the obligation of Ṣadaqa (Zubda.)

For a time less than a day Ṣadaqa is obligatory in spite of the perfume being in a large quantity and the besmearing having been a span or two wide. The time commencing from mignight and ending on noon will be treated a full day (Zubda).

RULE OF ACTION

By taking such meal which has been cooked with some fragrance therein, there is no obligation though the meal might have become aromatic and the fragrance might have been excelling. If the fragrance has been mixed after cooking the meal as we usually mix spices, cinnamon and cardamoms etc., there will also be no obligation by taking such meal. But indeed, taking an aromatic meal is a Makrūh act. On the other hand, if someone takes such a thing which has not been cooked but some fragrance has been mixed therein, as there are sauces and pickles, so in such a case if the fragrance is excelling, a Damm will be obligatory as Wājib provided the thing has been taken in a handsome quantity. In case such a thing has been taken in a little quantity Ṣadaqa will have to be given though the thing might not have become aromatic. Because, in this case the basis of the penalty is the ingredients and not the aroma. If such a meal has been taken little by little several times, Damm will be obligatory. If a fragrance is mixed with an uncooked meal (and then it is cooked) then in case of the meal being excelling (i.e. in larger quantity than the ingredients of fragrance) nothing will be obligatory though it might have been taken in a large quantity. But if the meal reamins aromatic it will stand Makrūh.

RULE OF ACTION

If someone has eaten a handsome quantity of a fragrant commodity like saffron and it is applied to a major part of his mouth, Damm becomes obligatory as Wājib. If a major part of his mouth is not affected, Ṣadaqa will have to be given. This rule of action pertains to taking pure fragrant thing which has not been mixed with some meal (Ghunya).

RULE OF ACTION

While wearing Iḥrām it is admissable to drink aerated water or any other beverage or syrup wherein no fragrance has been mixed. In a fragrance-mixed beverage, if fragrance is in a little quantity, Ṣadaqa will be Wājib but if a person drinks in several times in one sitting, Damm will be obligatory as Wājib. In case the fragrance is excelling Damm will be Wājib by taking the beverage only once in a good quantity. (Ghunya).

RULE OF ACTION

If some perfume has been applied to Ḥajar-e-Aswad (as some people apply perfume to it in the days of Ḥajj) and the observer of Ṭawāf is Muḥrim (with Iḥrām), its Istilām will not be lawful. The Muḥrim should make a gesture of Istilām with his hands and kiss them. If a Muhrim performed the Istilam of Ḥajar-e-Aswad and the perfume was applied to his face or hands, a Damm would be obligatory in case the perfume so applied was in considerable quantity; otherwise Ṣadaqa would have to be given (Ghunya.)

RULE OF ACTION

It is not admissible for a Muḥrim to lie or take rest on a perfume-applied bed. The penalty in this respect may be conjectured on fragrance-smeared clothes.

RULE OF ACTION

While wearing Iḥrām, it is forbidden to apply ḥenna to your head, hands or beard. If the ḥenna was applied to your full head, full beard or one fourth of your head or beard, a Damm became obligatory provided the ḥenna was thinly applied and not in a very thick form. In case of its being thick enough, two Damm would be obligatory; one of applying perfume and the other for covering your head or face. This is however subject to the condition that the applied ḥenna lasted for a full day or a full night. For a period lasting less than a day or a night, only one Damm and one Ṣadaqa would be obligatory as Wājib in the case of male persons while in the case of female persons only one Damm would stand obligatory as Wājib because of the fact that covering of head was not forbidden for females.

RULE OF ACTION

Damm is also obligatory as Wājib for applying ḥenna to full palm of a hand. If a woman applied ḥenna to the palm of her hand, Damm will be Wājib (Ghunya).

RULE OF ACTION

According to unanimous view of 'Ulamā it is Makrūh for a Muḥrim to eat a beetle leaf with fragrant tobacco or a cardamom. One should be very cautious in this respect as in the books of Fiqh (Islāmic Jurisprudence), there are some expressions which indicate Damm obligation for this Jināyat

RULE OF ACTION

If someone applies fragrant koḥl (antimony powder) to his eyes once or twice, a Ṣadaqa will be obligatory but in case it is applied more than twice, to offer a Damm will be Wājib. For the application of kohl without any fragrance there is neither any harm nor any obligation (Ghunya).

RULE OF ACTION

It is Makrūh to wear a garland of flowers in the state of Iḥram. People usually do not care in this connection. Intentional smelling of a fragrant fruit or flower is also Makrūh but it does not necessitate any obligation (Ghunya).

ULE OF ACTION

Suppose a person applied a little quantity of perfume to some different parts of his body. If these parts when added together become equal to a major part of his body, a Damm will be obligatory otherwise a Ṣadaqa will have to be paid (Zubda).

USE OF SEWN CLOTHES

If a person wore such clothes which were sewn or knitted or woven according to the shape of body and his wearing lasted for a full day or a full night, the Jināyat became perfect and a Damm stood obligatory. If his wearing lasted for a less time, only a Ṣadaqa would be Wājib. The difference of its being with and without excuse has already been detailed hereinbefore (Ghunya)

RULE OF ACTION

Suppose a person entered the state of Iḥrām while wearing sewn clothes. So to say he intended Ihrām with sewn clothes and pronounced Talbiya. Now, if after pronouncing Talbiya he continued wearing the sewn clothes for a full day, a Damm would be Wājib; otherwise for a less time a Ṣadaqa equivalent to Sadaqat-ul-Fitr became Wājib (Ghunya).

WEARING SOCKS OR SHOES

It is forbidden in Ihrām to wear the socks and the shoes

which may cover up to the raised up bone in the middle of your foot. (As it is usually covered by the English boots and by some of the locally made shoes). If someone continued to wear such shoes or socks for a full day or a full night, a Damm became Wājib; otherwise for a less time only a Ṣadaqa equal to a Sadaqat-ul-Fiṭr became obligatory (Ghunya).

THE JINĀYAT OF COVERING YOUR HEAD AND FACE

If a man covered his face or head or if a woman covered her face only with a piece of cloth etc. and continued covering for a full day or a full night, the Jināyat became perfect and a Damm became obligatory. In case of this covering for a less time, a Ṣadaqa would be Wājib. Women are required to cover their heads in the state of Iḥrām as necessarily as in usual circumstances. If they uncovered their heads they fell under no obligation because this covering of their heads was not a part of their Iḥrām. It is related to the common practices usually required from them.

RULE OF ACTION

If your head was covered while you were sleeping, a Ṣadaqa became obligatory as being awake and sleepy had no diffreence in this respect. But indeed, a sleeping person would not be sinful (Zubda).

RULE OF ACTION

If a person continued wearing sewn clothes for a full day, or covering his head or face for a full day and offered a Damm in expiation thereof, but at the same time he further kept the clothes in use as before, another Damm would have to be offered as expiation. In case of not offering the middling Damm only one Damm will suffice (Zubda).

RULE OF ACTION

To cover one fourth of your head or one fourth of your face is considered as to cover your full head or full face (Zubda)

THE JINĀYAT OF HAVING YOUR HAIR SHAVEN OR CUT

In case you have your hair cut or shaven for one fourth or more of your head or beard, or remove them by means of some medicine, or you pull them out; in each case, irrespective of its being committed wilfully or helplessly, the Jināyat is perfect and in penalty thereof a Damm is obligatory (Zubda).

RULE OF ACTION

Similarly, if you have your full armpit shaven or you shave all the hair below your navel or you have the hair of your full neck shaven, in each case a Damm is obligatory (Zubda).

RULE OF ACTION

In case you pruned the nails of all your four hands and feet in one sitting or you pruned all the nails of only one hand and one foot, the Jinayat became perfect and a Damm stood obligatory.

RULE OF ACTION

If you shaved or cut only two or three hair, you would have to give in expiation of every hair a Ṣadaqa of a handful of wheat or a piece of bread. In case of more than three hair a full Sadaqat-ul-Fitr would be Wājib.

RULE OF ACTION

If the hair fall without any act of Muḥrim, nothing is obligatory and if they fall with such an act of Muḥrim with which he has been entrusted by Allāh like ablution, one handful of wheat will then suffice the expiation of even 3 hair (Zubda).

RULE OF ACTION

Suppose a Muḥrim shaves one fourth or more of the head of another Muḥrim. In this case, the shaver is under obligation of Ṣadaqa and the one who got his head shaven is obliged to offer a Damm (Zubda).

TO KILL LICE

If a person killed a louse or put his clothes in sunshine so that the lice are killed or he washed his clothes in order to kill them, he sould be obliged to give a piece of bread in expiation of one and a handful of wheat in expiation of two or three lice. In case of more than three lice, in whatever number they may be he would fall under the obligation of Ṣadaqa i.e. half a Sā' (Zubda).

RULE OF ACTION

If a person put his clothes in sunshine or he washed them and thus the lice were killed but he had no intention to kill them, nothing became obligatory (Ghunya).

RULE OF ACTION

To get a louse of one's body killed by some one else or to catch it and throw it down alive on the ground or to give it to some other person in order to kill it; all such cases are equal and attract the obligation of penalty (Ghunya).

JINĀYAT PERTAINING TO SEXUAL INCLINATIONS

To kiss a woman or a young beardless lad lustfully or to touch anyone of them with sexual inclination all such acts attract the obligation of Damm. This is irrespective of one's being seminally discharged or not.

RULE OF ACTION

If a person had a sexual intercourse before Ṭawāf-e-Ziyāra, his Ḥajj stood nullified. Its Qaḍā became obligatory the next year or on the years thereafter. A Damm, that is to offer a sacrifice of a goa also stood Wājib. If both were Muḥrim, both would fall under t e obligation of offering a Damm separately It would not be l wful to abandon the practices of Ḥajj on account of the Ḥ ij thus being nullified. Indeed, all the practices of Ḥajj wo ld stand Wājib to be discharged like other usual Pilgrims. B t ven then, the Ḥajj obligations would not stand discharged. Its Qaḍā would be Wājib next year. If the nullified Ḥajj was a Farḍ Hajj, the obligation of its Qaḍa was obvious and if it was a Nafl Ḥajj, since it also became Wājib on being taken a start, thus its Qaḍā also became necessary (Ghunya).

RULE OF ACTION

If a person had a sexual intercourse after Waqūf-e-'Arafāt but before having his head shaven, his Ḥajj did not stand nullified. yet he would be bound to offer a Badana i.e., to offer a sacrifice of a full cow or a full camel (Ghunya)

RULE OF ACTION

If a person had a sexual intercourse after having his head shaven but before Ṭawāf-e-Ziyāra, his Ḥajj did not stand nullified in this case as well, yet in penalty thereof a goat would be Wājib. Some learned people in this case as well have defined Badana as Wājib (Ghunya).

TO HUNT WHILE WEARING IHRĀM

RULE OF ACTION

To hunt land animals, to injure them, to break their legs, to prune their feathers, to break their eggs, to milk them or to make a signal for their hunting or to lead a hunter towards them; all of these practices have also been forbidden while wearing Iḥrām. They all attract the obligation of penalty, details of which may be seen in detailed books.

RULE OF ACTION

Slaughtering and eating the meat of a goat, a cow, a camel, a buffalo, a hen or any other tame animal are lawfully permissible while wearing Iḥrām (Ghunya). But indeed, it is prohibited to slaughter a pigeon in every case, even if the pigeon is tame. This rule has been discussed in a separate article as many of the dwellers of Ḥaram consider it permissible to slaughter a tame pigeon, which is wrong.

RULE OF ACTION

To kill a locust while wearing Iḥrām is also forbidden. For killing one, two or three locusts the pilgrim has to give a Sadaqa in whatever quantity he likes. Caliph 'Umar said, "One date is better than a locust" (Mu'aṭṭa Mohammad). In case of more than three locusts half a Ṣā' of wheat is to be given (Zubda). The rule for killing a locust in Ḥaram is the same as its killing while wearing Ihram (Ghunya).

TO HUNT THE PREY OF ḤARAM OR TO CUT ITS TREE

RULE OF ACTION

Hunting in Ḥaram is forbidden (Ḥarām) for Muḥrim and non-Muḥrim (with and without Iḥrām) both. Mowing of the grass and cutting down the trees of Ḥaram are also prohibited. They attract penalties. In case of such happening some 'Ālim (learned man) should be consulted. Minā and Muzdalifa are included in the boundaries of Ḥaram and as such grass moving etc., must be avoided here. The open field of 'Arafāt is outside the precincts of Haram. There is no harm to mow grass here.

THE 2ND KIND OF JINĀYAT PERTAINING TO WĀJIBĀT OF ḤAJJ

Proceeding Beyond Mīqāt Without Iḥrām

RULE OF ACTION

Suppose an adult and sensible inhabitant of outside Mīqāt intends to enter Mecca. It matters naught whether his intention to enter Mecca is for the purpose of Ḥajj or 'Umra or for some other purpose. If he moves forward beyond Mīqāt towards Mecca without wearing Iḥrām he will stand sinful and it will be Wājib for him to go back to Mīqāt. If he did not return to Mīqāt and wore Iḥrām at a place beyond it, a Damm would be obligatory as Wājib on him and if he wore Iḥrām on returning to Mīqāt, Damm would be eliminated.

Note: Sea travellers of Ḥajj have an allowance of delaying Iḥrām-wearing till reaching Jedda, yet to wear Iḥrām earlier is preferable. On proceeding beyond Jedda, a Damm will be obligatory. The air-travellers should however wear Iḥrām while getting into the aircraft carrier. If they reached Jedda without Iḥrām, a Damm would be obligatory, because in the way they fly across tne Miqāt.

TO PERFORM ṬAWĀF WITHOUT ABLUTION OR WITH POLLUTION, MENSES OR BIRTH–BLOOD DISCHARGE AND TO REDUCE THE CIRCUITS OF ṬAWĀF

If at the time of performing Ṭawāf-e-Farḍ or Ṭawāf-e-Nafl your body or clothes were "Najis" (polluted), nothing would be obligatory but it would stand Makrūh (Zubda).

RULE OF ACTION

If a person performed full or a major part of Ṭawāf-e-Ziyāra without ablution he would give a Damm, and if he performed Ṭawāf-e-Qudūm or Ṭawāf-e-Wadā' or Ṭawāf-e-Nafl or less than a half of Ṭawāf-e-Ziyāra without ablution, he would have to give a Ṣadaqa equivalent to Ṣadaqat-ul-Fiṭr for every circuit of the performed Tawāf. If in all such cases he revised the Ṭawāf after an ablution the expiation and Damm would be eliminated ('Alamgīri).

RULE OF ACTION

If a person performed a full or a major part of Ṭawāf-e-Ziyāra with pollution, menses or birth-blood discharge, a Badana i.e., a full cow or a full camel would be obligatory as Wājib. If the Ṭawāf performed with such a state of impurity was Ṭawāf-e-Qudūm or Ṭawāf-e-Wadā' or Ṭawāf-e-Nafl, (the sacrifice of) a goat would be Wājib. In all such cases a revision of the Ṭawāf after due purification would eliminate the expiation (Ghunya).

RULE OF ACTION

The Ṭawāf with pollution, mensus or birth-blood discharge is Wājib to be revised, while the revision of the Ṭawāf performed without ablution is only Mustaḥab but in case of non revision it attracts the above mentioned penalty.

RULE OF ACTION

A Sa'i already performed after first Ṭawāf is not required to be revised, as the first Ṭawāf has already stood admitted and is being revised only on account of its being defective. This 2nd Ṭawāf is only to make good that loss (Zubda)

RULE OF ACTION

If a person performed Ṭawāf-e-Ziyāra without ablution in the days of Naḥr (Sacrifice), then he performed Ṭawāf-e-Wadā' in these very days of Naḥr with ablution, this would stand for Ṭawāf-e-Ziyāra. But, on the other hand it would not stand for Ṭawāf-e-Ziyāra if performed after the days of Naḥr and a Damm would be Wājib (Zubda).

RULE OF ACTION

If a person performed Ṭawāf-e-'Umra with pollution, menses or birth-blood discharge or without ablution, a Damm would stand obligatory irrespective of the Ṭawāf being complete or comprising a major part thereof or a minor part thereof confined to only one circuit (Zubda.) In case of revision of the Ṭawāf, Damm would be eliminated (Ghunya).

RULE OF ACTION

Abandoning of any Wājib of 'Umra does not attract the obligation of any Badana or Ṣadaqa; only a Damm (i.e. a goat or seventh part of a cow or camel) becomes obligatory. But in the Iḥrām of 'Umra a violation of the restrictions of Iḥrām attracts the obligation of a Damm or a Sadaqa as is attracted in the Iḥrām of Ḥajj (Zubda).

RULE OF ACTION

While performing Ṭawāf-e-Qudūm or Ṭawāf-e-Wadā', if a person missed one, two or three circuits thereof, he would fall under the obligation of one Ṣadaqa for each of the circuits. In case of his missing four or more circuits, a Damm would be obligatory. On the other hand, if a person missed Ṭawāf-e-Qudūm totally, nothing would be obligatory but it is considered as Makrūh and unpleasant (Zubda).

RULE OF ACTION

If a person abandoned Ṭawāf-e-Qudūm after giving it a start, a Damm would be obligatory in case of abandoning most number of its circuits; and in case of abandoning least number of its circuits he would be obliged to pay one Ṣadaqa for each abandoned circuit as in Ṭawāf-e-Ṣadr. The rule of action in this respect for a Nafl Ṭawāf would be on the lines of Ṭawāf-e-Qudūm (Ghunya, Shami).

JINAYAT PERTAINING TO SA'Ī

RULE OF ACTION

If a complete Sa'ī or a most number of its rounds is either abandoned without any excuse or performed while riding Ḥajj will stand accomplished. Damm as well will be eliminated on revision of the Sa'ī on foot. If this observance of Sa'ī while riding was out of some excuse, nothing would be Wājib. If only one or two or three rounds of a Sa'ī are abandoned or are observed while riding without any excuse, one Ṣadaqa for each round will be obligatory (Ghunya).

LEAVING 'ARAFĀT BEFORE SUNSET

RULE OF ACTION

If a person left 'Arafāt before sunset, a Damm would be obligatory despite the fact that he might have left 'Arafāt in order to take hold of stray camel or to look for a person. If indeed he returned before sunset, Damm would be eliminated but if he returned after sunset a Damm would stand (Zubda).

ABANDONING WAQŪF-E-MUZDALIFA WITHOUT EXCUSE

If a person abandoned Waqūf-e-Muzdalifa without any excuse, a Damm would be obligatory. In case he abandoned it out of some excuse; for instance a woman or a very old person or a weak person abandoned it due to rush of people, nothing would be obligatory (Ghunya).

MISARRANGED PERFORMANCE OF THE PRACTICES OF 10TH DHUL-ḤIJJA

RULE OF ACTION

Suppose a Mufrid or a Qārin or a Mutamattī' got his head shaven before offering sacrifice, or suppose a Qārin or a Mutamattī' offered sacrifice before Ramī; in all such cases a Damm would be obligatory, because a proper arrangement was obligatory to perform these practices. For a Mufrid however, this arrangement of performance is obligatory only in Ramī and Halaq (having his head shaven) as he is not obliged to offer a sacrifice. On the other hand, for a Qārin this arrangement is obligatory to perform Ramī, sacrifice and Ḥalaq. He should first perform Rami, then offer sacrifice and then should have his head shaven. In case of priority or delay, a Damm would be obligatory.

JINĀYAT PERTAINING TO RAMĪ

RULE OF ACTION

If Ramī for one day in full is abandoned or most of the pebbles are abandoned, a Damm will be Wājib. For instance, a person abandoned eleven pebbles in the Ramī of the first day and performed it with only ten pebbles, a Damm would be obligatory. If he abandoned the Ramī of more than one day or full four days, in that case as well only one Damm would stand obligatory (Zubda).

RULE OF ACTION

The Ramī of the 13th Dhul-Ḥijja standa obligatory only when the dawn of the 13th appears in Minā. In this case as well, if a person abandoned the Rami of the 13th Dhul-Ḥijja, a Damm would be obligatory (Zubda).

Note:

(1) For all rules of action wherein an obligation of Damm has been defined, it is necessary that the animal is sacrificed within the boundaries of Ḥaram. Offering sacrifice outside Haram does not stand admitted. Moreover, the sacrificed

animal is obligatory to be given as charity. It is not permissible for you to eat anything out of it by yourself or to give it to rich persons (Ghunya).

(2) If a person cannot afford Damm or Ṣadaqa on account of poverty, the expiation will continue to stand obligatory. He may discharge this obligation whenever he can afford. This in fact means that if a person commits, without any excuse, a Jināyat on which Damm or Ṣadaqa is Wājib the expiation will continue to stand as long as the obligation is practically discharged. He has no choice to keep fasts in exchange. On the other hand, if this perpretation of Jināyat is out of some excuse, keeping 3 fasts will also suffice instead of Damm or Ṣadaqa (Zubda).

(3) For Jināyat of Iḥrām, a Qārin falls under the obligation of two penalties, whether it may be the obligation of a Damm or the obligation of a Ṣadaqa, because of the fact that he enters the state of two Iḥrāms. But indeed if he passes by Mīqāt without Iḥrām, then only one Damm will be obligatory. Moreover, the Jināyat committed by a Qārin, in respect of Wājibāt of Ḥajj, attracts the obligation of only one penalty (Ghunya).

(4) The obligation of Damm for a Jināyat is not permissible to be discharged in the shape of hard cash equivalent to the price of Damm. It is obligatory to offer the sacrifice of animal in Ḥaram. But indeed, in cases where either offering a Damm or giving food in exchange has been left on one's own choice, Damm obligation can be discharged in the shape of hard cash equivalent to its price.

Masjid - e - Nimra in 'Arafat

CHAPTER FOURTEEN

The Places Worth Visiting at Mecca

1. BAIT-I-KHADIJA
   The house of Umm-ul-Mu'minīn Khadīja-tul-Kubrā where all her children by the Prophet were born, namely: Qāsim, Zainab, 'Abdulla, Ruqayya, Fātima and Umm Kulthūm. (a'lai hum-us-Salām). The Prophet stayed here prior to Hijra. After Bait-Allah this house is regarded as a very sacred one.

2; The place of birth of the Prophet: Now a library has been housed in it.

3. The House of Abū Bakr-aṣ-Ṣiddīq: It is situated in the locality of ZIQĀQ-I-SAWWĀGHĪN. It is here that 'Uthmān, Ṭalḥa and Zubair embraced Islām. Without a guide it is difficult to reach there.

4. DĀR-I-ARQAM
   In the beginning of Islām, the house of ARQAM MAKHZŪMĪ was the center of preaching. It was here that Ḥamza and 'Umar embraced the Faith. This house is adjacent to ṢAFĀ.

5. MASJID-I-JINN
   This mosque is situated in Sūq-i-Ma'la. It is also known by the name of Masjid-i-Bai'at, and Masjid-i-Hars. It was here that the Prophet took Bai'at from Jinns.

6. MASJID-I-SHAJARA
   This mosque is opposite the mosque of Jinn.

7. MASJID-I-BILĀL
   This mosque is situated on the hill of Abū Qubais. According to some authorities the miracle of 'the cleavage of Moon' (Shaqq-ul-Qamar) took place here.

The Mosque of Bilāl

8. MASJID-I-MUJTABĀ
This mosque is near the birth place of the Prophet.

9. MASJID-I-ṬUWĀ
It was here that the Prophet stayed when he offered 'Umra.

10. MASJID-E-Ā 'ISHA
This mosque is near Tan'īm. The Pilgrims and people of Mecca wear Ihram from this place for Ḥajj or 'Umra.

11. MASJID-I-AJIYĀD
It is situated in the locality of Jiyād.

12. MASJID-I-KHĀLID
It is situated in Jarat-ul-Bāb.

13. MASJID-I-KHAIF
It is situated in Minā, as already referred to.

14. MASJID-I-NASB
Also situated in Minā, near Masjid-i-Khaif.

15. JABAL-I-ABŪ QUBAIS
In the days of Ignorance, it was known as JABAL-I-AMĪN. This hill is in the southern direction of Ḥaram. The miracle of the cleavage of Moon is reported to have taken place here.

16. JABAL-I-NOOR
It is also known as Jabal-i-Ḥirā which is about three miles from Mecca. Here is the famous cave Ḥirā where the Prophet used to go for meditation prior to the Call.

17. JABAL-I-THAUR
This is the hill in the cave of which the Prophet and his dear companion Abū Bakr aṣ-Ṣiddīq (Allah be pleased with him) stayed for three days at the time of Hijra. It is about 7 miles from Mecca on the way to Medīna.

18. JANNAT-UL-MU'ALLA.

This is the oldest cemetery of Mecca. It is divided into two parts by a road passing through it. It contains the graves of Amīna, the mother of the Prophet, Khadīja and Asma, two wives of the Prophet, Abd-ur-Raḥmān, son of Abū Bakr, 'Abdulla, son of 'Umar, and Qāsim, the son of the Prophet and many more. (May Allah's peace be on them)

NOTE: All these places are not easy to be located without a guide. Some of these have become the victim of inevitable expansion of the Masjid-al-Ḥarām to accommodate Pilgrims from all over the world.

The Mosque of the Prophet in Medina:

This Mosque was built when the Prophet, God's peace be upon him, came to Medina as an emigrant. He himself participated in its construction by carrying stones and bricks. Its area, when completed, was 2,475 square meters.

In the Period of the Orthodox Caliphs

During the reign of 'Umar ibn al-Khattab, the second Caliph, the Mosque was expanded by 1,100 square meters, and in the reign of 'Uthman ibn 'Affan a further extension of 496 square meters was added.

In the Umayyad Period

During the reign of Caliph al-Walid ibn 'Abd al-Malik, the Mosque was expanded by 2,369 sq. m.

In the Abbasid Period

In the reign of Caliph al-Mahdi ibn al-Mansur, the Mosque was expanded by 2,450 sq. m.

In the Mamelukes Period

In the reign of King Ashraf Qaytbai an extension of 120 sq.m. was added.

In the Ottoman Period

During the reigh of Sultan 'Abd al-Majid II, the Mosque was expanded by 1,293 square meters. Thus the total area of the Mosque became 10,303 sq. m.

In the Saudi Period

In 1948 His Majesty the late King 'Abd al-'Aziz conveyed, in an address to all Muslims, the good tidings that he has decided to expand the Holy Mosque of the Prophet.

In 1950 implementation of the expansion project began, by demolishing the houses surrounding the Mosque. Compensations to the owners of those houses amounted to 30 million riyals.

In 1953 the ceremony for placing the cornerstone was held. Foundation excavations had begun in 1952. By the end of 1954 the construction of shops and residential quarters to the west of the Mosque was completed. The proceeds from these premises are waqf (endowment) for the Mosque.

In 1955 a great celebration marked the completion of the expansion project. The area of the Mosque became 16,326 sq.m., an increase of 6,023 sq. m. over its previous area. Two minarets, each 70 meters high and with a foundation 17 meters deep, were also added. The total cost of the construction project was 50 million riyals.

In recent years, the Mosque became too small for the number of people attending prayers due to the fact that the number of visitors has doubled. This motivated His Majesty King Faysal to undertake a further expansion of the Mosque. Studies were made, and as a first step, it was decided to allocate 50 million riyals in this year's budget 1973/74 for the acquisition of the houses which are to be demolished for this purpose. Most of those houses have already been demolished, and work is still underway.

Masjid - e - Nabvi

at night

CHAPTER FIFTEEN

VISIT TO MEDĪNA AL–MUNAWWARA

The City of the Prophet (peace be upon him)

The City of the Prophet, Medīna is located about 600 kilometeres to the north of Mecca. This is the city to which Prophet Muḥammad (peace be upon him) migrated from Mecca. The migration marks the beginning of the Islāmic calendar, al-Hijra, meaning the 'migration'. The city is called Munawwara meaning the 'lighted one', or the city of light, because of the Prophet (peace be upon him) and his association with it. It was from here that the light of guidance spread and brought mankind, from darkness into light. To visit the holy city, where the Prophet (peace be upon him) is resting, is one of the greatest blessings of Allāh. Next to Ḥajj, the highest pre-eminence and the the greatest blessings lie in paying a visit to the most Sacred Mosque of the greatest of the Prophets, the beloved Messenger of Allāh (peace be upon him). The love and respect of the Messenger of Allah, in fact, stands as the pre-requisite of Īmān, and as such one must feel the natural urge to visit the second most most holiest of the holy places after the Ka'ba. The fact is that after reaching the sacred territories, one does not come back without paying homage to the Holy Prophet. Furthermore, attendance of the Holy Mosque and offering salutation to the Prophet of Islām at his resting place bears so great a reward of blessings which cannot possible be achieved from afar.

Allāh's Prophet showered blessings on this city. It's sacredness and unlawfulness of hunting and lopping of trees and demarcation of its precincts renders it as Ḥarām (sacred). It is one of the two Ḥarmain, the first being the City of Mecca. It's holiness precedes all cities but the City of Mecca. According to the tradition 'Āmir b Sa'd reported on the authority of his father (Allāh be pleased with him) that Allāh's Messenger (peace

Masjid - e - Nabvi Exterior View 1

be upon him) I have declared sacred the territory between two lava plains of Medīna, so it's trees should not be cut down or it's games killed, and he also said : "Medīna is best for them if they knew. No one leaves it through dislike of it without Allāh putting in it someone better than he in place of him, and no one will stay here in spite of its hardships and distress without my being an intercessor or witness on behalf of him on the day of Resurrection". (Saḥīḥ Muslim).

Concerning the Mosque of the Holy Prophet in Medīna, Sahih Muslim quotes, "Abū Huraira (Allāh be pleased with him) when narrated it directed from Allāh's Apostle (peace be upon him) having said: 'A prayer in my Mosque is one thousand times more excellent than a prayer in any other Mosque except in Masjid-al-Ḥarām (Mosque of the Ka'ba) '. "

'Abdullāh b Zaid al-Manzinī (Allāh be pleased with him) reported Allah's Messenger (peace be upon him) as saying: "That which is between my house and my pulpit is a garden from the gardens of Paradise." This place in the Mosque is called Rauḍat-ul-Janna. (Saḥīḥ Muslim).

According to another Ḥadīth, Prophet Muḥammad was reported as having said,

مَنْ زَارَنِىْ بَعْدَ مَمَاتِىْ فَكَأَنَّمَا زَارَنِىْ فِىْ حَيَاتِىْ

Whosoever visited my grave after my death, it is like he visited me during my life.	Man zāranī ba'da mamāti, faka-annamā zārinī fī ḥayātī,

It is a source of great blessing to visit the Prophet's Mosque after (preferably) or before performing the Ḥajj or "Umra.

THE ETIQUETTES OF THE VISIT

As you approach Medina, it is better to take a bath or at least perform ablution before entering the city. One should put on new and clean clothes, wear perfume, and enter the Ḥaram with extreme politeness and humility as if one is granted the audience of the very person who has the beloved of Allāh and all humanity. Recite as much Darūd as possible and send Salām on the Prophet (peace be upon him).

A taxi service is available directly from the Airport to the Holy Mosque. At the time of entering the Holy City of Medīna, recite:

بِسْمِ اللّٰهِ الرَّحْمٰنِ الرَّحِيْمِ ط اَللّٰهُمَّ اَنْتَ السَّلَامُ وَمِنْكَ
السَّلَامُ وَاِلَيْكَ يَرْجِعُ السَّلَامُ فَحَيِّنَا رَبَّنَا بِالسَّلَامِ وَاَدْخِلْنَا
دَارَكَ دَارَ السَّلَامِ ط تَبَارَكْتَ رَبَّنَا وَتَعَالَيْتَ يَا ذَا الْجَلَالِ وَالْاِكْرَامِ
رَبِّ اَدْخِلْنِيْ مُدْخَلَ صِدْقٍ وَّاَخْرِجْنِيْ مُخْرَجَ صِدْقٍ وَّاجْعَلْ
لِّيْ مِنْ لَّدُنْكَ سُلْطَانًا نَّصِيْرًا ط وَقُلْ جَآءَ الْحَقُّ وَزَهَقَ
الْبَاطِلُ اِنَّ الْبَاطِلَ كَانَ زَهُوْقًا ط وَنُنَزِّلُ مِنَ الْقُرْاٰنِ مَا هُوَ
شِفَآءٌ وَّرَحْمَةٌ لِّلْمُؤْمِنِيْنَ وَلَا يَزِيْدُ الظّٰلِمِيْنَ اِلَّا خَسَارًا ط

In the name of Allāh, the most Merciful, the most Beneficent. O Allah! Thou art peace, and from Thee is peace and peace returns to Thee. Keep us, our Lord, with peace and allow us to enter Thy House of peace. Blessed art Thou and exalted is Thy Majesty, O Thou

Bismillāh-ir-Raḥman-ir-Raḥim. Allāhumma ant-as-salāmu wa mink-as-salāmu wa ilaika yarji'-us-salāmu faḥayyinā bis-salāmi wa ad-khilnā dāraka dār-as-sal-ām. Tabārak-ta Rabbanā wa ta'ālaita yā dhal-Jal-āli wal-Ikrām. Rabbi ad-khilnī mud-khala ṣidqin wwa akhrijnī

possessed of Glory and Honour. O my Lord! Let my entry be by the gate of Truth and my exit by the gate of Truth, and grant me from Thee an assisting power and say: Truth has arrived and falsehood has fled, verily falsehood is a fleeting thing. And we sent down in the Holy Qur'ān that which is healing and a mercy to those who believe and to the unjust it causes nothing but loss after loss."

mukhraja ṣidqin wwa'jalli mill-adunka sulṭānan-naṣīrā. Wa qul jā'al Ḥaqqu wa zahaq-al-bāṭil, inn-al-bāṭila kāna zahūqa. Wa nunazzilu min-al-Qur'āni mā huwa shifā'un wwa raḥamat-ul-lil-mu'minīna wa lā yazīd-uẓ-ẓālimīna illā khasārā.

During the stay in Medina Ṭayyaba (the pure city),

(i) recite many times salutations on the Prophet (peace be upon him).
(ii) try to offer all prayers in congregation in the Mosque of the Prophet,
(iii) Engage in worship in the later part of the night
(iv) Try to recite the Holy Qur'ān in Masjid-e-Nabvī
(v) Engage in I'tikāf in the Mosque
(vi) If possible offer Ṣalāt behind each pillar in Riāḍ-al-Janna
(vii) Avoid worldly matters in the Mosque.
(viii) Be present in the Mosque, glance at the sacred mausoleum and engage in worship as much as possible.
(ix) Visit Masjid-e-Qubā on Saturdays., if possible, and recite Fātiḥa for the first martyrs of Islām in Uḥud.

The eight pillars inside the Mosque have immense blessings of Allāh and His Messenger. They are:

(1) Ustawāna-Hannāna: (Ustawana means a pillar). Rasūl-Allāh used to stand near it and deliver the Khuṭba.

(2) Ustawāna 'Ā' isha: The Messenger of Allāh said about this Pillar, "If I were to disclose to you the blessings of this pillar, people will draw lots for the opportunity to pray near it"

(3) Ustawāna Abī Labāba: Abī Labāba was one of the companions of the Holy Prophet. In repentance a mistake committed by him, he tied himself to the pillar till the Prophet released him and prayed for his pardon from Allāh.

(4) Ustawāna Sarīrī: The Messenger of Allāh used to sit here and observe I'tikāf.

(5) Ustawāna 'Alī or Hāris: Here Caliph 'Alī (may Allāh be pleased with him) used to offer prayers and act as a guard as well.

(6) Ustawāna Wafūd: The Messenger of Allāh used to meet delegation here and teach people about Sharī'a.

(7) Ustawāna Maria'—tal-Baṣīr: It is also called, Maqām-e-Jibra'īl. The Angel Jibra'īl used to come here with revelations to the Prophet.

RULE OF ACTION:

For a person who is under the obligation of a fard Ḥajj, it is better to perform Ḥajj first and then to pay a visit to Medīna. Otherwise it is discretionary whether a person first pays a visit to Medīna and performs Hajj or his Ḥajj is followed by the visit to Medīna.

At the time of entering the gate of the Masjid, give alms, and put your right foot first (through the Gate of Jibra'īl if possible) and recite:—

بِسْمِ اللّٰهِ الرَّحْمٰنِ الرَّحِيْمِ

اَللّٰهُمَّ صَلِّ عَلٰى سَيِّدِنَا مُحَمَّدٍ وَّ عَلٰى اٰلِ سَيِّدِنَا مُحَمَّدٍ

اَللّٰهُمَّ اغْفِرْ لِيْ ذُنُوْبِيْ وَافْتَحْ لِيْ اَبْوَابَ رَحْمَتِكَ ۔ اَللّٰهُمَّ

اجْعَلْنِيْ الْيَوْمَ مِنْ اَوْجَهِ مَنْ تَوَجَّهَ اِلَيْكَ وَ اَقْرَبِ

مَنْ تَقَرَّبَ اِلَيْكَ وَ اَنْجَهِ مَنْ دَعَاكَ وَابْتَغٰى مَرْضَاتِكَ ۔

In the name of Allāh, the Most Merciful, and Compassionate. O Allāh, send salutations on our leader Prophet Muḥammad and on his off-spring. O Allāh, pardon my sins, and open for me the doors of Thy Mercy. O Allah, make for me this day the most attentive to Thee and closest to Thee and make me the most rewarded one of Thy pleasure, and the most successful of those who prayed to Thee and sought Thy will.

Bismillāh-ir-Raḥmān-ir-Raḥim. Allāhumma Ṣalli 'alā Sayyidinā Muḥammad wa 'alā āli Sayyidinā Muḥammad. Allāhummaghfirli dhunūbī waftaḥ lī abwāba Raḥmatika, Allāhummaj-a'lnil yauma min aujahī man tawajjaha ilaika wa aqrabī man taqarraba ilaika wa anjahī man da'ā'aka wabtaghā marḍatik.

You should then go to Riāḍ-al-Janna, the place between the Holy grave and the Mimber (the pulpit). Here you should offer two Rak'at of prayer of Taḥiyyāt-ul-Masjid. If you could not find any place in Riāḍ-al-Janna, then offer these two Rak'at anywhere in the Mosque.

Thank Allāh, after the prayer, for bestowing on you such a blessed opportunity in your life. Then recite the following Du'ā:

اَللّٰهُمَّ اِنَّ هٰذِهٖ رَوْضَةٌ مِّنْ رِّيَاضِ الْجَنَّةِ شَرَّفْتَهَا وَكَرَّمْتَهَا
وَمَجَّدْتَهَا وَعَظَّمْتَهَا وَنَوَّرْتَهَا بِنُوْرِ نَبِيِّكَ وَحَبِيْبِكَ مُحَمَّدٍ
صَلَّى اللّٰهُ تَعَالٰى عَلَيْهِ وَاٰلِهٖ وَسَلَّمْ ۔ اَللّٰهُمَّ كَمَا بَلَّغْتَنَا
فِى الدُّنْيَا زِيَارَتَهٗ وَمَاٰثِرَهُ الشَّرِيْفَةَ فَلَا تَحْرِمْنَا يَا اَللّٰهُ
فِى الْاٰخِرَةِ مِنْ فَضْلِ شَفَاعَةِ مُحَمَّدٍ صَلَّى اللّٰهُ عَلَيْهِ وَاٰلِهٖ
وَسَلَّمْ ۔ وَاحْشُرْنَا فِىْ زُمْرَتِهٖ وَتَحْتَ لِوَائِهٖ وَاَمِتْنَا عَلٰى مَحَبَّتِهٖ
وَسُنَّتِهٖ وَاسْقِنَا مِنْ حَوْضِهِ الْمَوْرُوْدِ مِنْ يَّدِهِ الشَّرِيْفَةِ شَرْبَةً
هَنِيْئَةً لَّا نَظْمَأُ بَعْدَهَا اَبَدًا ۔ اِنَّكَ عَلٰى كُلِّ شَىْءٍ قَدِيْرٌ ۔

O, Allāh! verily this place is one of Thy Gardens, Thou hast honoured it and made it eminent and great and lighted it with the light of Thy Prophet and Thy beloved Muḥammad, peace of Allāh be upon him and his posterity. O, Allāh! in like manner Thou hast brought us to visit the Holy Mosque of the Prophet (blessings and peace be upon him) and it's sacred signs and also his blessed monuments, in this world, deprive us not in the same manner, O Allāh! from his intercession in the next world. Collect us, (on the day of Judgement) in his community

Allahumma inna hadhihī raudatum-mir-Riadil-jannati sharraftahā wa karramtahā wa majadt-tahā wa 'azzamtahā binuri nabbiyyika wa ḥabibika Muḥammad Ṣallal-lāhu Ta'ālā 'alaihi wa ālihī wa'sallam. Allāhumma kamā ballaghtanā fid-dunyā ziyāratahū wa ma'-āth-irah-ush-sharīfata falā tuḥrimnā yā Allāh fil-ākhirati minfaḍli shafā'ati Muḥammad Ṣall-al-lāhu 'alaihi wa ālihī wa sallam. Waḥshurnā fī zumratihī wa taḥta lawā'ihī wa amitnā 'alā muḥabbatihī wa sunnatihī wasqinā min hauḍih-il-maurūdi min-yyadihi'sh-sharīfati sharbatan hanī'atan-llā-naẓma'u ba'

and under his banner. Cause us to die in his love and following his Sunna. Give us to drink from his cistern (by which we shall descend) a pleasant draught where after we shall never feel thirsty. Verily Thou hast power over all things.

dahā abadan, innaka 'alā kulli shai'in Qadīr.

AT THE HOLY MAUSOLEUM:

When you draw near to the Holy grave, stand facing it with humility, reverential silence and peace, with eyes lowered in awe and obiesance. When you face his grave with your back to the Ka'ba, reflecting that the Holy Prophet is resting with his face towards the Ka'ba, bear in mind nothing but the grand and lofty position of the Prophet in such a manner that he, the best of Allāh's creation, is well nigh (able) to see you. On no account should you raise your voice in greeting as long as you are near the grave. You should not touch the Hujra nor the lattice, nor should you kiss it, nor make a circumambulation of it. You should not offer prayers facing unto it. For all these are forbidden according to the consensus of the Imāms. You stand near the shrine as if you are in his presence in his life. With extreme politeness and humility, recite salutations on the best of Allāh's creation:

اَلسَّلَامُ عَلَيْكَ اَيُّهَا النَّبِيُّ السَّيِّدُ الْكَرِيْمُ وَالرَّسُوْلُ الْعَظِيْمُ
الرَّءُوْفُ الرَّحِيْمُ ط وَرَحْمَةُ اللهِ وَبَرَكَاتُهٗ ط اَلصَّلٰوةُ
وَالسَّلَامُ عَلَيْكَ يَا سَيِّدَنَا وَنَبِيَّنَا وَحَبِيْبَنَا وَقُرَّةَ اَعْيُنِنَا
يَا رَسُوْلَ اللهِ ط اَلصَّلٰوةُ وَالسَّلَامُ عَلَيْكَ يَا نَبِيَّ اللهِ ط
اَلصَّلٰوةُ وَالسَّلَامُ عَلَيْكَ يَا حَبِيْبَ اللهِ ط اَلصَّلٰوةُ وَالسَّلَامُ

عَلَيْكَ يَا خَيْرَ خَلْقِ اللّٰهِ ؕ اَلصَّلٰوةُ وَالسَّلَامُ عَلَيْكَ
يَا شَفِيْعَ الْمُذْنِبِيْنَ عِنْدَ اللّٰهِ ؕ اَلصَّلٰوةُ وَالسَّلَامُ عَلَيْكَ
يَا مَنْ اَرْسَلَهُ اللّٰهُ تَعَالٰى رَحْمَةً لِّلْعٰلَمِيْنَ ؕ اَلصَّلٰوةُ وَالسَّلَامُ
عَلَيْكَ يَا مُحَمَّدَ بْنَ عَبْدِ اللّٰهِ بْنِ عَبْدُ الْمُطَّلِبِ بْنِ هَاشِمٍ
يَا طٰهٰ يَا يٰسٓ يَا بَشِيْرُ يَا سِرَاجُ يَا مُنِيْرُ يَا مُقَدَّمَ جَيْشِ
الْاَنْبِيَاءِ وَالْمُرْسَلِيْنَ ؕ وَهَا اَنَا يَا سَيِّدِىْ يَا رَسُوْلَ اللّٰهِ
قَدْ جِئْتُكَ هَارِبًا مِّنْ ذَنْبِىْ وَ مِنْ عَمَلِىْ وَمُسْتَشْفِعًا وَمُسْتَجِيْرًا
بِكَ اِلٰى رَبِّىْ فَاشْفَعْ لِىْ يَا شَفِيْعَ الْاُمَّةِ يَا كَاشِفَ الْغُمَّةِ
يَا سِرَاجَ الظُّلْمَةِ اَجِرْنِىْ بِهٖ يَا اَللّٰهُ مِنَ النَّارِ ؕ يَا نَبِىَّ
الرَّحْمَةِ يَا رَسُوْلَ اللّٰهِ اَتَيْنَاكَ زَائِرِيْنَ ؕ وَ قَصَدْنَاكَ
رَاغِبِيْنَ ؕ وَعَلٰى بَابِكَ الْعَالِىْ وَاقِفِيْنَ وَ بِحَقِّكَ عَارِفِيْنَ
فَلَا تَرُدَّنَا خَائِبِيْنَ وَلَا عَنْ بَابِ شَفَاعَتِكَ مَحْرُوْمِيْنَ ؕ
يَا سَيِّدِىْ يَا رَسُوْلَ اللّٰهِ اَسْأَلُكَ الشَّفَاعَةَ وَاَسْأَلُ اللّٰهَ تَعَالٰى
لَكَ الْوَسِيْلَةَ وَالْفَضِيْلَةَ وَالدَّرَجَةَ الرَّفِيْعَةَ وَالْمَقَامَ الْمَحْمُوْدَ
وَالْحَوْضَ الْمَوْرُوْدَ وَالشَّفَاعَةَ الْعُظْمٰى فِى الْيَوْمِ الْمَشْهُوْدِ ؕ
اَنْتَ الْمُشَفَّعُ اَنْتَ الَّذِىْ تُرْجٰى شَفَاعَتُكَ عِنْدَ الصِّرَاطِ اِذَا
مَا زَلَّتِ الْقَدَمُ ؕ اَشْهَدُ اَنَّكَ يَا رَسُوْلَ اللّٰهِ قَدْ بَلَّغْتَ

الرِّسَالَةَ وَأَدَّيْتَ الْأَمَانَةَ وَنَصَحْتَ الْأُمَّةَ وَكَشَفْتَ
الْغُمَّةَ وَجَلَيْتَ الظُّلْمَةَ وَجَاهَدْتَ فِي سَبِيلِ اللهِ حَقَّ
جِهَادِهٖ وَعَبَدْتَ رَبَّكَ حَتّٰى أَتَاكَ الْيَقِيْنُ جَزَاكَ اللهُ
تَعَالٰى عَنَّا وَعَنْ وَالِدَيْنَا وَعَنِ الْإِسْلَامِ خَيْرَ الْجَزَاءِ
اَلصَّلٰوةُ وَالسَّلَامُ عَلَيْكَ يَا سُلْطَانَ الْأَنْبِيَاءِ الْمُرْسَلِيْنَ
وَرَحْمَةُ اللهِ وَبَرَكَاتُهٗ -

Peace be on you, O Prophet! the generous leader, the great Prophet, kind, merciful and the mercy of Allah and His blessings and peace be on you, O our leader! our Prophet! O the coolness of our eyes! O Messenger of Allah! Blessings and peace be on you O Prophet of Allāh! blessings and peace be on you, O beloved of Allāh!

Blessings and peace be on you, O the best of Allāh's creation! Blessings and peace be on you, O the intercessor of the sinners with Allāh! Blessings and peace be on you, O, you whom Allāh has sent as a Mercy for the Worlds!

Blessings and peace be on you O Moḥammad bin Abdullāh, bin Abdil— Muṭṭalib bin Hāshim! O Ṭāhā! O Yāsīn! O Bashīr! O Sirāj! O Munīr! O

Assalāmu 'alaika ayyuhannabī-yy-us-sayyid-ul-karīm warrasūl--al-'Aẓīm-ur-Raūf-ur-Raḥīm-wa-Raḥ-matu-llāhi wa Barakātuh. Aṣṣalātu wassalāmu 'alaika yā Sayyidanā wa Nibīyyinā wa Ḥabībinā wa qurrata 'a'yuninā yā Rasūl-Allāh, Aṣṣalātu was-salāmu 'alika yā Nabīyy-Allāh, Aṣṣalātu wassalāmu 'alika yā Ḥabīb-Allāh,

Aṣṣalātu wassalāmu 'alaika yā khaira khalqillāh, Aṣṣalātu wassalāmu 'alaika yā shafī'al-mudhnibīna 'ind-Allāh, Aṣṣal-ātu wassalāmu 'alaika yā man arsalahu-llahū Ta'ālā Raḥma-tan-llil-'ālamīn. Aṣṣalātu-wassalā-mu 'alaika yā Moḥammad-abna 'Abdillāhibini 'Abdil-Muṭṭalibi bin Hās-him. Yā Ṭahā yā Yāsīn, ya Bashīr, ya Sirāj, ya Munīr ya Muqaddama jaishal anbayā'i wal-mursalīn. Wahā anā yā Sayyidī Yā Rasūl-Allāhi qad

the Chief of the Prophets and Messengers! Here I am O my leader! O Rasūl-Allāh! a fugitive from my sins and my deeds, and hopeful of your intercession to my Lord, so intercede for me, O the Intercessor of the Umma! O the remover of the darkness! O the lamp in the darkness! O Allāh! save me from Hell fire. O the Prophet of Mercy! O Rasūl-Allāh we come to you visiting, intending anxiously to see you, and at your highly esteemed gate we are standing in front of you recognizing you as you deserve, so do not disappoint us, and do not deprive us at your door from your intercession. O our leader! O Rasūl-lāh! I ask for your intercession and I ask Allāh for you to grant the most excellent reward that He hast ever granted to any of the Prophets and grant you O Rasūl-Allāh the excellence and raise you to glorious station, and the cistern, the descending place, and the great intercession at the day of witness. you are the choicest, and you are the one that we all look up to for intercession at the path on which we might tumble. I testify that you, O Messenger of Allāh, have communicated

ji'tuka hāribam-min dhambi-wa min 'amalī wa mustashfi-'an wa mustajīram-bika ilā-Rabbī fashfa'lī yā shafī-ul-ummati yā kāshif-ul-ghummati yā sirāj-uẓ-ẓulmati ajirni bihī yā Allāh min-an-nār. Yā Nabīyya-ar-raḥmati yā Rasūl-Allāhi -atainaka zāi'rīn, Wa qaṣadnāka rāghibīn, Wa'alā bābik—al'ālī wāqifīn wā biḥaqqika 'ārifīn fala taruddana khā'ibīn wa lā 'an babi shafā'atika maḥrūmīn yā Sayyidī yā Rasūl-Allāhi as'aluk-ash-shafā'ata was as'alullāha Ta'āla lak-al-wasīlata wal faḍīlata wad-darajāt-ar-rafia-'ata wal maqām-al-Maḥmūd wal-ḥauḍ -al-maurūda wash-shafā'at-al-'Uẓmā fil yaumil-mashhūd. antal mushaffa'u antal-ladhī turjā shaf-ātuka 'ind-aṣ-ṣirāti idha ma zallat-il-qadam. Ashhadu annaka yā Rasūl-Allāhi qad ballaght-ar -risālata wa addait-al-amānata wa naṣaḥt-al-ummata wa kashaft-al-ghummata wa jalait-aẓ ẓulmata wa jāhadtta fī sabīli-llāhi ḥaqqa jihādihī wa 'abadtta Rabbaka ḥattā atak-al-yaqīn. Jazāk-llāhu Ta'āla 'anna wa'an walidianā wa 'an-il-Islāmi khaira-al-jazāi Assalātu wassalāmu 'alika yā Sulṭān-al-anbiā wal-mursalīna wa Rahmatullāhi wa Barakātuh.

light and have called to the path of Allāh with wisdom and good admonition, and you have worshipped your Lord till the truth came unto you. May Allāh award you on our behalf, and from our parents, and from Islām, the best of awards Blessings and peace be on you O the Chief of Prophets and Messengers and Allāh's mercy and His blessings.

Then turn to the right and salute Abū Bakr, the man of truth (may Allāh be pleased with him). There are two more great personalities of Islam resting beside Rasūl-Allāh, Abū Bakr Ṣiddīque and 'Umar Ibn-al-Khaṭṭāb. Recite in front of the grave of Abū Bakr:

اَلسَّلَامُ عَلَيْكَ يَا سَيِّدَنَا اَبَا بَكْرِ نِ الصِّدِّيقِ ط اَلسَّلَامُ عَلَيْكَ
يَا خَلِيفَةَ رَسُولِ اللهِ عَلَى التَّحْقِيقِ ط اَلسَّلَامُ عَلَيْكَ يَا صَاحِبَ
رَسُولِ اللهِ ثَانِيَ اثْنَيْنِ اِذْ هُمَا فِي الْغَارِ اَلسَّلَامُ عَلَيْكَ يَا مَنْ
اَنْفَقَ مَالَهُ كُلَّهُ فِي حُبِّ اللهِ وَحُبِّ رَسُولِهِ حَتّٰى تَخَلَّلَ بِالْعَبَا
رَضِيَ اللهُ تَعَالٰى عَنْكَ وَاَرْضَاكَ اَحْسَنَ الرِّضَا وَجَعَلَ الْجَنَّةَ
مَنْزِلَكَ وَمَسْكَنَكَ وَمَحَلَّكَ وَمَاْوٰكَ ط اَلسَّلَامُ عَلَيْكَ يَا اَوَّلَ
الْخُلَفَاءِ وَتَاجَ الْعُلَمَاءِ وَصِهْرَ النَّبِيِّ الْمُصْطَفٰى وَرَحْمَةُ
اللهِ وَبَرَكَاتُهُ ـ

Peace be on you, O Abū Bakr the truthful! Peace be on you

Assalāmu 'alaika yā Sayyidanā Abā Bakri-nis-Siddīque. Assa-

of Allāh! Peace be on you O the companion of the Messenger of Allāh and "the Second of the Two when the two were in the cave."

Peace be on you, O you who had spent all of his property in love for Allāh and in the love for His Messenger, till he retired apart with his cloak! May Allāh be pleased with you and please you with the best of pleasures, and may Allāh make the Garden your abode, and resort. Peace be on you, O the first Caliph! the crown of the learned and the father in law of the Prophet the pure and May Allāh's mercy and blessings be on you.

illāhi 'al-at-tahqīq. Assalāmu 'alaika yā ṣāhiba Rasūl-Allāhi thāni-yathnaini idhumā fil-ghār. Assalāmu 'alaika yā man anafaqa mālahū kullahū fī-ḥubbillāhi wa ḥubbi Rasūlihī ḥattā takhallalu bil'abā, raḍi-Allāhu Ta'ālā 'anka wa arḍāka aḥsana-ar-riḍā, wa ja'al-al-jannata, manzilaka wa maskanaka wa maḥallaka wa ma'wāk. Assalāmu 'alaika yā awwal-al-khulafāi wa tāj-al-'ulamā'i wa ṣihr-an-nabiyy-il-Muṣṭafā, wa Raḥmatullāhi wa Barakātuh.

SALUTATION TO 'UMAR IBN-AL-KHAṬṬĀB

By moving further to the right at an arm's length, pay salutations to 'Umar Ibn-al-Khaṭṭāb (may Allāh be pleased with him) and recite:

اَلسَّلَامُ عَلَيْكَ يَا عُمَرَ بْنَ الْخَطَّابِ ط اَلسَّلَامُ عَلَيْكَ يَا نَاطِقًا
بِالْعَدْلِ وَالصَّوَابِ ط اَلسَّلَامُ عَلَيْكَ يَا حَنَفِيَّ الْمِحْرَابِ ط اَلسَّلَامُ
عَلَيْكَ يَا مُظْهِرَ دِيْنِ الْاِسْلَامِ ط اَلسَّلَامُ عَلَيْكَ يَا مُكَسِّرَ الْاَصْنَامِ
اَلسَّلَامُ عَلَيْكَ يَا اَبَا الْفُقَرَاءِ وَالضُّعَفَاءِ وَالْاَرَامِلِ
وَالْاَيْتَامِ ط اَنْتَ الَّذِیْ قَالَ فِیْ حَقِّكَ سَيِّدُ الْبَشَرِ لَوْ كَانَ
نَبِیٌّ مِّنْ بَعْدِیْ لَكَانَ عُمَرَ بْنَ الْخَطَّابِ ط رَضِیَ اللّٰهُ تَعَالٰی

عَنْكَ وَ اَرْضَاكَ اَحْسَنَ الرِّضَا وَجَعَلَ الْجَنَّةَ مَنْزِلَكَ وَمَسْكَنَكَ
وَمَحَلَّكَ وَمَاْوٰكَ ط اَلسَّلَامُ عَلَيْكَ يَا ثَانِيَ الْخُلَفَاءِ وَ تَاجَ
الْعُلَمَاءِ وَصِهْرَ النَّبِيِّ الْمُصْطَفٰى وَرَحْمَةُ اللهِ وَبَرَكَاتُهٗ ۔

Peace be on you, O Umar bin al-Khaṭṭāb! Peace be on you who spoke just and right! Peace be on you, O decorator of Miḥrāb! Peace be on you O overpowering for Islām! Peace be on you, O smasher of the idols! Peace be on you, O the patron of the needy, the weak, the widows and the orphans! You are the one about whom the leader of mankind has said, "if there was to be another Prophet after me it would have been 'Umar-Ibn-al-Khaṭṭāb." May Allāh be pleased with you and may He grant you the best of the contentment and make the paradise your abode and place of resort. Peace be on you O the Second of the Caliphs and the crown of the learned and the father-in-law of the chosen Prophet. The mercy of Allāh and His blessings be on you.

Aṣsalāmu 'alaika yā 'Umar-abn-al-Khaṭṭāb. Assalāmu 'alaika yā nāṭiqam-bil-'adli waṣ-ṣawāb. Assalāmu 'alaika yā ḥanafiyy-al-miḥrāb. Assalāmu 'alaika yā muẓhira dīn-il-Islām. Assalāmu 'alaika yā mukassir-al-aṣnām. Assalāmu 'alaika yā ab-al-fuqarā'i waḍḍu'afā'i wal-arāmili wal-aitām Ant-al-ladhī qāla fī ḥaqqika sayyid-ul-bashari, "Lau kāna nabiyyum-mim-ba'di lakāna 'Umar-abn-al-Khaṭṭab," raḍī-Allāhu Ta'ālā 'anka wa arḍaka aḥsan-ar-riḍā wa ja' al-al- jannata manzilaka wa maskanaka wa maḥallaka wa ma'wāk.
Assalā-mu 'alaika yā thānī-al-khulafā-i wa tāj-al-'ulamā'i wa ṣihr-an-babiyy il-Muṣṭafā, wa Raḥma-tullāhi wa Barakātuh.

Then move forward a bit to the right and recite the following Du'ā:

اَلسَّلَامُ عَلَيْكُمَا يَا وَزِيْرَىْ رَسُوْلِ اللهِ ط اَلسَّلَامُ عَلَيْكُمَا

يَا مُعِيْنَيْ رَسُوْلِ اللّٰهِ ، اَلسَّلَامُ عَلَيْكُمَا يَا ضَجِيْعَيْ رَسُوْلِ اللّٰهِ
اَلسَّلَامُ عَلَيْكُمَا يَا رَفِيْقَيْ وَ مُشِيْرَيْ رَسُوْلِ اللّٰهِ صَلَّى اللّٰهُ
عَلَيْهِ وَسَلَّمَ وَالْمُعَاوِنَيْنِ لَهٗ عَلَى الْقِيَامِ فِي الدِّيْنِ
وَالْقَائِمَيْنِ بَعْدَهٗ بِمَصَالِحِ الْمُسْلِمِيْنَ جَزَاكُمَا اللّٰهُ اَحْسَنَ
جَزَاءِ اَلسَّلَامُ عَلَيْكُمَا وَرَحْمَةُ اللّٰهِ وَ بَرَكَاتُهٗ -

Peace be on both of you, O premiers of Rasūl-Allāh Peace be on both of you O companions of Rasūl-Allāh! Peace be on both of you O co-reposers of Rasūl-Allāh! Peace be on both you O friends and co-ordinators of Rasūl—Allāh! Peace be on him! O, the helpers for him on maintenance of Islām! O the bystanders after him for the benefit of the Muslims! May Allāh grant both of you the best of reward-Mercy and Allāh's blessings be on both of you!

Assalāmu 'alaikumā yā wazīrai Rasūlillāh, Assalāmu 'alaikumā yā mu'īnai Rasūlillāh, Assalāmu alaikumā yā ḍajī'ai Rasūlillāh, Assalāmu 'alaikumā yā Rafīqai wa Mushīrai Rasūlillāh sallallāhu 'alaihi wa sallam, wal mu'āwinaini lahū 'alal-qiyāmi fid-dīni wal-qā'imaini ba'dahū bimaṣaliḥ-il-Muslimīna jazakum-Allahu aḥsana jazā Assalamu 'alaikumā wa Raḥmatullāhi wa Barakātuh.

Now you move towards Rasūl-Allāh, and, standing facing the Holy Prophet you should pray to Allāh whatever you can. Particularly you should invoke Allāh's mercy and His blessings for yourself, your parents and the rest of the Muslims in the world. Try to cimmunicate as if you are in the presence of the Prophet, pray to Allāh as much as you can, here in this place, where thousands of angels are showering Allāh's mercy and his blessings on the Holy Prophet. Here you can recite and hold your tears if you can!

اَللّٰهُمَّ اِنَّكَ قُلْتَ وَقَوْلُكَ الْحَقُّ وَلَوْ اَنَّهُمْ اِذْ ظَلَمُوْٓا اَنْفُسَهُمْ

جَاءُوكَ فَاسْتَغْفَرُوا اللّٰهَ وَاسْتَغْفَرَ لَهُمُ الرَّسُولُ لَوَجَدُوا اللّٰهَ
تَوَّابًا رَّحِيمًا ۝ لَقَدْ جَاءَكُمْ رَسُولٌ مِّنْ اَنْفُسِكُمْ عَزِيزٌ عَلَيْهِ مَا
عَنِتُّمْ حَرِيصٌ عَلَيْكُمْ بِالْمُؤْمِنِينَ رَءُوفٌ الرَّحِيمُ ۝ فَاِنْ
تَوَلَّوْا فَقُلْ حَسْبِيَ اللّٰهُ لَآ اِلٰهَ اِلَّا هُوَ عَلَيْهِ تَوَكَّلْتُ وَهُوَ
رَبُّ الْعَرْشِ الْعَظِيمِ ۝ وَقَدْ جِئْنَاكَ سَامِعِينَ قَوْلَكَ طَائِعِينَ
اَمْرَكَ ۝ اَللّٰهُمَّ رَبَّنَا اغْفِرْ لَنَا وَلِاِخْوَانِنَا الَّذِينَ سَبَقُونَا
بِالْاِيمَانِ وَلَا تَجْعَلْ فِي قُلُوبِنَا غِلًّا لِّلَّذِينَ اٰمَنُوا رَبَّنَا
اِنَّكَ رَءُوفٌ الرَّحِيمُ ۝ اِنَّ اللّٰهَ وَمَلٰٓئِكَتَهٗ يُصَلُّونَ عَلَى النَّبِيِّ
يَا اَيُّهَا الَّذِينَ اٰمَنُوا صَلُّوا عَلَيْهِ وَسَلِّمُوا تَسْلِيمًا ۝ اَللّٰهُمَّ
صَلِّ وَسَلِّمْ وَبَارِكْ عَلَيْهِ ۝ اَللّٰهُمَّ اَنْ تَرْزُقَنِي اِيمَانًا كَامِلًا
ثَابِتًا تُبَاشِرُ بِهٖ قَلْبِي وَيَقِينًا صَادِقًا حَتّٰى اَعْلَمَ اَنَّهٗ
لَا يُصِيبُنِي اِلَّا مَا كَتَبْتَ لِي وَعِلْمًا نَافِعًا وَّقَلْبًا خَاشِعًا
وَّلِسَانًا ذَاكِرًا وَّوَلَدًا صَالِحًا وَّرِزْقًا وَّاسِعًا وَّحَلَالًا
طَيِّبًا وَّتَوْبَةً نَّصُوحًا وَّصَبْرًا جَمِيلًا وَّاَجْرًا عَظِيمًا
وَّعَمَلًا صَالِحًا مَّقْبُولًا وَّتِجَارَةً لَّنْ تَبُورَ يَا نُورَ
النُّورِ يَا عَالِمَ مَا فِي الصُّدُورِ اَخْرِجْنِي وَجَمِيعَ الْمُسْلِمِينَ
مِنَ الظُّلُمَاتِ اِلَى النُّورِ فِي الدُّنْيَا وَالْاٰخِرَةِ وَتَوَفَّنِي
مُسْلِمًا وَّاَلْحِقْنِي بِالصَّالِحِينَ بِرَحْمَتِكَ يَا اَرْحَمَ الرَّاحِمِينَ

يا رب العالمين ۔ ربنا آتنا فى الدنيا حسنة وفى الآخرة
حسنة وقنا عذاب النار ۔ سبحان ربك رب العزة
عما يصفون وسلام على المرسلين والحمد لله رب
العالمين ۔

O Allah! Thou hath said, and Thine word is true. "And if they are cruel to themselves, and they come to you in order to ask forgiveness from Allāh and you want pardon for them (for their sins) then they will find Allāh, the acceptor of repentance, the Merciful, Verily a Messenger has come to you (O people), from among you, on whom is heavy that which may give you hardships, he is greedy for your well being, (he is) affectionate and merciful. So if they turn away from thee (O Prophet), so say Allāh is sufficient for Me, none is worthy of worship except Him, on Him I have trusted and He is the owner of the Great Throne". We have come to Thee hearing Thy words, obeying They orders, O Allāh! our Lord forgive us, and our brothers, those who have preceded us in faith and donot make us in our hearts malicious to those who believe in faith. Our Lord verily

Allāhumma innaka qulta wa qauluk-al-ḥaqqu, "wa lau annahum idh ẓalamū anfusahum jā'uka fastaghfarullāha wastaghfara lahum-ur-Rasūlu lawajudullāha Tawwābar-Raḥīma. Laqad jā'akum Rasūlum-min anfusikum 'azīzun 'alaihi mā a'nittum hariṣun 'alaikum bil-mu'minīna Raūf-ur-Raḥīm. Fa in tawallau faqul ḥasbi-Allāhu lā ilāha huwa'alaihi tawakkaltu wa huwa Rabbul-'arshil-'Aẓīm." (Qur'ān). Wa qad_ji'nāka sami'inā Qaulaka tā'i'īna amraka ,Allāhumma Rabbanaghfirlanā wali-ikhwānin-al-ladhīna sabaqūnā bil-īmāni wa lā taj'-'al fī qulūbinā ghillanllilladhīna āmanū. Rabbanā innaka Raūf-ur-Raḥīm. Inn-Allāha wa malā'ikatahū yuṣallūna 'alan- nabīyyi, yā ayyuh'all-ladhīna āmanū ṣallu 'alaihi wa sallimū taslīmā. Allāhumma ṣalli wa sallim wa bārik 'alaih. Allāhumma an tarzuqanī īmānan kāmilan thābitan tubāshiru bih qalbī wa

Thou art kind and merciful. Verily Allāh and His Angels recite salutation on the Prophet, O ye who believe, recite on him your salutations. O Allāh recite Peace and Blessings on him. O Allāh! I ask Thee that Thou grant me perfection in faith and steadfastness in faith such that it brings contentment in my heart and the true belief, until I know whatever Thou hast written for me will reach me and grant me the beneficial knowledge and a fearful heart and a praising tongue for Thou, and good sons and bountiful sustenance pure and Ḥalāl and true repentance, good patience and good deeds, great awards and trade which knows no loss. O the light of light! the one who knows what is in hearts, bring me forth from darkness to light in this world and the next and cause me to die a Muslim and join me with the pure people. O the most Merciful of Mercifuls! O the Lord of the Worlds! Our Lord grant us goodness in this world and goodness in the next world and save us from Hell-fire. Holy is your Lord, the Lord of honours, pure from what the unbelievers describe.

yaqīnan ṣādiqan ḥattā a'lama annahū lā yuṣībunī illā mā katabta lī wa'ilman-nāfi'an wwa qalban khāshi'an wwa ṣāliḥan wwa rizqan wwāsi'an wa ḥalālan ṭayyiban wwa taubatan-naṣūḥan wwa ṣabran jamīlan wwa ajran 'aẓīman wwa 'amalan ṣāliham—maqbūlan wwa tijārtan-llantabūra, yā nūr-an-nūri yā 'ālima mā fis-ṣudūri akhrijnī wa jamī'al-Muslimīna min-aẓ-ẓulu-māti il-an-nūri fid-duniyā wal ākhirati wa tawaffanī Musliman-wwalḥiqnī biṣṣāliḥīn, bi-Raḥmatika yā Arḥam-ar-Rāhimīn, yā Rabb-al-'ālamīn.

Rabbanā ātinā fid-dunyā ḥasanatan wwa fil-ākhirati ḥasanatan wwaqinā adhab-an-nār. Subḥāna Rabbika Rabb-il-'izatti 'ammā yaṣifūn, Wa salāmun 'alal-mursalīna wal-ḥamdu lillāhi Rabb-il-'ālamīn.

And peace be on the Prophets and all praise to Allah alone, the Lord of the Worlds!

Then turn your face towards Ka'ba and recite:

اَللّٰهُمَّ لَا تَدَعْ لَنَا فِيْ مَقَامِنَا هٰذَا الشَّرِيْفِ ذَنْبًا اِلَّا
غَفَرْتَهٗ وَلَا هَمًّا يَا اَللّٰهُ اِلَّا فَرَّجْتَهٗ وَلَا عَيْبًا يَا اَللّٰهُ
اِلَّا سَتَرْتَهٗ وَلَا مَرِيْضًا يَا اَللّٰهُ اِلَّا شَفَيْتَهٗ وَعَافَيْتَهٗ
وَلَا مُسَافِرًا يَا اَللّٰهُ اِلَّا نَجَّيْتَهٗ وَلَا غَائِبًا يَا اَللّٰهُ اِلَّا
رَدَدْتَّهٗ وَلَا عَدُوًّا يَا اَللّٰهُ اِلَّا خَذَلْتَهٗ وَدَمَّرْتَهٗ
وَلَا فَقِيْرًا يَا اَللّٰهُ اِلَّا اَغْنَيْتَهٗ وَلَا حَاجَةً يَا اَللّٰهُ مِنْ
حَوَائِجِ الدُّنْيَا وَالْاٰخِرَةِ لَنَا فِيْهَا صَلَاحٌ اِلَّا قَضَيْتَهَا وَيَسَّرْتَهَا
اَللّٰهُمَّ اقْضِ حَوَائِجَنَا وَيَسِّرْ اُمُوْرَنَا وَاشْرَحْ صُدُوْرَنَا وَتَقَبَّلْ
زِيَارَتَنَا وَاٰمِنْ خَوْفَنَا وَاسْتُرْ عُيُوْبَنَا وَاغْفِرْ ذُنُوْبَنَا وَاكْشِفْ
كُرُوْبَنَا وَاخْتِمْ بِالصَّالِحَاتِ اَعْمَالَنَا وَرُدَّ غُرْبَتَنَا اِلٰى
اَهْلِنَا وَاَوْلَادِنَا سَالِمِيْنَ غَانِمِيْنَ مَسْتُوْرِيْنَ مِنْ عِبَادِكَ
الصَّالِحِيْنَ ۝ مِنَ الَّذِيْنَ لَا خَوْفٌ عَلَيْهِمْ وَلَا هُمْ يَحْزَنُوْنَ
بِرَحْمَتِكَ يَا اَرْحَمَ الرَّاحِمِيْنَ يَا رَبَّ الْعَالَمِيْنَ ۝

O Allāh! leave not any of our sins but that Thou hast forgiven it, in this honourable place

Allāhumma lā tada' lanā fī maqāminā hādh-ash-sharīfi

dhamban illā ghafartahū wa

nor any worry that Thou hast quelled it, nor any imperfection that Thou hast covered it, nor any patient but that Thou hast granted him recovery and well being nor any traveller that Thou hast redeemed him, nor any missing one that Thou hast caused him to come back, nor any enemy (for Muslims) that Thou hast downcast him, and destroyed him, nor any destitute that Thou hast but enriched him, nor any of the needs of this world or the other world that which benefits us, that Thou hast fulfilled it, and eased it. O Allāh fulfill our needs and ease our affairs and open our chests to (divine guidance), and accept our visit and secure us from fears and cover our imperfections and dispel our afflictions and cause our actions to end well, and return us to our families safe, and protected, (make us) from your good slaves, from those who have no fear nor any worry with Thy Mercy, the most Merciful of Mercifuls, The Lord of the Worlds!

lā hamman yā Allāh illā farrajtahū wa lā aiban ya Allāh illā satartahū, wa lā mariḍan yā Allāh illā shafaitahū wa 'āfaitahū, wa lā musāfiran yā Allāh illā najaitahū, wa lā ghā'iban yā Allāh illā radadttahū, wa lā 'uduwwan yā Allāh illā khadhaltahū wa dammartahū, wa lā faqīran yā Allāh illā aghnaitahū, wa lā ḥājatan yā Allāh min ḥawāij-id-dunyā wal-ākhirati lanā fīhā ṣalāḥun illā qadaitahā wa yassartahā. Allāhummaqḍi ḥawā-'ijanā, wa yassir umūranā, washraḥ ṣudūranā, wa taqabbal ziyāratanā, wa āmin khaufanā, wastur 'uyubanā, waghfir dhunūbanā wakshif kurūbanā, wakhtim biṣ-ṣāliḥāti a'mālanā, wa rudda ghurbatanā ilā ahlinā wal auladinā sāliminā ghānimīna mastūrina min 'ibādik-aṣ-ṣāliḥīn. Min-al-ladhīna lā khauf-un 'alaihim wa lā hum yaḥzanūn.. Bi Raḥmatika yā Arḥam-ar-Rāḥimīn, yā Rabb-al-'ālamīn.

Then move to the place where Revelation from Allāh used to descend on the Prophet, and recite fof the angels who are near to Allāh (Jibra'īl etc.):

اَلسَّلَامُ عَلَيْكَ يَا سَيِّدَنَا جِبْرَائِيْلَ ط اَلسَّلَامُ عَلَيْكَ يَا سَيِّدَنَا
مِيْكَائِيْلَ ط اَلسَّلَامُ عَلَيْكَ يَا سَيِّدَنَا اِسْرَافِيْلَ ط اَلسَّلَامُ عَلَيْكَ
يَا سَيِّدَنَا عِزْرَائِيْلَ ط اَلسَّلَامُ عَلَيْكُمْ يَا مَلَائِكَةَ اللّٰهِ
الْمُقَرَّبِيْنَ مِنْ اَهْلِ السَّمٰوَاتِ وَالْاَرَضِيْنَ كَافَّةً عَامَّةً
اَلسَّلَامُ عَلَيْكُمْ وَرَحْمَةُ اللّٰهِ وَبَرَكَاتُهٗ ط

Peace be on you,
O our chief Jibrā'īl!
Peace be on you,
O our chief Mīkā'īl!
Peace be on you,
O our Chief Isrāfīl!
Peace be on you,
O our chief 'Izra'il
Peace be on you all,
O the near ones
To Allāh from among the dwellers of the Heavens and the Earth, all of you!
Peace be on you all
and His Mercy and
Blessings.

Assalāmu 'alaika yā sayyidan Jibra'il Assalāmu 'alaika ya sayyidanā Mīkā'īl, Assalāmu 'Alaika yā sayyidanā Israfīl, Assalāmu 'alaika yā sayyidanā 'Izrā'īl, Assalāmu 'alaikum ya malā'ikat--Allāh-il- muqarrabīna min ahl-is-samawāti wal-arḍīna kāffatan 'āmma, Assalāmu 'alaikum wa Raḥmatullāhi wa Barakātuh.

It is reputed that the daughter, Fāṭima, of the Prophet (may Allāh be pleased with her), is also resting at the back of the Holy Grave. As you enter through Bāb-i-Jibrā'īl, and walk towards the Grave of the Prophet, her resting place (Hujra) lies on your right. Stand there with utmost respect and recite for her:

اَلسَّلَامُ عَلَيْكِ يَا سَيِّدَتَنَا فَاطِمَةَ الزَّهْرَاءِ يَا بِنْتَ رَسُوْلِ اللّٰهِ
اَلسَّلَامُ عَلَيْكِ يَا بِنْتَ نَبِيِّ اللّٰهِ ط اَلسَّلَامُ عَلَيْكِ يَا بِنْتَ

حَبِيْبِ اللّٰهِ ۔ اَلسَّلَامُ عَلَيْكِ يَا بِنْتَ الْمُصْطَفٰى ۔ اَلسَّلَامُ عَلَيْكِ
يَا خَامِسَةَ اَهْلِ الْكِسَاءِ ۔ اَلسَّلَامُ عَلَيْكِ يَا زَوْجَةَ اَمِيْرِ
الْمُؤْمِنِيْنَ سَيِّدِنَا عَلِيِّ نِ الْمُرْتَضٰى كَرَّمَ اللّٰهُ تَعَالٰى وَجْهَهٗ ۔
اَلسَّلَامُ عَلَيْكِ يَا اُمَّ الْحَسَنِ وَالْحُسَيْنِ السَّيِّدَيْنِ الشَّهِيْدَيْنِ
الْكَوْكَبَيْنِ الْقَمَرَيْنِ النَّيِّرَيْنِ سَيِّدَا شَبَابِ اَهْلِ الْجَنَّةِ فِى
الْجَنَّةِ اَبِىْ مُحَمَّدِ نِ الْحَسَنِ وَ اَبِىْ عَبْدِ اللّٰهِ الْحُسَيْنِ رَضِىَ
اللّٰهُ تَعَالٰى عَنْهُمَا وَعَنْكِ وَ اَرْضَاكِ وَ اَحْسَنَ الرِّضَا وَ جَعَلَ
الْجَنَّةَ مَنْزِلَكِ وَ مَسْكَنَكِ وَ مَحَلَّكِ وَمَاْوَاكِ ۔ اَلسَّلَامُ عَلَيْكِ
وَعَلٰى اَبِيْكِ الْمُصْطَفٰى وَبَعْلِكِ عَلِيِّ نِ الْمُرْتَضٰى وَابْنَيْكِ
الْحَسَنَيْنِ وَرَحْمَةُ اللّٰهِ وَ بَرَكَاتُهٗ ۔

Peace be on you all and his Mercy and His blessings. Peace be on you, O our chief Lady Fāṭima Ẓahara, O the daughter of Rasūl-Allāh! Peace on you O the daughter of Prophet of Allāh! Peace be on you O the daughter of the beloved of Allāh! Peace be on you O the daughter of the chosen one! Peace be on you, O the Fifth of the family of wrappers. Peace be on you, O wife of the fourth Caliph of the Muslims, our

Assalāmu 'alaiki yā sayyidat-anā Fāṭima-taẓẓahrā'i yā Binta Rasūl-illāh, Assalāmu 'alaiki yā Binta Nabīyyillāh, Assal-āmu 'alaiki yā Binta Ḥabīb-illāh, Assalāmu 'alaiki yā Bintal-Muṣṭafā, Assalāmu 'alai-ki yā Khāmisata ahl-il-kasāi, Assalāmu 'alaiki yā zaujata Amīr-il-Mu'minīna Sayyidinā 'Alī-yyi-nil-Murtaḍā (Karra m allāhu Ta'ālā wajhah). Assalā-mu 'alaiki yā Ummal-Ḥasani Wal – Ḥusain-is-sayy-dain-ish-shahīdain-il-kaukabain-il- qam-arain-il-nayyaraini, sayyida

leader 'Alī Murtaḍā, on whom Allāh has especially bestowed his countenance (attention)! Peace be on you, O the mother of Ḥassan and Ḥussain, the two chiefs of the two martyrs, the two stars, the two bright moons, the leaders of the youth, of the paradise in paradise, Abī Moḥammad Ḥasan, and Abī 'Abdullāh Ḥusain! May Allāh be pleased with both of them and with you in the best way and may He make paradise your abode your house, your resort. Peace be on you and on your father, the chosen one, and on your husband 'Alī Murtaḍā and on your sons the two Ḥusnains and Allāh's Mercy and His Blessings.

shabābi ahl-il-jannati fil-jannati, abī Muhammadi-nil-Ḥasani raḍiallāhlu Ta'āla a'nhumā, wa 'anki wa arḍaki aḥsan-ir--riḍā wa ja'al-al-jannata manzilaki wa maskanaki wa maḥallaki wa ma'-wāk. Assalāmu 'alaiki wa 'alā abīk- il-Musṭafā wa ba'-liki 'Alīyyi -nil-Murtaḍā, wabnaik-il-Ḥasanaini wa Raḥmatullāhi wa Barakātuh.

JANNAT–UL–BAQĪ'

This is a cemetery is the east of Medīna Ṭayyaba. Therein lie many companions of the Messenger of Allāh, his pure wives, and his sons and daughters, his relatives, aunts and uncles and the third Caliph 'Uthmān (may Allāh be pleased with all of them).

You should visit this cemetery while you are in Medīna and recite Fātiḥa for them. Recite the following Du'ā:

اَلسَّلَامُ عَلَيْكُمْ يَا اَهْلَ الْبَقِيْعِ يَا اَهْلَ الْجَنَابِ الرَّفِيْعِ
اَنْتُمُ السَّابِقُوْنَ وَنَحْنُ اِنْ شَاءَ اللّٰهُ بِكُمْ لَاحِقُوْنَ ۝ اَبْشِرُوْا

بِاَنَّ السَّاعَةَ اٰتِيَةٌ لَّا رَيْبَ فِيْهَا وَاَنَّ اللّٰهَ يَبْعَثُ مَنْ فِى
الْقُبُوْرِ ط اٰنَسَكُمُ اللّٰهُ تَعَالٰى وَ شَرَّفَكُمُ اللّٰهُ تَعَالٰى بِقَوْلِ
اَشْهَدُ اَنْ لَّا اِلٰهَ اِلَّا اللّٰهُ وَحْدَهٗ لَا شَرِيْكَ لَهٗ وَ اَشْهَدُ
اَنَّ مُحَمَّدًا عَبْدُهٗ وَرَسُوْلُهٗ ط

Peace be on you, O the dewllers of Baqī! O the dwellers of the high post near Allāh! You are the forerunners and we shall, Inshā Allāh, join you. Be pleased that the Day of Judgement is nigh, no doubt in that and Allāh will raise the dwellers of the graves. He hath made acquaintance with you and honoured you with His great words, that I witness that there is none worthy of worship except Allāh. He is the only one, who has no partner and I witness that Muḥammad is his slave and His Messenger.

Assalāmu 'alaikum yā ahl-al-Baqī', ya ahl-al-janab-ir-rafī', antum-us-sābiqūna wa naḥnu Inshā 'Allāhu bikum lāḥiqūn. Abshirū bi-ann-assā'āta ātiyatunllā raiba fīhā wa ann—Allāha yab'athu man fil-qubūr. Anasakumullāhu Ta'ālā wa sharrafakumullāhu Ta'ālā biqauli ashhadu an-llā ilāha ill-Allāhu waḥdahū lā sharīka lahū wa ashhadu anna Muḥammadan 'abduhū wa Rasūluh.

MARTYRS OF UḤUD

In the mountains bordering Medīna, is the famous mount of Uḥud. Here the first battle was fought against the non-believers. Here lie the first martyrs of Islām. You should go and visit the battle ground, recite Fātiḥa for the martyrs. The first martyr of Islām, Ḥamza (may Allāh be pleased with him), the beloved uncle of the Prophet (peace be on him), fought here bravely and gave his life to save the honour of Islām.

Recite this Du'ā followed by Fātiḥa:

اَلسَّلَامُ عَلَيْكَ يَا سَيِّدَنَا حَمْزَةَ بْنَ عَبْدِ الْمُطَّلِبِ ، اَلسَّلَامُ
عَلَيْكَ يَا عَمَّ رَسُوْلِ اللّٰهِ ، اَلسَّلَامُ عَلَيْكَ يَا عَمَّ نَبِيِّ اللّٰهِ
اَلسَّلَامُ عَلَيْكَ يَا عَمَّ حَبِيْبِ اللّٰهِ ، اَلسَّلَامُ عَلَيْكَ يَا عَمَّ
الْمُصْطَفٰى ، اَلسَّلَامُ عَلَيْكَ يَا سَيِّدَ الشُّهَدَاءِ وَيَا اَسَدَ اللّٰهِ
وَيَا اَسَدَ رَسُوْلِهٖ ، اَلسَّلَامُ عَلَيْكُمْ يَا شُهَدَاءُ يَا سُعَدَاءُ
اَلسَّلَامُ عَلَيْكُمْ بِمَا صَبَرْتُمْ فَنِعْمَ عُقْبَى الدَّارِ ، اَلسَّلَامُ عَلَيْكُمْ
يَا شُهَدَاءَ اُحُدٍ كَافَّةً عَامَّةً وَرَحْمَةُ اللّٰهِ وَبَرَكَاتُهٗ ،

Peace be on you, O our chief Ḥamza bin Abdul-Muṭṭalib! Peace be on you, O the uncle of the Messenger of Allāh! Peace be on you, O the uncle of the Prophet of Allāh! Peace be on you, O the uncle of the beloved of Allāh! Peace be on you, O the uncle of the chosen one of Allāh! Peace be on you, O the chief of the Martyrs, and the lion of His Messenger! Peace be on you all, O the martyrs, O the fortunate ones! Peace be on you all, that you all persevered with patience and earned the blessed house of the next world. Peace be on you all, and Allāh's mercy and His Blessings.

Assalamu: 'alaika yā Sayyi-danā Ḥamzat-abna 'Abdil-Muṭṭalib, Assallāmu 'Alaika yā 'amma Rasūlillāh, Assalāmu 'alaika yā 'amma Ḥabībillāh, Assalāmu 'alaika yā 'amm-al-Muṣṭafā, Assalāmu 'alaika yā sayyid-ash-shuhadā'i, wa yā Asadillāhi wa yā asada Rasūlih, Assalāmu 'alaikum bimā ṣabartum fanimā 'uqbad-dār, Assalāmu 'alaikum yā shuhada'a Uḥudin kāffatan 'āmma wa Raḥmatullāhi wa Barakātuh.

Then recite Sūra Fātiḥa, and face towards the Ka'ba and recite:

اَللّٰهُمَّ يَا رَبَّ الْعَالَمِيْنَ يَا رَجَاءَ السَّائِلِيْنَ وَ اَمَانَ
الْخَائِفِيْنَ وَ حِرْزَ الْمُتَوَكِّلِيْنَ يَا حَنَّانُ يَا مَنَّانُ يَا دَيَّانُ
يَا سُلْطَانُ يَا سُبْحَانُ يَا قَدِيْمَ الْاِحْسَانِ ط يَا اَللّٰهُ الرَّبُّ
الْاَعْلٰى ط فَاطِرُ السَّمٰوٰتِ وَ الْاَرْضِ ط يَا اَللّٰهُ يَا سَامِعَ
الدُّعَاءِ اِسْمَعْ دُعَاءَنَا وَ تَقَبَّلْ زِيَارَتَنَا وَ اٰمِنْ خَوْفَنَا
وَاسْتُرْ عُيُوْبَنَا وَاغْفِرْ ذُنُوْبَنَا وَارْحَمْ اَمْوَاتَنَا وَ تَقَبَّلْ
حَسَنَاتِنَا وَ كَفِّرْ سَيِّئَاتِنَا وَ اجْعَلْنَا يَا اَللّٰهُ عِنْدَكَ مِنَ
الْعَائِذِيْنَ الْفَآئِزِيْنَ الشَّاكِرِيْنَ الْمَجْبُوْرِيْنَ مِنَ الَّذِيْنَ
لَا خَوْفٌ عَلَيْهِمْ وَ لَا هُمْ يَحْزَنُوْنَ ط بِرَحْمَتِكَ يَا اَرْحَمَ
الرَّاحِمِيْنَ يَا رَبَّ الْعَالَمِيْنَ ط

O Allāh! The Master of the worlds, O listener of the requests, and security for the fearfuls! O Merciful! O loving! O the generous! O the Emperor! The Glorious! The Ancient Bestower! O Allāh! the shaper of the Heavers and the Earth! O Allāh! O listener of the prayers! listen to our prayers and accept our visit and shelter us from our fears, and cover our frailties, and forgive our sins, and be merci-

Allāhumma yā Rabb-al-'ālamīna yā Rajā'-as-sā'ilīna wa amānal-khā'ifina wa ḥirz-al-mutawakkilīna, yā Ḥannānu, yā Mannānu, yā Dayyānu, yā Sulṭānu, yā Subḥānu, yā Qadīm-al-Iḥsān. Yā Allāh-ur-Rabb-ul a'lā, Fāṭir-us-samāwāti wal-arḍ. Yā Allāh yā Samī'ad-duā', isma' duā'anā wa taqabbal ziyāratanā, wa āmin khaufanā, wastur 'uyūbanā waghfir dhunūbanā, warḥam amwātanā, wa taqabbal ḥasanātinā,

ful to our deeds, and accept our good deeds and forego our misdeeds. And make us, O Allāh! the sheltered ones, the successful ones, the grateful ones, the ones who deserve Thy Mercy, and make us like those who have no fears nor worries, with Thy Mercy, the Most Merciful of Mercifuls, O the Lord of the Worlds!

wa kaffir sayyiātinā, waj'alnā yā Allāhu 'indaka min-al-ā'izin-al-fā'izīna-sh-shākirīn-al-majbūrina min-al- ladhīna lā khaufun 'alaihum walā hum yaḥzanūn, bi-Raḥmatika yā Arḥam-ar-Rāḥimīna yā Rabb-al-'ālamīn.

MASJID QIBLATAIN

This is the famous Mosque, where the revelation came to the Prophet (peace be on him) to turn the face in prayers to the Ka'ba. It was here the famous event in Islamic history took place of turning from one Qibla i.e. Jerusalem to the other i.e. Mecca and hence the name "Qiblatain". Visit this Mosque, preferably on a Tuesday, offer two rak'at and recite:

اَللّٰهُمَّ إِنَّ هٰذَا مَسْجِدُ الْقِبْلَتَيْنِ وَمُصَلّٰى نَبِيِّنَا وَحَبِيْبِنَا
وَسَيِّدِنَا مُحَمَّدٍ صَلَّى اللّٰهُ عَلَيْهِ وَاٰلِهٖ وَسَلَّمَ ۔ اَللّٰهُمَّ
اِنَّكَ قُلْتَ وَقَوْلُكَ الْحَقُّ فِيْ كِتَابِكَ الْمُنَزَّلِ عَلٰى صَدْرِ نَبِيِّكَ
الْمُرْسَلِ : قَدْ نَرٰى تَقَلُّبَ وَجْهِكَ فِي السَّمَآءِ فَلَنُوَلِّيَنَّكَ قِبْلَةً
تَرْضٰهَا ، فَوَلِّ وَجْهَكَ شَطْرَ الْمَسْجِدِ الْحَرَامِ ۔ اَللّٰهُمَّ كَمَا
بَلَّغْتَنَا فِي الدُّنْيَا زِيَارَتَهٗ وَمَاٰثِرَهُ الشَّرِيْفَةَ فَلَا تَحْرِمْنَا
يَا اَللّٰهُ فِي الْاٰخِرَةِ مِنْ فَضْلِ شَفَاعَةِ مُحَمَّدٍ صَلَّى اللّٰهُ عَلَيْهِ
وَاٰلِهٖ وَسَلَّمَ وَاحْشُرْنَا فِيْ زُمْرَتِهٖ وَتَحْتَ لِوَآئِهٖ وَاَمِتْنَا

عَلٰى مُحَبَّتِهٖ وَسُنَّتِهٖ وَاسْقِنَا مِنْ حَوْضِهِ الْمَوْرُوْدِ بِيَدِهِ
الشَّرِيْفَةِ شَرْبَةً هَنِيْئَةً مَرِيْئَةً لَا نَظْمَأُ بَعْدَهَا اَبَدًا،
اِنَّكَ عَلٰى كُلِّ شَيْءٍ قَدِيْرٌ ۔

O Allāh! This is the Mosque of Qiblatain. It is the place of worship of our Prophet, Our beloved, our leader Muḥammad (peace and blessings of Allāh be upon him and His family), O Allāh, Thou sayeth in Thine Book, and Thy word is the Truth, in the book which descended on Thy Prophet, Thy Messenger. "We have seen you (O Muḥammad), turning your face over and over again towards the heaven. Now, therefore, We turn you towards the Qibla that you like the best; so turn your face towards the Masjid-al-Ḥarām." O Allāh! In the like manner Thou hast brought us to visit the Holy Mosque of the Prophet (peace and blessings be upon him and his family) and its sacred signs and also his blessed Monuments, in this world, deprive us not in the same manner, O Allāh! from his intercession in the next world. Collect us (on the day of Judgement), in his community and under his banner. Cause us to die in his love and following his

Allāhumma inna hādha Masjid-ul-Qibla-tain wa Muṣallā Nabīyyinā wa Ḥabībinā wa Sayyidinā Muḥammad, ṣall-Allāhu 'Alaihi wa ālihī wa sallam, Allāhumma innaka qulta wa qauluk-al-Ḥaqqa fī Kitābik-al-munazzali 'alā ṣadri Nabīyyik-al-Mursal, "Qad narā taqalluba wajhika fis-samā'i falā-nuwalli-yannaka Qiblatan tarḍāhā, fa-walli wajhaka shaṭr-al-Masjid-al-Ḥarām." Allāhumma kamā ballaghtanā fiddunyā ziārata-hū wa ma'āthirah-ush-sharīfata falā tuḥrim-nā yā Allāh fil-ākhirati min faḍli shafā'ati Muḥammad, ṣall-Allāhu 'alaihi wa ālihī wa sallam, waḥshurnā fī zumratihī wa taḥta liwā'ihī wa amitnā 'alā muḥabbati-hī wa Sunnatihī wasqinā min hauḍ-il-maurūdi bi-yadihi-sh-sharīfati sharbatan hanī'atan-llā naẓma'u ba'dahā abadan, innaka 'alā kulli sha'in Qadīr.

Sunna. Give us to drink from his cistern (by which we shall descend) a pleasant draught whereafter we shall never feel thirsty. Verily Thou hast Power over all things.

VISIT TO MASJID—E—QUBĀ

It is advisable to visit the Masjid—e—Quba on a Saturday morning according to the Sunna of Prophet Muḥammad (peace be upon him). It is said that a Nafl prayers of two Rak'at here carries a reward equal to that of an 'Umra. After the prayer, recite the following Du'ā:

اَللّٰهُمَّ اِنَّ هٰذَا الْمَسْجِدَ مَسْجِدُ قُبَاءٍ وَ مُصَلّٰى نَبِيِّنَا وَحَبِيْبِنَا
وَسَيِّدِنَا مُحَمَّدٍ صَلَّى اللّٰهُ عَلَيْهِ وَسَلَّمَ ط اَللّٰهُمَّ اِنَّكَ قُلْتَ
وَقَوْلُكَ الْحَقُّ فِيْ كِتَابِكَ الْمُنَزَّلِ عَلٰى صَدْرِ نَبِيِّكَ الْمُرْسَلِ لَمَسْجِدٌ
اُسِّسَ عَلَى التَّقْوٰى مِنْ اَوَّلِ يَوْمٍ اَحَقُّ اَنْ تَقُوْمَ فِيْهِ ط فِيْهِ رِجَالٌ
يُّحِبُّوْنَ اَنْ يَّتَطَهَّرُوْا ط وَاللّٰهُ يُحِبُّ الْمُطَّهِّرِيْنَ ط اَللّٰهُمَّ طَهِّرْ
قُلُوْبَنَا مِنَ النِّفَاقِ وَاَعْمَالَنَا مِنَ الرِّيَا وَفُرُوْجَنَا مِنَ الزِّنَا
وَاَلْسِنَتَنَا مِنَ الْكِذْبِ وَالْغِيْبَةِ وَ اَعْيُنَنَا مِنَ الْخِيَانَةِ
فَاِنَّكَ تَعْلَمُ خَائِنَةَ الْاَعْيُنِ وَمَا تُخْفِى الصُّدُوْرُ ط رَبَّنَا ظَلَمْنَا
اَنْفُسَنَا وَاِنْ لَّمْ تَغْفِرْلَنَا وَتَرْحَمْنَا لَنَكُوْنَنَّ مِنَ الْخَاسِرِيْنَ ط

O Allāh! This Mosque is Mosque of Qubā, It is the place of worship of our

Allāhumma inna hādh-al-Masjida Masjidu Qubā wa Muṣallā Nabiyyinā wa Habībinā

Masjid
- e -
QUBĀ

Exterior

Prophet, our beloved, our leader, Muhammad (peace and blessings of Allāh be upon him). O Allāh! Thou sayeth in Thine Book, and Thy word is the Truth, in the Book which descended on Thy Prophet, Thy Messenger, "The Mosque is to be made on the foundation of fear of Allāh, so that you may stand in it (in prayer) from the very first day deservingly. In it there are men who love righteousness of faith and Allāh loves the righteous ones." O Allāh! Sanctify our hearts from infidelity, and our deeds from pretensions, and our chastity from adultery, and our tongues from lies and backbiting, and our eyes from dishonesty. Of course, Thou knowest the dishonesty of eyes and whatever (evil) is hidden in the hearts. Our Lord! We have been cruel to ourselves and if Thou did not forgive and have mercy on us, we will be from among the losers.

wa Sayyidinā Muhammad Ṣallallāhu 'alaihi wa sallam, Allāhumma innaka qulta wa qauluk al-haqqa fi kitabik – al-munazzafi 'alā Nabiyyik-al-Mursal, " 'lā - Masjidun ussisa 'al-at-taqwā min awwali yaumin aḥaqqun. an taqūma fīh, fihī rijālun-yyuḥibbūna an-yyataṭahharū, wallāhu yuḥibb-ul-mutahharīn." Allāhumma tahhir qulūbanā min-an-nifāqi wa a'mālanā min-ar-riyā' wa furūjanā min-az-zinā wa alsinatanā min-al-kidhbi wal-ghībati wa a'yunanā min-al-khiyānati fa-innaka ta'lamu khā'inat'al-a'yuni wa mā tukhf -is-ṣudūr, Rabbanā ẓalamnā an-fusanā wa in-l l am taghfir-lanā wa tarḥamnā la-nak-ūnanna min-al-khāsirīn

FAREWELL TO MEDĪNA-AL–MUNAWWARA:

When departing from Medīna al-Munawwara, it is Mustaḥab to come to the Mosque of Prophet Muḥammad (may Allāh's peace and blessings shower on him) to say a farewell Salām in a very polite manner, the same as the one offered on arrival here. Offer Salām to the Prophet, and his two Companions, Abū Bakr Siddīque and 'Umar bin al-Khattāb(may Allāh be pleased with them both). Pray for your children, your family, friends, and all Muslims of the world, near Maqām-i-Jibrā'īl, which is said to be a place where prayers are accepted.

Finally come back to the front of the Mosuleum, and recite the following Du'ā:

اَلْوَدَاعُ يَا رَسُوْلَ اللهِ، اَلْفِرَاقُ يَا نَبِيَّ اللهِ، اَلْأَمَانُ يَا حَبِيْبَ
اللهِ لَاجَعَلَهُ اللهُ تَعَالٰى اٰخِرَ الْعَهْدِ لَامِنْكَ وَلَامِنْ
زِيَارَتِكَ وَلَامِنَ الْوُقُوْفِ بَيْنَ يَدَيْكَ اِلَّا وَمِنْ خَيْرٍ وَّ
عَافِيَةٍ وَّصِحَّةٍ وَّسَلَامَةٍ اِنْ عِشْتُ اِنْ شَآءَ اللهُ تَعَالٰى
جِئْتُكَ وَاِنْ مُتُّ فَاَوْدَعْتُ عِنْدَكَ شَهَادَتِيْ وَاَمَانَتِيْ وَعَهْدِيْ
وَمِيْثَاقِيْ مِنْ يَوْمِنَا هٰذَا اِلٰى يَوْمِ الْقِيَامَةِ وَهِيَ شَهَادَةُ اَنْ لَّآ
اِلٰهَ اِلَّا اللهُ وَحْدَهٗ لَاشَرِيْكَ لَهٗ وَاَشْهَدُ اَنَّ مُحَمَّدًا عَبْدُهٗ
وَرَسُوْلُهٗ، سُبْحَانَ رَبِّكَ رَبِّ الْعِزَّةِ عَمَّا يَصِفُوْنَ. وَسَلٰمٌ
عَلَى الْمُرْسَلِيْنَ. وَالْحَمْدُ لِلّٰهِ رَبِّ الْعَالَمِيْنَ، قَالَ رَسُوْلُ اللهِ
صَلَّى اللهُ عَلَيْهِ وَسَلَّمَ مَنْ زَارَ قَبْرِيْ وَجَبَتْ لَهٗ شَفَاعَتِيْ وَ
قَالَ النَّبِيُّ صَلَّى اللهُ عَلَيْهِ وَسَلَّمَ: مَنْ زَارَنِيْ بَعْدَ مَمَاتِيْ
فَكَاَنَّمَا زَارَنِيْ فِيْ حَيَاتِيْ۔

Farewell O Rasūl-Allāh! O beloved of Allāh! May Allāh not make this visit to you the last one; except with goodness,

Al-wadā' yā Rasūl-Allāh, Al-firāqu yā Nabiyy-Allāh, Al-amānu yā Ḥabīb-Allāhi, lā ja'la-hullāha Ta'ālā ākhir-al-'Ahdi lā

security, health and peace. If I live, by the will of Allāh, I will come again, and if I die, then I keep in security with you my witness, my promise and assurance from this day to the day of judgement, that "there is none worthy of worship except Allāh, the One who has no partner, and I witness the fact that Muḥammad is His slave and Messenger" Praise to the Lord, the Reverend, Who is free of what the infidels ascribe to Him, and peace be on Prophets, and All praise is to Allāh, the Sustainer of the Worlds. Rasūl Allāh (peace and blessings of Allāh be upon him) said, "Whoever visits my grave, his intercession becomes compulsory on me", and the Prophet (peace be upon him) also said, "Whosoever visits me after my death, it is as if he visited me during my life."

minka wa lā min ziyāratika wa lā min-al-wuqūfi baina yadaika illā wa min khairin wwa 'āfiyatin wwa ṣiḥḥātin wwa salāma, in 'ishtu in-shā' Allāhu Ta'ālā ji'tuka wa in-mmuttu fa-audatu 'indaka shahādatī wa amānatī wa āhdī wa mīthāqī min-yyauminā hādhā · ilā yaum-il-qayāmati wa hiya shahādatun an-llā ilāha ill-Allāhu waḥdahū lā sharīka lahū wa ash-hadu anna Muḥammadan 'abduhū wa Rasūluh, Subḥāna Rabbika Rabb-il-'izzati 'ammā yaṣifūn, wa salāmun 'al-al-Mursilīna wal-ḥamdu lillāhi Rabbil 'ālamīn. Qāla Rasūl-Allāhi Ṣall—Allāhu 'Alaihi wa sallam: Man zāra qabrī wajabat lahū shafa'atī wa-qāl-an-Nabīyyu Ṣallallāhu 'alaihi wa sallam: Man zāranī ba'da mamātī fa-ka-annama zāranī fī ḥayātī.

We request the readers of this Guide to let us know the errors and omissions so that the same may be corrected in the next edition for the benefit of all Muslims who intend to go on Ḥajj and/or 'Umra.

We also request you to remember to pray for strengthening our Iman and for the acceptance of our humble efforts in providing this information, the main aim being to make easier for our Muslim brothers and sisters to go through this Sacred Journey with the least amount of inconvenience. May Allāh, because of this sincere effort, make our passage through the Day of Resurrection much easier than we can imagine. We pray to Almighty Allāh that may He accept our humble efforts and also the Ḥajj of all Muslim brothers and sisters in His way.

CHAPTER SIXTEEN

PLACES WORTH VISITING

IN AND AROUND MEDINA

JANNAT–UL–BAQI'

It is the old cemetery of Medīna. A list of the Companions of the Prophet, his wives and the followers of the Companions and their followers and host of other pious Muslims who are having eternal rest in this cemetery is given below:

" ' Uthmān, all the wives of the Prophet except Khadīja and Maimūna, Ruqayya daughter of the Prophet, 'Abbās, the uncle of the Prophet, 'Abd-ur-Rahmān bin 'Auf, Sa'd bin abi Waqqāṣ, 'Abdullā bin Mas'ūd , Hasan bin 'Alī bin Ḥusain, 'Uthmān bin Math'ūn etc.

After praying at the graves of the Prophet and his two Companions in the Masjid-e-Nabvī, JANNAT-UL-BAQĪ' should also be visited, preferably on Fridays and to offer FĀTIHA there is MUSTAḤAB.

MARTYRS OF UHUD

At a distance of three miles from Medina is the famous mountain of UḤUD about which the Prophet is reported to have said: UḤUD is the mountain which loves us and we love it In another Ḥadīth it is reported like this: UHUD is one of the Rukn of Paradise. The second battle of the days of the Prophet was fought here. A visit to the graves of the Martyrs of Uḥud, to the mountain of Uḥud, and its surrounding mosques is recommended for Thursday after Fajr prayer. The shrine of SAYYID USH-SHUHĀDĀ Ḥamza, the uncle of the Prophet is located here. 'Abdulla bin Jassh and Mus'ab bin 'Umair are also buried here

Offer FĀTIḤA and salutations on the graves of all these here. Then offer Salām to the rest of the UHUD Martyrs. About seventy of them are buried here.

MASJID–I–QUBĀ

This is the first mosque in Islām. After migration and before arrival in Medīna the Prophet stayed there for 15 days. The Prophet himself laid the foundation of this mosque with his own pious hands and participated in its construction as an ordinary labour. In praise of this Mosque, Allāh declared in the Holy Qur'ān:

لَمَسْجِدٌ أُسِّسَ عَلَى التَّقْوٰى مِنْ أَوَّلِ يَوْمٍ أَحَقُّ أَنْ تَقُومَ فِيهِ ط
فِيهِ رِجَالٌ يُحِبُّونَ أَنْ يَتَطَهَّرُوا وَاللّٰهُ يُحِبُّ الْمُطَّهِّرِينَ ۝

Certainly a mosque founded on observance of righteousness from the first day is more deserving that thou shouldst stand in it. In it are men who love to purify themselves. And Allāh loves those who purify themselves.

La-masjidun ussisa 'alat-taqwā min awwali yaumin aḥaqqu an taqūmu fīh fīhi rijālunyyuḥibbūna an-yyataṭahharū wallāhu yuḥibb-ul-mutahhirīn.

After MASJID–I–ḤARĀM, MASJID–I–NABVĪ, and MASJID–I–AQṢĀ, this mosque is the holiest among the mosques of Islām. The Prophet used to visit it at least once a week. The Prophet is reported to have said, "Offering of two RAK'AT of NAFL in this mosque is equal in thawāb to an 'Umra." It is better to first offer two RAK'AT of TAḤAYYAT-UL–MASJID and then offer two RAK'AT for earning the reward equal to an 'Umra.

MASJID–I–JUM'A

After a stay of fourteen days, the Prophet left Qubā for Medīna. On his way, when he reached the locality of Banū

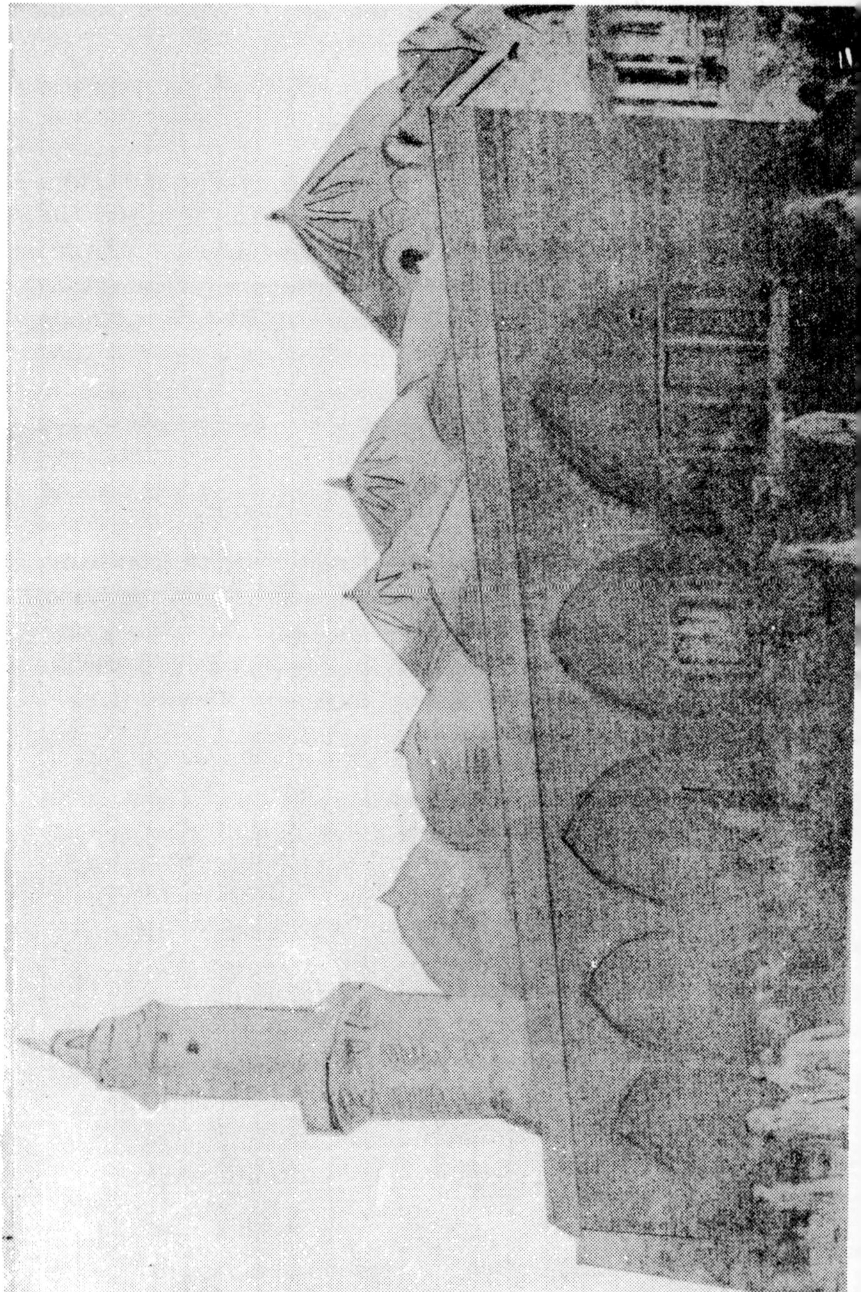

Sulaim, it was the time of Jum a prayer. The Prophet delivered the first KHUTBA in Islām there and led the Jum'a prayer.

MASJID–I–MUṢALLĀ

This mosque is situated in Medīna itself in south-west saari' MANAKH. The Prophet used to offer two 'ĪDAIN here (Muṣallā means 'Īdgāh). It is also known as MASJID–I–GHAMĀMA (clouds), for most probably, prayer for rain (ṢALĀT–I–ISTISQĀ) was also offered here.

MASJID–I–SUQYA

On his way to the Battle of BADR, the Prophet offered ṢALĀT by the side of a well known by the name of BI'R–I–SUQYA.

MASJID–I–AḤZĀB (Fath)

On the western side of JABAL–I–SALI'A. At the time of the Battle of the Ditch, the Prophet prayed there for three days for victory and the Muslims were rewarded likewise.

MASJID–I–QIBLATAIN

Situated on the hilltop near the valley of "ATĪQ," north-west of Medīna. It contains two MIḤRĀBS, one in the direction of BAIT–AL–MAQDAS (Jerusalem) and the other towards MECCA. Some Companions were offering ṢALĀT there at the time of the Revelation dealing with the change of QIBLA. So they now turned their faces towards Mecca. Hence the name MOSQUE OF TWO QIBLAS.

Mosques

MASJID—I—ABŪ BAKR

Near Masjid-i-Ghamāma towards south. Abū Bakr (Allāh be pleased with him) is reported to have offered some prayer, there during his Caliphate or prior to that.

MASJID—I—'ALĪ

'ALĪ (Allāh be pleased with him) is reported to have offered the 'ĪD prayer there during the seige of the house of 'Uthmān (Allāh be pleased with him).

MASJID—I—'UMAR

Near Masjid—i—Ghamāma on way to Masjid—i—Qubā on your left

MASJID—I—ZUBABA

On way to UḤUD, the Prophet pitched his tent here and also offered SALĀT

MASJID—I—BANĪ ZAFAR or BADHLA

It is situated in an easterly direction from BAQĪ'. Here was a stone which had the imprint of the hoof of the female mule which the Prophet was riding.

MASJID—I—BANĪ ḤARAM

On the way to Masjid—i—Fatḥ, on the right side of Jabal-i-Fath, on the right side of Jabal-i-Sali'a valley. In its cave the Prophet used to take rest at night during the Battle of the Ditch.

MASJID–I–IJĀBA

North of Baqī'. Once the Prophet visited the spot and offered prayers there for a considerable time.

MASJID–I–UBAYY

Adjacent to Baqī'. Near to it was the house of Ubayy bin Ka'ab, a Companion of the Prophet. The Prophet used to visit the house often and offered ṢALĀT there. There are many more mosques in Medīna. It is better to visit them, if time permits, and offer two RAK'AT Nafl at each place and to pray to Allāh.

WELLS OF MEDĪNA

BI'R–I–ARIS

Near MASJID–I–QUBĀ. Its water was very sweet and clear. Once the Prophet along with his bosom friend, Abū Bakr sat on its brim.

BI'R–I–ROMA

It is situated in the valley of 'ATĪQ,' west of MASJID–I–QIBLATAIN. Its water was very sweet and clear. The Muslims were in dire need of it. 'Uthman (Allāh be pleased with him), on the expressed wish of the Prophet, purchased it in 20,000 Dirhams from its Jewish owner and dedicated it to the Muslim community of Medīna.

BI'R–I–GHARS

At a half mile distance in a northern direction of MASJID–I–QUBĀ.

BI'R—I—BUDA'A

Near the Syrian Gate, situated in a Garden. With the grace of the Prophet, its water was famous for curing the sick of diseases

BI'R—I—BUSSA

Near Baqī'. It is reported that once the Prophet washed his hands with its water.

BI'R—I—HAA

In front of MAJĪDĪ Gate, outside the northern boundary. It was the property of ABŪ Ṭalḥa Ansārī. When the Qur'ānic verse

لَنْ تَنَالُوا الْبِرَّ حَتّٰى تُنْفِقُوا مِمَّا تُحِبُّونَ ؕ

You cannot attain to righteousness unless you spend out of what you love.	Lan tanā-lul-birra ḥattā tunfiqū mimmā tuḥibbūn.

was revealed, Ṭalḥa dedicated the well to his relatives with the approval of the Prophet (peace be upon him).

BI'R—I—'EHN

East of Masjid—i—Qubā, near the mosque of SHAMS. The Prophet is reported to have made ablution with its water.

Some of these places are easier to reach without a guide. To some, the Taxi drivers will take you during the Ziāra and some of these are probably closed.

APPENDIX I

FOREIGN EMBASSIES IN JEDDA

AFGHANISTAN	–	Kilometre 3, Medina Road Al-Kadesia St., tel. 53142
ALGERIA	–	Medina Road, Ahrned Shawki Street, tel. 53202
ARGENTINA	–	Villa Bakr Khomais, South of British Embassy, tel. 52666.
AUSTRALIA	–	Off Al-Hamra Road, Ruwais P.O. Box 4876, tel. 513, 52329.
AUSTRIA	–	Medina Road, Kilometre 4, Opposite King Saud Mosque, tel. 52548
	–	Commercial Office: Sharbatly Bldg. 4th Floor, Apartment No. 61, tel. 26622, 20134.
BAHRAIN	–	Al-Ruwais near the old Royal Palace, tel. 51905
BANGLADESH	–	(Temporary Address): Red Sea Palace Hotel, tel. 28555, 28950, 28787
BELGIUM	–	Medina Road Kilometre 2, Shakeeb Amawi Building, tel. 53196.
BRAZIL	–	Villa No. 1, West of Medina Road, East of Qasr Al - Hamra, tel. 54574.
CAMEROUN	–	Villa Abdul Aziz Jokhdar Kandara, Al-Maik Street Adjoining Airport Street, Al-Qasr, – Behind Arramad Hospital, tel. 28260/53444.
CANADA	–	6th Floor, Commercial & Residential Centre. King Abdul Aziz Street, tel. 34598, 34111, 34597.
CHAD	–	Kilo 5, Medina Road, tel. 53662

CHINA	–	Villa Amir Mansour, Mohamed Abdul Wahhab Street, Baghdadia tel. 29147, 22605, 33997/29147
	–	Commercial Office: Apts: 503-504, Maghraby Building, Jadid Street, tel. 32860.
DENMARK	–	Commercial & Residential Centre, King Abdul Aziz Street, 9th Floor, tel. 33044/33416.
EGYPT	–	Airport St., Sharafia, tel. 21011, 21200, 21268.
ETHIOPIA	–	Sons of Amar Mansour Bldg., Mohamed Abdul Wahhab Street, Baghdadiya, tel. 23013.
FINLAND	–	Villa Zogheibi, Ministry of Defence Office Street, Sharafiya, tel. 53192, 54177.
FRANCE	–	Sheikh Mohamed Bin Abdul Wahhab St., tel. 21233/21447/34064/23803/24890
GABON	–	Sharafia, Khalid Bin Al-Waleed St., tel. 53497.
GAMBIA	–	Villa Jamil Mustapha Nazir (near Residence), Sharafiya, tel 53292, 52528, 27044.
GERMANY	–	Medina Road M. Mustafa Ashoor Building, tel. 53545, 53344.
GHANA	–	Medina Road, Kilometre 4, Off Palestine Road, tel. 52779.
GREECE	–	Kandara Palace Hotel, Villa 13, tel. 34370.
GUINEA	–	11 Abou Feras Street at Ruwais, tel. 53718.
INDIA	–	Building of Sheikh Mohamed Ibrahim Masoud near Baghdadiya, Medina Road, tel. 21602/21603.

INDONESIA	–	Villa Abdul Malik Bin Ibrahim, Gabali Street No. 9, Baghdadiya, tel. 21681/21497.
IRAN	–	Medina Road, Abou Al-Tayeb Street, East tel. 53145/51424/53143/53474.
IRAQ	–	Medina Road Kilometre 5, tel. 52948/52949.
ITALY	–	Ahmed Abdullah Amoudi Bldg. Sharafiya tel. 21451/21452/21448.
JAPAN	–	Palestine Road, tel. 52402/52405.
JORDAN	–	Khozam Palace-Sea Port Road, tel. 23241, 23022.
KENYA	–	12, Medina Street, Dukki, Cairo, tel. 859455, 859456
KOREA	–	North Hamra Palace, tel. 53218/51700/21654.
KUWAIT	–	Sharafiya, 17 Ali Bin Abi Taleb Street, tel. 53163/53237.
LEBANON	–	Villa Bokhan, Kilometre 3, Medina Road, tel. 52488/52696.
LIBYA	–	Medina Road Kilometre 5; Olayan Al-Hashidi Building, Near Prince Khalid Al-Faisal Palace, tel 51273.
MALAYSIA	–	Shuhada Street, Kilometre 3, Medina Rd. tel. 52371/53866.
	–	Commercial Section: Flat 511 & 512, 5th Floor, Commercial and Residential Centre, King Abdul Aziz Street, tel. 24481.
MALI	–	3-B, Bahjat Street, Zamalik, Cairo, tel. 816108/816107.
MAURITANIA	-	Villa Misfer Kilometre, 3, South Airport Road Fence, University Street, Mecca Rd, tel. 28171.

MEXICO	—	Beirut, Lebanon
MOROCCO	—	Medina Road, Al-Hamra Street behind King Saud Mosque, tel. 52568.
NETHERLANDS	—	Kilometre 1, Medina Road, tel. 53611/53612.
NIGER	—	Villa Al-Sheikh Mohd. Ibrahim Masoud, Palestine Street, Near American·Embassy, tel. 51551.
NIGERIA	—	Sayed Abdallah Abbas Sherbatly Bldg. Baghdadiya (Behind Kutbi Fuel Station, near the Royal Saudi Ministry of Foreign Affairs) Medina Road, tel. 32533,/32835.
NORWAY	—	8, El-Guezira Street, Zamalek, Cairo, tel. 808824/808456/51478
OMAN	—	Medina Road, Ruwais Kilometre 2, opposite American Cultural Centre, tel. 53618/19
PAKISTAN	—	92, Sea Port Road, opposite Qasr Khozam, tel. 27333/27569.
PHILIPPINES	—	Kilometre 5, Medina Road (Near the Villa of HH Prince Muhsin bin Abdul Aziz), tel. 53343/53255/53266.
QATAR	—	Medina Road, North of Ministry of Communications Office, tel. 52538/53973.
SENEGAL	—	Medina Road, behind Telephone Bldg. (Formerly Ashoor's Bldg.), tel. 54465.
SOMALIA	—	Kilometre 2, Medina Road, tel. 51495, 53025.
SPAIN	—	Mecca Road Kilometre 4, Tunsi Bldg., tel. 23226
SUDAN	—	Medina Road, tel. 20560/33682/33681.
SWEDEN	—	Baghdadia (Corner of Medina Road and Sharafiya Airport Street), tel. 21416/21417.

SWITZERLAND	–	Off Medina Road Kilometre 2, tel. 51387
SYRIA	–	Al-Huda St., Al-Sharafiya, tel. 51049
TCHAD	–	Medina Road, Kilometre 5, behind Telephone Building, 53662/52349
THAILAND	–	Madaris Street, Baghdadiya (Near the Office of Royal Protocol), tel. 31344
TUNISIA	–	Badana St., Mecca Road Kilometre 3, tel. 32133/33574
TURKEY	–	Al-Musaidiya St., Medina Road, Kilometre 7, tel. 54873
UGANDA	–	Medina Road, Khalid bin Walid Street, Sharafiya, tel. 52386.
UNITED ARAB EMIRATES	–	'Uthman Bin 'Affan Street No. 58, Sharafiya, tel. 53770/54067.
UNITED KINGDOM	–	Ruwais, tel. 52544/52628/52768/52849/52974.
	–	Commercial Section: Dutch Bank Bldg. 4th Floor, tel. 27122, 27406/27306.
UNITED STATES OF AMERICA	–	Palestine Road, Ruwais tel. 52188, 53299, 52589/53410/54110 52996.
	–	Commercial Centre: Jedda Palace Hotel, tel. 24226/32949,51694/54291.
URUGUAY	–	Beirut, Lebanon.
VENEZUELA	–	Property of Sheikh Saleh Rajah, Hamra Palace Street, tel. 51124/32949/24226.
YEMEN	–	Airport Street, tel. 24291/25540/51124.
ZAIRE	–	Opp U.S. Embassy, tel. 52977, 52973, 52979

SAUDI MISSIONS ABROAD

AFGHANISTAN: Zarghouna Wat, Kaboul; Tel. 20548

ALGERIA: Chemin des Glycines, Residence Casiopee, Alger; Tel. 603243.

AUSTRIA: Wallnerstrasse 3/V, Vienne I; Tel. 638274

BELGIUM: 160, Avenue F. Roosevelt, Bruxelles 5; Tel. 495725.

EGYPT: Villa 12, Rue al-Kamel Muhammad, Zamalek, Le Caire: Tel. 802073/4

ETHIOPIA: Old Airport (zone), P.O. Box 1104, Addis Abeba; Tel. 48010

FRANCE: 1. Rue Andre'-Pascal, Paris 16e; Tel. 8704251

GHANA: House No F. 868/1, off Antonments Road, P.O. Box 670, Accra; Tel. 76651

GREECE: 59, Rue Marathonodromon, Psychico, Athenes; Tel. 676911

GUINEA: Conakry

INDIA: 6, Tilak Marg, New Delhi 1

INDONESIA 3 Djalan Imam, Bondjal, Djakarta, Tel. 46342

IRAN: Ave. Villa, Ave. Nasser, No 29, B.P. 2903, Teheran; Tel. 626354

IRAQ: Waziria , Baghdad; Tel. 20036/7

ITALY: Viale Regina Margherita 260, Roma; Tel. 868161

JAPAN: No 4-18, 3-Chome, Moto Azabu, Minato-Ku, Tokyo: Tel. 4085158/9

JORDAN: Abou Bakr Street, Jabal Amman, Amman; Tel. 24341

KUWAIT: Shaikh Fahed as-Salim Building, al-Hilali Street, Sharq, P.O. Box 20498, Kuwait; Tel. 33001/531155

LEBANON: Al-Manara, Bilis St, Beyrouth; Tel. 346173/346172

LIBYA: Sh. Kayrauan, Tripoli; Tel. 30486

MALAYSIA, Federation of: Police Cooperative Building, Fifth Floor, P.O. Box 2002 1, Sulaiman Road, Kuala Lumpur; Tel. 21387/8

MALI: B.P. 81, Bamako; Tel. 4568

MOROCCO: 43, Place de l'Unite' Africaine, Rabat: Tel. 30171

NIGERIA: 182, Awolowo Road, Ikoyi, P.O. Box 2836, Lagos; Tel. 20397

PAKISTAN: F-151,Block 2, Khaled Ben Waleed Road, P.E.C.H.S., Karachi; Tel. 47156/20156

Senegal: Rue Beranger Feraud, Masclary, Dakar; Tel. 20140/1

SPAIN: Hermanos Becquer, 4, Madrid; Tel. 2762204/03/02

SUDAN: 12/1/39, New Extension Khartoum: Tel. 41986

SWEDEN: Villa Hasselbacken, Hazeliusbacken 18, Stockholm 11521; Tel. 635775

SWITZERLAND: Kramburgstrasse 12, 3006 Berne; Tel. 441555/6

SYRIA: Avenue Al-Jala', Damas; Tel. 334914/5

TUNISIA: 16 Rue d'Autriche, Belvedere, Tunis; Tel. 281295

TURKEY: Abdallah Ceydet Sokak 18, Cankaya, Ankara; Tel. 122115

U.A.R: See Egypt.

UNITED KINGDOM: 27, Eaton Place, London S.W. 1; Tel. BEL 8431/2/3/4

U.S.A.: 1520-18th Street, N.W., Washington D.C. 20036; Tel 483-2100

VENEZUELA: Edificio Mobile, Oficina 300, Ave., Caracas; Tel. 324168/9

FOR FURTHER INFORMATION

1. Saudi Arabian Information Office, 1156 15th St. N.W, Washington D.C., 20005 D.C.

2. Dr. Ahmad Sakr, Permanent Representative of World Muslim League in the U.S.
   P.O. Box 140, Lombard, Ill 60148
   Phone: 312/627.8894

3. Dr. M.A. Rauf, Director, Islamic Centre,
   2551 Massachusetts Ave., N.W.
   Washington, D.C. 20008.
   Phone: 202/332.3451

APPENDIX II

SAUDIA OFFICES

CITY	ADDRESS	TELEPHONE	CABLE
JEDDA			
	Executive Office Airport Road	25222	SAUDAIR
	Reservations	21222	
	City Ticketing Office	24222	
	Airport Information (Arr, Dep.)	22111	
	Executive Ticketing Office	24407/31925	
	Oasis Hotel Ticketing Office	27836/31921	
	Airport Inbound Cargo	24438/31626	
	Airport Outbound Cargo	31804	
	Medina Road Ticketing Office	53765 (Resvn)	
MECCA			
	Al–'Umra Entrance	23200	
	Mecca Hotel	23211	
	Bougari Building	23222/23232	
MEDINA			
	Booking & Sales Office	24411/15	SAUDAIR
	Bab–al–Majeedi	23825 Airport	
	P.O. Box 671	24120 Cargo	
		21101 Res.	

APPENDIX III

LIST OF HOTELS

Name & address	Cable	Phone(s)	Information
JEDDA			
1. Asia Hotel King A. Aziz St. Amoodi Building	Asia Palace	25111 26218	Central air-conditioning, tariff on application
2. Al–Attas 'Arafat Road P.O. Box 1299 (Telex) Attastel SJ 023	Hanytel	20400	100 rooms, all air-conditioned, rates on application.
3. Al–Attas Oasis 'Arafat Road P.O. Box 1789 (Telex) Attastel SJ 023	Oasistel	20211 20418 20617	128 rooms, AC with Bath & Phone, Service 15%, Oriental & Europian, Rest, Roof Garden, Car Park.
4. Baha-ud-din King Faisal St. Fahad Building		25844 25958 31506	DB&B 50, SB&B 35
5. Al–Harmain (Downtown) Bab Sharif King A. Aziz St. P.O. Box 85		26655 34167 26823	DFB 45-57, DB&B 30–40, SFB 35–42 SWB&AC 35–50, DWB&AC 45–65, Service 10%;
6. Al–Harmain Palace Near the Airport		3790 2652	DFB 104, DB&B 60, SFB 40, SB&B 40, Suite 90 per day

7. Jeddah Palace Bab Mecca King Abdul A. Aziz St. P.O. Box 473	Jeddah Palace	32255 32387 32572	85 rooms,Suite, AC, Private Bath & Phone, Bank Conerence Room,Barber, Service 15%, SWB 70–75, DWB 90-100.
8. Kandara Palace Airport Road P.O. Box 473	Kandara Palace	25700 23155 26235	150 rooms, 20 suited, swimming pool, Bank, Conference Rooms for 500 SWB 50-95, DWB -120
9. Quraish Palace Behind Municipality Muhalla Ash Sham		29497 29627	DFB 95, DB&B 50 SFB 52, SB&B 30.
10. Red Sea Palace King A. Aziz St. P.O. Box 824	Respotel	28950 28555 28787	100 rooms, Terrace SB&B 45-75 DB&B 80-120 Service 10% AC, All with Phone and Bath.

MECCA

1. Africa Bab 'Umra, As-suq-as-saghir		26067 36873 36880	AC, Hot water, Singles, Doubles & Suites, no attached bath.
2. Aziz Khogeer Hotel Babal Malik Al-Jiyad	Aziz Khogeer	36331 35020 34919	AC, Hot water, Singles, Doubles & 4-Bed suites, Separate Bath.
3. Hotel Al-Fath Shar'a al-Malik		31242 31353	63, DWB SR 90 7 TWB SR 120 Service - 10%

4.	Al-Haram Ibrahim-Al-Khalil St.	Al-Rebab	27720 27721 23712	25 singles SR: 80, 172 DWB SR:160 5 suites SR: 300, AC, Service 10%, Hot water.
5.	Intercontinental P.O. Box 1496 Um-mul-jud, Jedda Road Telex —	Inhotel-Cor Mecca	34425 34274 34125 39615 34656 31570	44 SWB - SR:150 104 DWB-SR:200 20 suites-SR 325 5 villas - SR: 650 Service - 15%
6.	Shobra Hotel Al-Ashraf Bldg Al-Jayad	Shobrad	28242 28241 28240	80 DWB - SR 160 5 suites, AC, Hot water, Service 10%
7.	Tysir Hotel Sharnia	Al-Tysir	22881 22930	25 SWB - SR 60 60 DWB - SR 90 12 suites - SR 130 AC, Hot water Service 10%

NOTE: All first class hotels have good restaurants.

Abbreviations:

SWB — Single with bath; DWB — Double with bath,
DFB — Double full board; DB&B — Double Bed & Breakfast
SFB — Single full board;
TWB — Treble with bath SB&B — Single Bed & Breakfast

OTHER HOTELS

Phone and Address

JEDDA

1. Airport Jedda 33155/33261/33489
Airport Road, al– Kharjiya

2. al–Amin 33191
King Abdul Aziz Street

3. al–Andalus 34493
Shari al–Jadid

4. 'Arafat 32248
Bab–ush–Sharif, Muhalla al–Bahr

5. Al–Atlas 23361
Shara' Jadid, near Masjid Hanafi

6. Bahauddia 23851/23852
Jawar Fara' Muassasa al-Naqd

7. Ba Ghaffar 33261/33155
—

9. Al–Hamra ....—
Airport Road

9. Intercontinental 29231
—

10. International 29022/29814/29412
Bab Jadid, Abood Bajabir Bldg.

11. Istanbul 26377/26578/26756
Bab-ush–Sharif, King Abdul Aziz St.

12. al–Jazeera 22365
King Abdul Aziz Street

13. al–Khayam 29893/33560
King Faisal Street

14. Makarram 32300
Bab-ush-Sharif, King Faisal St.

15. Medina 33650/32392
Shara' Zahab (jadid)

16. Middle–East 33837/26883
King Abdul Aziz St. Near Riadh Bank

17. al–Nahda (Saudia) 239/23788
Shari'–ul–Mina, al–Balad

18. al–Najd 26926
Bab Sharif, King Abdul Aziz St.

19. al–Qudas 33477
Shara' Jadid, Near Post Office

20. al–Rihab 33216/32302
Shara' Jadid, al–Khaskiya

21. al–Riyadh 33950/33944/33962
Ash. Sharfiya, Airport Road

22. as–Salam. 27869/22776
Bab–ush–Sharif, King Abdul Aziz St.

23. Shaheen. 26582
King Abdul Aziz St. Mufti Bldg. (Auqaf)

24. at–Taj. 21720/21511
Mecca Road, Kilo 1.

25. at–Taj(New) 26814/26815
Airport Road

26. at–Taj New. 21288/21479
Passport Office Road

27. al–Tai Palace. 21288
Airport Road

28. al–Undlas 34493
Shara' Zahab

MECCA

1. al–Amin 28394
Al–Jayad, Near Hospital

2. Badar. 25467
Abrahim–al–Khalil Road

3. al–Ghazzawi al–Hafiz. 31242/31353/31464
Sug–as–Saghir

4. Hura 35632
Shara' al–Jaffali

5. Kandara. 27483
—

6. al–Ka'ki 27604/27605
Al–Jayad

7. Farooq Jamil al–Khoqeer 27514/27515/27517
Almira Bldg. Al–Mudi'

8. Mecca 32381/27161/23222/24797
Bub–ul–'Umra, Al–Shabika

9. Medina 24948
Suq–as–Saghir

10. Mufti 24163
Al–Malik St, Al–Bugri Bldg.

11. Om–al–Qura 27652
Bab–ul–'Umra, Suq–as–Saghir

12. al–Qaltan 22425/34462
Al–Ghazza St.

13. ar–Razooqi . . . . –
Bab–ul–'Umra

14. ar–Rihab . . . . –
al–Shabika

15. as–Safa 25601/24748
Ash–Shamia, Asma Bldg.

16. as–Salam 22880/22926
Al–Ghazza

17. Tayyaba 29478/36868
Bab–ul–Malik, Al–Jayad

18. Zamzam 29201/21524/20450
Shara' al–Marwa

MEDINA **Phone and Address**

1. al–Ansar 24420
–

2. Abu Khalid 54926
King Abdul Aziz Street

3. 'Arafat 24882
Bab–ul-Haidari, Hajari Bldg.

4. Al–Ayan 22489
–

5. Baha–ud–Din 25224/21340
Bab–al–Majidi

6. Dar–ul–Ansar 21743
–

7. Dar–ul–Hijra 22667
King Abdul Aziz Street

8. Dar–ul–Hina 23638
Bab–ul–Majidi

9. Dar–ul–Iman 21743
Shari' as–Sunbala

10. Dar–ur–Rawda. 22991
King Abdul Aziz Street

11. Ghassan. 23130
King Abdul Aziz Street

12. al–Haram 24525/23200/25525
Shari' as–Sahiba

13. al–Hijaz 21110/21120
Shari' as–Sunbala

14. al–Ibrar. 21119
Bab–us–Salam

15. Indijani 21540
Bab–ul–Majidi

16. al–Joud. 25925
King Abdul Aziz Street

17. al–Khair Palace. 25110/24686
King Abdul Aziz Street

18. A.A. Khogeer 25173
Near Baqi'

19. Kirama 21075
King Abdul Aziz Street

20. Mecca 27011
Bab–ul–Majidi

21. Medina Palace 21020/24961
Shari' as–Sunbala

22. Middle East 28003
Abi Zar

23. Nowafak 21929

24. an–Nasr 21189
Shari' as–Sunbala

25. an–Nour 23164
–

26. al–Ohud 22510/22520
Near Baqi'

27. al–'Omran. 21449
–

28. al–Qasar–al–Ansar. 24420/25420
Shari' al–Himi

29. al–Qudas. 21822/22000/25522
Shari' al–Ghaiba

30. al–Rawa 21016
. . . . King Abdul Aziz Street

31. ar–Rihab. 22000
Shari' as–Saha

32. al–Sa'd Palace. 21423
Shari al–Roomiya

33. al–Sa'daa 22923/22943
King Abdul Aziz Street

34. Shaheen. 21190/25600
King Abdul Aziz Street

35. Taiba. 23270

36. Taiba Palace 24201
Near Baqi'

37. al–Tunis 21489
Shari' Roomiya

38. al–Tayseer 22541/21429
Shari' as–Sunbala

39. al–Wafa. 21590
King Abdul Aziz Street

40. al–Wahid Palace 22130
King Abdul Aziz Street

41. al–Zahra 21230
Shari' as–Sunbala

42. as–Zahur Palace 22815
King Abdul Aziz Street

APPENDIX IV

AIRLINES AND AGENTS

IN JEDDA: **Agents for**

1. Al Huseini Travel Agency
King Abdul Aziz Street . . : . . . . P.I.A.
P.O. Box Box 1702, Ph:27429, ... Varig
23294, Cable Speedwell.

2. Aouini Hussein and Co. . . . . Air Cameroun, Air France
King Abdul Aziz Street . . . . .Afrique, Royal Air Maroc
P.O. Box 8, Ph: 26329 . . . . U.T.A.

3. Alitalia
Al–Mufti Building. . . . . .Alitalia
King Abdel Aziz Street,
P.O. Box 2910, Ph: 22107, 25238
Cable Alitaliairlines

4. Areen Travel, Al Jawrara Bldg. . . . . Ethiopian Airlines
Medina Road, P.O. Box 266 . . . . .Sabena, Tunis Air
Ph: 33125/6/7/8, Cable. . . . . T.M.A.
Areentravel

5. Ghazi I. Shaker and Bros. . . . . M.E.A.
King Abdel Aziz St. Ph: 21140/1
Airport Ph: 24840

6. Darwish Travel Agency . . . . Alia
King Abdel Aziz St., P.O. Box 1719
Ph: 23324

7. Haji Abdulla Alireza & Co. . . . . Air Algerie
King Abdel Aziz St., P.O. Box 8 . . . . K.L.M.
Ph: 26329

8. Hatim Travel Agency. . . . . .Air India
Prince Faisal Bldg.
King Abdel Aziz St.
P.O. Box 419, Ph: 31026
Cable: Loulou.

9. Saddik & Mohamed Attar Co. . . . . Ariana Afghan Airlines,
. . . . British
King Abdel Aziz St.. . . . . . . .Airways, East African Airways
P.O. Box 439, Ph: 23437, 23244 . . . Ghana Airways, Iraqi
. . . . Airways
Cable: Attarco. . . . . .Kuwait Airways, SAS, Swissair

10. Saudi Arabian Markets . . . . Air Canada
P.O. Box 65, Ph: 23142 . . . . . . Overseas National Airways
Airport, Ph: 26787 . . . . Sudan Airways
Cable: Markets

11. Saudi Travel & Tourist Bureau . . . . . . .British Caledonian,
. . . . Egypt Air
Prince Faisal Building . . . . Iran Air, Japan Airlines
King Abdel Aziz St. Ph: 21172. . . . .Libyan Arab Airlines,
. . . . Somali
Cable: Maysser . . . . Airlines, THY.

12. T.M.A. Attar Building . . . . T.M.A.
King Abdel Aziz St, P.O. Box 266
Ph: 28446, 33814, Cable: Tramedair

13. Yemen Airways Corporation. . . . . Y.A.C.
Al–Moghrabi Building
King Abdel Aziz St.
P.O. Box 4693, Ph: 33169
Cable: Yemenair

IN MECCA:

1. Arab Commercial Enterprises .... Pan. Am.
   Ibrahim Jaffali Building
   P.O. Box 586, Ph: 24240
   Cable: Comment

2. Saddik and Mohamed Attar Co. ....British Airways
   P.O. Box 22, Ph: 26046 .... SAS, Swissair
   Cable: Attarco

IN MEDINA:

1. Al–Kuraishi .... Saudia
   Bab Al–Majeedi

APPENDIX V

RATES FOR VARIOUS SERVICES

POST:

	Letter Air Mail	Post Card	/Aerogramme
U.K.	16 Qursh	10 Qursh	10 Qursh
U.S.A.	23 Qursh	10 Qursh	10 Qursh
Inland	4 Qursh	3 Qursh	4 Qursh

TELEGRAPH:

U.K.	29 Qursh (1 Rial 9 Qursh) per Word
U.S.A	40 Qursh (2.0 Rials) per Word
Inland	4 Qursh per word

TELEPHONE:

U.K.	50 Rials per 3 minutes
U.S.A.	60 Rials per 3 minutes
Inland	Free local service
	SR 1.20–6.00/3 minutes

AIR CARGO

	45 Kg or more	Less than 45 Kg
U.K.	8.05 Rials/Kg.	10.70 Rials/Kg.
USA	18.05 Rials/Kg.	23.70 Rials/Kg.
Inland		0.50 Rials/Kg.

AIR TRAVEL (DOMESTIC)

Jedda-Medina	First Class	82.00 Rials
	Economy	55.00 Rials
	Tourist	52.00 Rials

The above rates are for one way travel. Return tickets will be twice the cost of one-way.

NOTE: These rates are from various sources and are liable to fluctuations. These should be taken as approximate figures and verified at the time of purchase or request for a service from the appropriate agency or authority thereof.

Please also note that while we have made every effort to provide readers with accurate information, the Author and Publisher can accept no responsibility for possible inaccuracies and omissions.

APPENDIX VI

GENERAL TELEPHONE DIRECTORY

SERVICES AND EMERGENCY TELEPHONE NUMBERS THROUGHOUT KINGDOM

Trunk Calls 90
International Calls 91
Trunk Complaints 92
Traffic Accidents. 93
Telephone Faults. 94
Telephone Information. 95
Ambulance. 97
Fire Brigade 98
Police 99

LONG DISTANCE CODE NUMBERS

Riyadh 011
Jedda 021
Dammam/Alkhobar 031
Mecca 022
Medina 041

DAMMAM/AL-KHOBAR

Customs 3176/3119
Elec. (Power Failure) 23444
Water trouble 21399
Police Dammam 22440
Police Alkhobar 42290
Telephone Maintenance 21206

AIRLINES

Airport Enquiries 41000
Saudia Traffic. 6167
Lost Confirm 5273
Booking. 42000/41697/41697
ITA Booking 4156/2436/2435
Gulf Air. 44342/41930/41931
Air France 3284
PIA 4263/5186/4193/52033
ITA Enquiries. 5284/41931
Swiss Air 2303
KLM. 4462/2655/2656
TMA. 3146
Pan Am 5289/5290
TWA. 2653
Darwish Airways. 4291
Middle East Airways 2365
Lufthansa 4274/4273/43800
Syrian Airlines 5137
Kuwait Airways 42102
Olympic Airways. 44416

CAR RENTAL

Ren-A-Car (M. Mahrus) Al-Khobar
. . . . 44390/44642

HOSPITALS

Central Dammam 22640
Al-Madama Dispensary 21050
As Salama Hospital 41011
Ash Sharq Hospital 43355
Central Hospital 41450
Fakhri Hospital. 42322
Al-Manæ' Hospital
for eye, dental 42330
Al Jazira Clinic 21439

HOTELS

Al-Dossary 25563
Dammam. 21738/21926
Al-Haramain. 26670/26421
Al Gusaibi 42466/42160
Al-Khaja Al-Khobar 43122
Gulf Flowers 23691/22170

PHARMACIES

Al-Abli 41819
Al-Safa 41615
Al-Wafa 52661
Dammam. 22312

Al-Gossaibi	21455
Al-Harmain	22920
Al-Khafaji	21163
Al-Amal	42207
Saudi-Arabia	42458
Al-Fardous	43608
Al-Khobar	42193
Middle East	41612

JEDDA

Elec. Power Failure	23044
To report an accident to Police	32101
To report city water trouble	27177
Telephone Services	23795
Telephone maintenance	21200
Long distance supervisor	63670
France	21233/34064/53357/53351

AIRLINES

Nanaba Airlines	23956
Jedda Airport	22111/28717
Airport Enquiries	32231
(KLM)	24684/25505
Air France	22882/32468
British Airways	22937/22986
Egypt Air	21144
Korean Airlines	25612
Kuwait Air	28349
Lufthansa	23224
British Airways	22937/22986
Egypt Air	21144
Korean Airlines	25612
Kuwait Air	28349
Lufthansa	23224
M.E.A.	21933
Olympic Airways	22228
Pan American	31151/23731
Royal Jordanian (Alia)	21327
Sebena Belgian Airways	23404/22002
Syrian Arab Airlines	25612
Tunis Air	22448/22474
T.W.A.	22228

BANKS

American Express	31151/2373
Arab	22896/23349
British	23251/23621
Dutch	29635/26266
First Nat. City	33767/24155/24374
Indo-China	23344
Lebanese	23285/22462
National Com.	22863/23122/23347
Al-Jazira	24844-26049
Riyadh	22418/22634/32416
Saudi Arabian	21188
S.A.M.A	31122/31130
	31306
Suleiman Al-Rajihi	23815

CAR RENTALS

Arabian Car Rental	33965
Sahary CarCorporation	21032/20400
Avid Rent-A-Car	52930
Saudi Hotel	24051/35051

CUSTOMS

Director-Jedda Customs	31748
Jedda Port Customs	31222

HOSPITALS

Jedda Clinic	27715
Lebanese	52955/23708
Whittaker	51313/51122
Al-Maghrabi	23680/27159
Dar El Shifa	27444
Jedda	27444
Public Eye	24926/7
General	25694/21369
Central	21133
Maternity Clinic	22526
Khalid Idriss	23555
Obstetrics	33606
Al-Rahbani	53633

PHARMACIES

Batarjee	23515/23259
Red Sea	20180
Middle East	29986
Muhammad Tamer	23982/22313
Moondial	29081

MECCA

Customs	28505/28504
Electricity	21022/21203
Passport	22755/22116
Police	25109/25212

Rabita … 24288/20552
Traffic Police … 26050/20/20460
Water … 23993

BANKS

Arab … 23455/23456
National Commercial … 21404/21405
Riadh … 20996/21378

DISPENSARIES

Al-Hafayer … 29487/25526
Indian … 25659
Al-Misfala … 23625
Al-Mo'abada … 22590
Pakistani … 29236

DRUG STORES

Al-Amal … 28020
Ba-Qader … 36924
Ba Wazir … 28131/23441
Ba Zaid … 22608
El-I'tabia … 20465
Al-Ghazza … 22118
Al-Hikmeh … 23971
Al-Khoqir … 23842/22869
Al-Mansour … 22682
Najm-al-Hada … 20868
Al-Rashidi … 29364
Al-Shams … 23426
Al-Sharq … 22614/23880
Al-Shifa … 24843
Al-Srour … 21039
Al-Tunisi … 26209

HOSPITALS

Jayad … 26111/26644/24883
King Faisal … 21633/25215
King Abdul Aziz … 26411/27091
Maternity … 24802/22050
National … 27170/26170
National Maternity … 36569/27169

PHARMACIES

Al-Batarji … 21673
Ba Wazir … 27636
Fahmi … 28059
Ibrahim Tiro … 25036
Mecca … 27130
Al-Nasr … 25651
Sawwaf … 28049
At-Tahir … 27587/27585

MEDINA

Customs … 21515/24103
Electricity … 22232
Islamic University … 24051
International calls … 25452/21976
Passport … 24557/24112
Police … 25515/25660
Rabita … 23252
Traffic Police … 24626/25720
Trunk controller … 25502

BANKS

National Commercial … 25344/25345
Riadh … 21212

HOSPITALS

Central … 25221/25231
King … 25532/24910
Maternity … 25406/24761
Pakistani … 24884

PHARMACIES

Al-Amal … 23880
Al-Ahli … 25150
Al-Batarji … 24802
Al-Fardaws … 24842
Al-Harmain … 22478
Al-Jaziran … 24875
Al-Kawthar … 23523
Al-Rawda … 23045
Salah … 23530
Al-Salam … 22220
Al-Shifa … 21519
Taiba … 22689
Al-Zahra … 22557

RIYADH

Elec. (Power Failure) … 29866
Airport Information … 61400
Trunk Controller … 20094/2703

BANKS

Banque du Caire … 28003/28033
Riyadh … 24011/24522/25688

First National City	24000/20270
The Arab Bank	24111/24855
The National Bank ex.	24044/25081

HOSPITALS

Riyadh General	51900
King Abdul Aziz	28555
Maternity and Children's	51122
Al-Watany	61211
Al-Ahli	22221
Obeid	62695
Al-Nasiriya	25600
Public Security	61911
Military	62311
King Faisal Specialist	35555/35041
Lost Property	61804

HOTELS

Al-Haramain	29009/25738/23831
Middle East	29011/29023
Al-Nasr	23082/282416
Airport	62193/63483
Al-Rawdha	28415
Yamama	28200
Zahrat Al-Shark	31278
Sahara Palace	61500
Al-Saudia	24051
El-Khreigi	39919
Al-Kads	23025
Intercontinental	34500
Semiramis	27757

MINISTRIES

Ministry of Information	25500
T.V. Station ex.	25500
Ministry of Petroleum	31133
Ministry of Pilgrimage	22200
Ministry of Commerce	21116
Ministry of Foreign Affairs	51322/51310
Ministry of Interior	24100
Passports	20505
Ministry of Defense	21115
Ministry of Agriculture	22200
Ministry ofHealth	24800
Ministry of Labor	27100
Ministry of Finance	27000
Information	29928
Ministry of Education	23600
Ministry of Communication	24400
General Administrative Institute	61600
Offices of the United Nations	26807/26771/25075

PHARMACIES

Arafat	24310
Al-Batafji	22043
Al-Hayat	217,9
Al-Kawthar	22825
Al-Khayyam	27250
Al-Mahaz National	61757
Shabeeb	25775
Tamr	24646

SUPERMARKETS

Spinneys	28493
Green Valley	27627
Al-Taj	24220
Al-Mallouhi	25746

APPENDIX VII

USEFUL WORDS AND PHRASES

Please	من فضلك	Min faḍlak
Thank you	شكرًا	Shukran
Welcome!	اهلًا وسهلًا	Ahlan wa sahlan!
Yes	نعم - ايوا	Na'am; aiwa
No	لا	Lā
Don't mention it	عفوًا	'Afwan
Sorry, excuse me	متاسف	Mut'assif
How are you?	كيف حالكَ	Kaif ḥālak (to a man);
	كيف حالكِ	Kaif ḥālik (to a woman)
Well	طيب، كويس	Ṭayyib; kuways
Good-morning	صباح الخير	Sabāḥ al-khair
Good-morning (reply)	صباح النور	Ṣabāḥ an-nūr
Good evening	مساء الخير	Masā' al-khair
Goodbye	فى امان الله	Fī amān Allāh
Goodbye (reply)	مع السلامه	Ma'a as-salāma
Hullo, welcome	مرحبا	Marḥaba
Tell me	قلى	Qullī
This	هٰذا	Hādha
That	ذلك	Dhālika
How much?	كم، قدش	Kam?; qiddash?
Expensive	غالى	Ghāli
Also	ايضًا	Ayḍan
What's the matter?	ايش فى	Aish fī?
Where is...?	فين	Fain...?
On your left	على شمالك	'Alā shimāluk
On your right	على يمينك	'Ala Yāminik
Straight on	دغرى	Dogrī
When...?	امته	Emta...?
Go!	امشى	Imshī
Come!	تعال	Ta'ālāl
I do not have...	ماعندى	Mā'iandī
Give me!	اعطينى	'Aṭainī
Bring me!	جيب لى	Jib.
Stop!	قف	Qif!
Do you speak English?	تكلم انگليزى	Tatakallam inglizī?
I don't speak Arabic.	ما تكلم عربى	Mā atakallam 'arabī
I do not know...	ما اعرف	Mā 'ārif...

It doesn't matter	ماعلش	Mā'alash
Look!	شوف	Shūf!
Money	فلوس	Flous
Petrol	بنزين	Benzīn
Oil	زيت	Zait
Car	سيارة	Sayyāra
Hotel	هوتيل	Hutail
Market	سوق	Sūq
Tea	شاى	Shāhi
Coffee	قهوه	Qahwa
Milk	حليب	Halīb
Sugar	شكر	Sukkar
Here	هنا	Hunā
There	هناك	Hunāk
Is it possible?	ممكن	Mumkin?
It is possible (perhaps)	يمكن	Yumkin
Suitcase	شنته	Shanta
Airport	مطار	Maṭār
Ticket	تذكره	Tadhkira
Harbour, port	ميناء	Mīna'
Hospital	مستشفى	Mustashfa
Police station	مركزالبوليس	Markaz-al-bulīs
Street	شارع	Shār'a
Town, city	مدينه	Madīna

NUMBERS

1 Waḥad	2 Itnin	3 Thalātha	4 Arb'a	5 Khamsa
6 Sitta	7 Sab'a	8 Tamānya	9 Tis'a	10 'Ashara
15 Kamsatāsh	20 'Ashrīn	50 Khamsīn	100 Mia	1000 Alf

DAYS OF THE WEEK

Sunday	يوم الاحد	Yaum al-aḥad
Monday	يوم الاثنين	Yaum al-itnin
Tuesday	يوم الثلاثه	Yaum ath-thalātha
Wednesday	يوم الاربعه	Yaum al-irb'a
Thursday	يوم الخميس	Yaum al-khamīs
Friday	يوم الجمعه	Yaum al-jum'a
Saturday	يوم السبت	Yaum as-sabt